in Ontario

Tracey Arial

Travel better, enjoy more

ULYSSES

Travel Guides

Offices

CANADA: Ulysses Travel Guides, 4176 St. Denis Street, Montréal, Québec, H2W 2M5, ☎ (514) 843-9447 or 1-877-542-7247, ⇝(514) 843-9448, info@ulysses.ca, www.ulyssesguides.com

EUROPE: Les Guides de Voyage Ulysse SARL, BP 159, 75523 Paris Cedex 11, France, ☎ 01 43 38 89 50, ⇝01 43 38 89 52, voyage@ulysse.ca, www.ulyssesguides.com

U.S.A.: Ulysses Travel Guides, 305 Madison Avenue, Suite 1166, New York, NY 10165, ☎ 1-877-542-7247, info@ulysses.ca, www.ulyssesguides.com

Distributors

U.S.A.: The Globe Pequot Press, 246 Goose Lane, Guilford, CT 06437 - 0480, ☎1-800-243-0495, Fax: 800-820-2329, sales@globe-pequot.com

CANADA: Ulysses Books & Maps, 4176 St. Denis Street, Montréal, Québec, H2W 2M5, ☎ (514) 843-9882, ext.2232, 800-748-9171, Fax: 514-843-9448, info@ulysses.ca, www.ulyssesguides.com

GREAT BRITAIN AND IRELAND: World Leisure Marketing, Unit 11, Newmarket Court, Newmarket Drive, Derby DE24 8NW, ☎ 1 332 57 37 37, Fax: 1 332 57 33 99, office@wlmsales.co.uk

SCANDINAVIA: Scanvik, Esplanaden 8B, 1263 Copenhagen K, DK, ☎ (45) 33.12.77.66, Fax: (45) 33.91.28.82

SWITZERLAND: OLF, P.O. Box 1061, CH-1701 Fribourg, ☎ (026) 467.51.11, Fax: (026) 467.54.66

OTHER COUNTRIES: Contact Ulysses Books & Maps, 4176 St. Denis Street, Montréal, Québec, H2W 2M5, ☎ (514) 843-9882, ext.2232, ☎ 800-748-9171, Fax: 514-843-9448, info@ulysses.ca, www.ulyssesguides.com

Canadian Cataloguing-in-Publication Data (see page 4)
© November 2001, Ulysses Travel Guides.
All rights reserved. Printed in Canada
ISBN 2-89464-443-4

The splendor of Silence,
of snow-jeweled hills and of ice.

Ingram Crockett
Orion

Author
Tracey Arial

Copy Editing
Eileen Connolly

Computer Graphics
André Duchesne

Editor
Jacqueline Grekin

Page Layout
Raphaël Corbeil

Photography
Cover page
Superstock

Publisher
Pascale Couture

Cartographer
Patrick Thivierge

Acknowledgements

Author: Thanks to Gilles Sauvageau, a technician with Igloo Vikski, the Canadian distributors of Fischer skis and Swix wax; Lucie Leclerc-Rose from the Canadian Olympic Association; Jim Reid from the Conservation Lands of Ontario; Julie from Conservation Nature Tours; J.D. Downing from the American Cross Country Skiers (AXCS); Dr. William Pruitt from the University of Manitoba; Dr. Hardy Granberg from the University of Sherbrooke; and John Gallagher from CANSI. Thanks also to dad, Pedro, Paul, Arial, the rest of my family and all my friends who joined me to explore the trails.

Ulysses Travel Guides: We acknowledge the financial support of the Government of Canada through the Book Publishing Industry Development Program (BPIDP) for our publishing activities. We would also like to thank the Québec government – SODEC income tax program for book publication.

Canadian Cataloguing-in-Publication Data

Arial, Tracey, 1963-

Cross-Country Skiing and Snowshoeing in Ontario

(Ulysses Green Escapes)
Includes index.

ISBN 2-89464-443-4

1. Cross-Country Skiing – Ontario – Guidebooks. 2. Snowshoes and snowshoeing – Ontario – Guidebooks. 3. Trails – Ontario – Guidebooks. 4. Ontario – Guidebooks I. Title. II. Series.

GV854.8.C3A742001   796.93'2'09713   C2001-941623-7

Table of Contents

List of Maps

Map Symbols

❓	Information centre	❤	Park
🅿	Parking	══ 🎿	Cross-country skiing trail
👫	Restroom	▬▬ 🥾	Snowshoeing trail
⛺	Picnic area	= = = = =	Other trail
⛺	Campground		

Symbols

⇄	Fax number
☎	Telephone number
(A)	Accommodations on site
(L)	Lessons on site
(R)	Rentals on site
●	Easy trail
■	Intermediate trail
◆	Difficult trail
♥	Favourite location

Cross-country skiing available

Snowshoeing available

Write to Us

The information contained in this guide was correct at press time. However, mistakes can slip in, omissions are always possible, places can disappear, etc. The authors and publisher hereby disclaim any liability for loss or damage resulting from omissions or errors.

We value your comments, corrections and suggestions, as they allow us to keep each guide up to date. The best contributions will be rewarded with a free book from Ulysses Travel Guides. All you have to do is write us at the following address and indicate which title you would be interested in receiving (see the list at the end of the guide).

Ulysses Travel Guides

4176 St. Denis Street
Montréal, Québec
Canada H2W 2M5

305 Madison Avenue
Suite 1166, New York
NY 10165

www.ulyssesguides.com
E-mail: text@ulysses.ca

Table of Distances (km)
Via the shortest route

© ULYSSES

	Chicago (IL)	Hamilton	Kingston	Kitchener-Waterloo	London	Montréal (QC)	New York (NY)	Niagara Falls	Ottawa	Sault Ste. Marie	Sudbury	Toronto	Thunder Bay
Hamilton	788												
Kingston	1100	338											
Kitchener-Waterloo	767	69	369										
London	661	140	451	110									
Montréal (QC)	1383	621	299	650	738								
New York (NY)	1294	765	583	838	911	618							
Niagara Falls	896	77	408	156	227	689	690						
Ottawa	1242	480	203	511	600	202	719	544					
Sault Ste. Marie	780	748	894	777	699	1003	1498	814	806				
Sudbury	1079	460	609	490	572	700	1212	529	508	302			
Toronto	855	75	263	123	198	547	829	144	410	696	411		
Thunder Bay	1058	1469	1623	1496	1414	1638	2212	1534	1516	723	1019	1421	
Windsor/Detroit (MI)	460	318	626	306	191	912	1018	413	773	584	751	386	1310

Example: The distance between Montréal and Toronto is 547km.

 *Where is Ontario?*

©ULYSSES

Ontario	
Capital:	Toronto
Population:	11,669,300 inhab.
Area:	1,068,630 km²
Currency:	Canadian Dollar

Introduction

People have been cross-country skiing and snowshoeing in Ontario for thousands of years because these two modes of transportation are the best ways to get through the snow easily, pleasantly and quickly.

Whether you want to get some exercise outdoors in the fresh air or simply tour around exploring trees, animals, rock formations and natural history, these are the sports for you.

This book details more than 200 of Ontario's most interesting cross-country skiing and snowshoeing locations. In some cases, the location is part of a long trail, such as the Bruce Trail. In most cases, however, we've listed a prime location, such as a conservation area, provincial park, nature reserve, ski centre or private property. We've also provided a description of the trails, grooming practices and services you'll find in each area, as well as the costs associated with such services. Private clubs run several of the sites listed within this guide, although most welcome day visitors for a fee.

Two of the areas mentioned here are so isolated that no roads lead to their entrances and they can only be accessed by train, while three others require guests to ski in to their accommodations where the trails begin. Yet another requires skiers to drive across an ice road to reach the trails. Another site lies at the end of a road, past a long slippery hill that makes leaving at the end of the day an additional challenge. All of these special conditions have been clearly indicated, so you can plan your skiing or snowshoeing adventure knowing that you'll face few surprises along the way.

We hope that you'll discover that many of these locations have something in common: excellent trails. These are Ontario's best trail networks for skiing and snowshoeing, primarily because local people who love snow have spent an incredible number of hours maintaining the tracks. The work of many people, most of whom are volunteers, goes into clearing and marking trails for skiing or snowshoeing. They've cleared, marked, and sometimes groomed, scarified and trackset the trails you'll be visiting. In many cases, volunteers also raised the money for lights that enable you to ski at night.

If you're lucky, you'll meet a good number of volunteers on the trails. You'll find that, although they're a mixed group of people of all ages and inclinations, they'll be friendly and encouraging. It's thanks to them that you can explore Ontario's most impressive landmarks, such as the Niagara Escarpment, the Oak Ridges Moraine, the Elora Gorge, the Sleeping Giant, the La Cloche Mountains and the shores of the five Great Lakes.

Chapter Overview

To help you identify areas that match your own passions, the chapter entitled **Cross-Country Skiing and Snowshoeing in Ontario** provides a big-picture look at Ontario. Along with the size and climate of each area, it mentions major physical landforms and unique historical landmarks throughout the province. We've also listed the province's cross-country skiing and snowshoeing clubs, so that anyone interested in getting more involved with the sport, whether to race or simply tour on weekends, can easily find out how to do so.

The **Practical Information** chapter helps you get ready for a season of cross-country skiing and includes a checklist of the most important items you'll need for a day or overnight trip.

The rest of the book is divided into seven major geographical regions: Greater Toronto, The Niagara Peninsula, Southern Ontario, Central Ontario, Eastern Ontario, Northeastern Ontario and Northwestern Ontario.

The **Greater Toronto** chapter includes Aurora, Bolton, Bradford, Brampton, Brantford, Cambridge, Oshawa, Port Hope, Pickering, Markham, Milton, Mississauga, Newmarket, and the city of Toronto. Lake Ontario, the Niagara Escarpment and the Oak Ridges Moraine are the most important physical features in the region.

The **Niagara Peninsula** includes Burlington, Grimsby, Hamilton, Niagara Falls, Niagara-on-the-Lake, St. Catharines, Stoney Creek and Welland. This area is sheltered by the Niagara Escarpment and includes the Welland Canal, Carolinian forests and an unusually rich variety of bird species.

Southern Ontario falls between Lake Erie and Lake Huron. Major cities in the area include Goderich, Guelph, Kitchener, Leamington, London, Orangeville, Sarnia, Stratford, Tobermory, Wasaga Beach, Windsor and Woodstock. This relatively flat region is known for Carolinian forests, oak savanna, vast farms, sandy beaches and flowing rivers.

Central Ontario includes the Kawartha Lakes region, Algonquin Park and the northern coast of Georgian Bay. Major cities are: Barrie, Bracebridge, Collingwood, Gravenhurst, Haliburton, Huntsville, Lindsay, Midland, Orillia, Peterborough, and the Town of the Blue Mountains. This area is the best-known cross-country destination, thanks to its plentiful snowfall and stunning scenery.

Eastern Ontario is the area north of Lake Ontario that borders on Québec. Major cities are: Belleville, Brockville, Cornwall, Gananoque, Kanata, Kingston, Nepean, Ottawa, and Trenton. This ancient marine bed is now known for pink granite, rock paintings, abandoned mines, farming estates, vast marshes and the Rideau Canal.

Northeastern Ontario includes the northern coast of Georgian Bay and Lake Huron north to James Bay. Major cities include: North Bay, Sault St. Marie, Sudbury and Timmins. This region, which also includes Manitoulin Island, has become known for a landscape of rock ridges, raging lakes and rivers, and stunted trees made famous by the Group of Seven.

Northwestern Ontario is the area north of Lake Superior through to Lake of the Woods and the Manitoba border. Major cities include: Atikokan, Dryden, Fort Frances, Kenora, Marathon, Nipigon and Thunder Bay. Only a few trails have pierced this vast mysterious region of impenetrable rock, huge canyons and waterfalls, making it a prime location for daring adventurers.

The **Multi-Region Trail** chapter provides basic information about any trail that crosses regional borders.

How to Use This Guide

Each centre listed in this guide features a **symbol** indicating whether cross-country skiing, snowshoeing, or both are available at that location. You'll then find a comprehensive description of each location, including everything needed to plan a trip.

The **location** of each centre is precisely indicated and includes the **number of trails** normally maintained.

We've also indicated the **total distance**—in km and miles—a skier or snowshoer would travel by following these trails. **All of these trails are looped unless we've indicated that they are linear.** In the few locations that require skiers to ski along the same sections two or three times to follow the looped trails, these sections are counted two or three times in the total figure. **Please note that distances provided for linear trails are one-way.**

Three **levels of difficulty** define the trails. **Easy** trails can be completed by just about anybody, including a four-year-old child or a parent pulling a pulka. On the signs along the trail and on placards with maps, easy trails are marked in green or with a green circle that has a curved line through the centre. In this guide they are indicated with a circle (●).

Intermediate trails are a bit more challenging, with hills and turns that provide a bit more to test a skier's skills. Trail signage identifies intermediate trails in blue or with a blue square that has a bent line through the middle. In this guide they are indicated with a square (■).

Difficult trails attract experienced skiers and snowshoers, and include challenging climbs and twisting uneven paths. They often include sections that are dangerous for those with less experience. These difficult trails are marked in black or with signs indicating black diamonds with jagged lines running through the middle. In this guide they are indicated with a diamond (◆).

Learning to associate the circle with easy, the square with intermediate and the diamond with difficult can help ensure that you always pick the right trail for your skill level, no matter which location in Ontario you decide to visit.

We've also indicated the percentage of trails that are **groomed**, a process that involves using snowmobiles or other tractor-like equipment to flatten the snow into a wide flat smooth surface for classic and freestyle cross-country skiing or extremely easy snowshoeing.

Many groomed trails are also **trackset**, either for classic cross-country skiing alone or for both classic and freestyle cross-country skiing on one trail. Track-setting a trail involves using

equipment to mark two indented parallel grooves into the middle or along the edge of a trail. Some trails are double trackset to enable skiers to travel in either direction or to enable faster skiers to pass quickly. Newer wider trails have grooves at the edge of a flat scarified section enabling classic and skating cross-country skiers to ski together.

We have added an additional **lighting** heading to any location that has at least one trail lit to enable visitors to ski at night between late December and mid-March. If this heading does not appear, no night skiing is available.

If you are likely to view interesting wildlife, rock formations, waterfalls, birds and other **interesting features** along the trails during the winter, we've listed them. We've also included a **winter bird checklist** in an appendix.

The cost of using a trail or parking at a location is indicated next to the **fee** heading. Please note that in some cases, access to trails is reserved for members. We've indicated where this is the case and provided membership costs.

Some areas offer other winter activities, such as tobogganing or skating. These are

Introduction

indicated in a heading called **other activities**.

Certain centres offer services such as equipment rental **(R)**, cross-country skiing or snowshoeing lessons **(L)**, or accommodations on site **(A)**. These three features are indicated under the **services** heading. In some cases, the costs associated with such services are also provided. Any additional features offered, such as parking, toilets, snack bar or waxing centre, are listed in the **amenities and other services** category.

Finally, for each destination you'll find instructions on **getting there**, as well as **contact information** for the club or organization in charge of maintaining the trails.

Included among the centres are some resorts and inns with their own private trails. Note that in some of these cases, most of which are in central Ontario, access to trails is restricted to overnight guests. We've indi-cated at the top of each description where this is so.

Some of the locations that we are particularly enthusiastic about include a descriptive paragraph that tells you a bit more about the development of the area and the trails, so that you'll know what to expect when you get there.

For those of you who don't have the time to explore each area, we've identified 28 of our favourite cross-country skiing locations, which are indicated by a heart symbol **(♥)**. These locations are guaranteed to be worth travelling to, either because of a stunning winter waterfall, a scenic view or an unusual experience. While all the areas listed are definitely worth-while, these are the best of the best.

We hope that, with this guidebook, you'll have a meaningful personal journey visiting the natural splendour of Ontario this winter.

Favourite Trails

The following trails are our favourites. In the text, they are marked with the following symbol: (♥)

Southern Ontario

The Niagara Peninsula

Greater Toronto

Central Ontario

Eastern Ontario

Northeastern Ontario

Northwestern Ontario

Multi-Region Trails

Trail Rating Information

● **Easy** trails can be completed by just about anybody, including a four-year-old child or a parent pulling a pulka.

■ **Moderate** trails are a bit more challenging, with hills and turns that provide a bit more to test a skier's skills.

◆ **Difficult** trails are a bit more challenging, with hills and turns that provide a bit more to test a skier's skills.

Cross-Country Skiing and Snowshoeing in Ontario

Cross-country skiing and snowshoeing are ideal winter recreational pursuits for anyone interested in nature exploration, improved health and physical fitness, or friendly competition.

In Ontario, the season begins as soon as there is snow, usually by mid-December until at least late March, and sometimes into April. One enthusiastic club north of Thunder Bay begins their season in September with a race on a sawdust-covered trail.

Cross-country skiing and snowshoeing both rely on low-cost, durable, portable equipment. They are also both incredibly easy for novices to learn, yet provide lots of stimulation for intermediate-level participants and enough challenge for athletes who use the sports to build endurance during their winter training regimes. Many runners train on snowshoes, for example, while other athletes rely on cross-country skiing for a strong cardiovascular workout that burns up to 800 calories an hour.

No matter what your skill set or desired activity level, there's a location in Ontario that will cater to you. In many cases, a local ski or snowshoe club is involved in grooming a variety of trails suitable for different skills and conditions. Some of these clubs also offer lessons to help you improve your form and group excursions to provide you with social opportunities. There are also many events and races throughout Ontario, ranging from the extremely competitive to the family-oriented, including those that are geared to women, children or other special groups so that participants of all levels can have fun and improve their skills.

Anybody can benefit from a few hours of cross-country skiing or snowshoeing while chatting with companions, watching a variety of winter birds or concentrating on racing form, and Ontario's an ideal place to participate!

Cross-Country Skiing

In cross-country skiing, long, thin skis support the weight of a person above the snow to enable fast, easy travel from place to place throughout the winter. Bindings attach boots to the ski only at the toe, leaving the heel free so that foot manoeuvres easily. This "free heel" is the primary difference between cross-country and alpine skiing techniques. The sport is also sometimes called Nordic skiing because of its origins in Sweden, Norway and Scandinavia.

Types of Trails

In Ontario, cross-country skiers have access to three types of cleared and marked trails: ungroomed, groomed, and groomed and trackset. Ungroomed trails are suitable for backcountry skiers who use very heavy equipment, including extra-wide light skis, to blaze their own track or to follow in the track of previous backcountry skiers. Groomed trails are single-track, flat, wide, smooth surfaces, which are often open to cross-country skiers and snowshoers. Groomed and trackset trails include at least one track defined either by two indented parallel grooves or by a flat, smooth surface that has been scarified to loosen the snow and permit grip. Modern trails now include at least two tracks side by side—one flat, scarified groomed track with no grooves and another track with two indented parallel grooves.

Styles

There are several different styles of cross-country skiing, beginning with the traditional form called "classic," which is now often practiced on the same trail next to "freestyle" skiers who skate from one ski to another. Then there's the form of free-heel alpine skiing called "telemarking," which is traditional "ski jumping" with a new reputation and better equipment. "Backcountry skiing" is reserved for those who like to make their own trails, and is often practiced by dog-lovers who "skijor." Parents with very small children will enjoy "pulking," and those who appreciate target shooting might want to try their hand at the "biathlon." A short description and history of each of these forms follows.

Classic

Classic cross-country skiing consists of using your legs and poles to push and glide along a track consisting of two parallel grooves that are slightly wider than skis or along a packed surface with no grooves at steep hills, curves or inclines.

The classic skiing techniques of diagonal stride and double poling are possible only because the middle portion of the ski, from just in front of the toe piece to just past the heel plate, grips the snow. The stiffness and bend (camber) in the ski combined with a skier's weight enables the grip section to touch the snow lightly enough so that the skis glide easily, yet also heavily enough to enable the skier to push on the snow to move forward. This push action can be improved with a temporary wax layer (see p 62) that grips the snow, although waxless skis have moulded scales to create a similar effect.

Cross-Country Skiing and Snowshoeing

— Caribou

When stood on end, classic skis are long enough to reach the wrist of a skier's outstretched arm, while the poles should reach a bit above a skier's armpit.

Freestyle (also known as "skating")

The freestyle or skating style consists of using short, wide skis and poles to continually glide from one foot to another in the shape of a "V" along a wide, packed trail.

Skating is also known as the "Norwegian two-step" because its continual movement is reminiscent of dancing. No grip region is necessary for this style.

When stood on end, skating skis are long enough to reach 3 to 4cm (1 to 1.5in) above the head of a skier, while the poles should reach the skier's chin. They are much stiffer than classic skis.

Telemark

The Complete Ski Runner, Arnold Lunn's 1913 classic guide to cross-country skiing technique, uses the name Telemark, which originally referred to a district in Norway, to describe a way of going up or down steep hills with a free-heel. The word now takes in a

distinct style of free-heeled alpine skiing that includes ski jumping. True enthusiasts enjoy the style in the backcountry, although they also practice at alpine resorts—without using the tow or chair lifts to climb.

Telemark skis are heavier, shorter and wider than classic cross-country skis, although they have the camber and stiffness to create a grip region.

Backcountry

Backcountry skiers use sturdy heavy skis and classic techniques, along with snow poles with wide baskets to explore untracked areas. Although the track created as a backcountry skier travels through untouched snow can be used to head back to the starting point in nice weather conditions, wands with flags, a compass, and survival skills become important if a storm hits or if winter camping is on the agenda.

Skijoring

A dog pulling a cross-country skier on classic skis is called "skijoring." The dog, which must weigh at least 13.6kg (30lbs), wears a sled-dog harness connected to a lead that attaches to a belt around the skier's waist. Modern skijoring equipment includes the harness, belt and strap in one woven piece, with a three-point buckle to attach the harness to the dog and a one-point buckle to attach the belt to the skier's waist. Those who skijor usually prefer ungroomed or single-track narrow trails.

Pulking

A classic skier who needs to pull small children or supplies can use a small sled with a long lead and waistband called a "pulk." The bottom of the pulk is constructed with extrusions that fit the grooves in a classic track or the tracks left behind by a backcountry skier.

Biathlon

Biathlon combines classic cross-country techniques and equipment with rifle shooting in an ancient form of hunting, although today's prey is usually limited to mechanical targets.

History

Compelling archaeological evidence—including petroglyphs in Rodoy, Norway and the remains of tools that resemble skis—dates cross-country skiing in the Nordic states back to at least 2,000 BC. The activity is now an essential element of Nordic folk tales, many

of which tell how famous heroes on skis successfully whisked important people from the clutches of certain death. This form of transportation first began evolving into a sport in 1767, when competitions were held between the companies charged with guarding the border between Norway and Sweden. By 1843, the first cross-country skiing race was held in Norway.

North Americans weren't introduced to cross-country skiing until 1849, when California miners used skis to travel from gold claim to gold claim. John "Snowshoe" Thompson became famous after spending 20 years—from 1856 until 1876—delivering mail to the miners on cross-country skis called "Norwegian snowshoes." Since the 3m-long (10ft) and 11cm-wide (4.5in) skis were made from oak, they were heavy, weighing a total of 9.3kg (25lbs). The average weight of cross-country skis these days is about 750g (1.7lbs) and the heaviest backcountry telemark pair weighs 1,700g (3.8lbs).

The new trend didn't reach Ontario until 1887, when a local newspaper published a picture of a man skiing on 3m-long (10ft) Norwegian snowshoes in High Park, Toronto. That was also the same year that Lord Frederick Hamilton—brother-in-

Ontario's Cross-Country Skiing Performance at Winter Olympic Games

1928: St. Moritz, Switzerland
Merritt Putman, from Toronto, placed 40th in the 18km race.

1932: Lake Placid, New York, U.S.A.
Three Ottawa natives participated in the 18km: William (Bud) Clark, John Taylor and John Currie. David Douglas, also from Ottawa, qualified for the 50km, but didn't finish.

1936: Garmish-Parenkirchen, Germany
William (Bud) Clark, from Ottawa, placed 48th in the 18km race.

1952: Oslo, Norway
Claude Richer, from Ottawa, placed 52nd in the 18km race.

1968: Grenoble, France
Dave Rees, from North Bay, placed 46th in the 50km, 58th in the 30km, and 61st in the 15km races. Rees also competed in the 10km men's relay.

1972: Sapporo, Japan
Helen Sander, from Dunrobin, placed 40th in the 10km and 41st in the 5km women's races. Malcome Hunter, from Ottawa, placed 43rd in the 30km and 45th in the 15km men's races.

1976: Innsbruck, Austria
Sue Holloway, from Ottawa, placed seventh in the 5km women's relay. Reijo Puiras, from Thunder Bay, placed 56th in the 15km men's race.

1988: Calgary, Alberta, Canada
Al Pilcher, from Orangeville, placed ninth in the 10km men's relay, 39th in the 30km and 46th in the 15km. Angela Schmidt-Foster, from Midland placed ninth in the 5km women's relay. Jean McAllister, from Ottawa, placed 46th in the 5km and 32nd in the 20km freestyle women's races.

1992: Albertville, France
Angela Schmidt-Foster, from Midland, placed 29th in the 15km, 39th in the 5km and 51st in the pursuit. Al Pilcher, from Orangeville, placed 45th in the 30km and 52nd in both the 10km and the pursuit. Wayne Dustin, from Sault Ste. Marie placed 48th in the 30km and 64th in the 10km. Darren Derochie, from Onaping placed 61st in the 50km. Dustin and Derochie's team also finished 11th in the 5km relay.

law and aide to then Governor-General Lord Lansdowne—reputedly brought Russian skis to Ottawa. By 1895, skiers were seen throughout Toronto and Ottawa, particularly in Rockcliffe Park. Eventually, the activity became extremely popular in the two cities and led to the development of recreational skiing clubs for enthusiasts who wanted to practice and learn new skills. The Toronto Ski Club began operating with six members in 1908 and grew to include 44 members two years later. The Ottawa Ski Club began in 1910 as a club of "ski jumping" enthusiasts who used two types of techniques—the Christiana turn and the Telemark turn—to go down hills. Today, alpine skiers rely on techniques related to the Christiana turn, which does not require a free-heel, while telemark skiing has turned into a sport all its own. Eventually the Ottawa club created a "cross-country running" division that relied on what we now call classic cross-country ski techniques.

At about this same time, Canada's earliest cross-country skiing pioneer was introducing the sport to northern Ontario while selling logging and construction material to crews working for the Temiskaming and Northern Ontario Railway. Although Herman "Jackrabbit" Smith-Johannsen was born in Norway in 1875, he became one of Canada's most famous citizens, thanks to his tireless promotion of cross-country skiing. He built Canada's first official trails, slalom courses and ski jumps in the Laurentians in Québec; helped develop the cross-country trails at Blue Mountain in Collingwood, Ontario in the late 1930s; raced until he was 75 years old; skied past the age of 100; and continued inaugurating ski events until 1986, when he died at the age of 112. The children's "Jackrabbit" ski programs and festivals at ski centres throughout Canada honour his memory.

As skiers throughout central and eastern Canada and the northeastern United States kept creating new recreational clubs, club members sought out similar groups in other cities so that they could compete against one another and also trade information, techniques and ideas. Eventually, an umbrella organization called the Northern States Ski Association (NSSA) was created. By 1913, the NSSA was comprised of 32 affiliated clubs.

Although the clubs began meeting for purely recreational reasons, it wasn't long before members began

Cross-Country Skiing and Snowshoeing

organizing ski competitions. The Canadian Ski Championships took place in Montréal on February 13, 1909, although it included only ski jumping (today's telemarking). The Ottawa club organized Ontario's first "cross-country running" race in 1914. The 19km (12mi) race took place on January 25 and most competitors took two hours to complete the course. After that, ski competitions included both "ski jumping," now known as telemarking, and ski running, today's classic touring.

When it came to promotional efforts, most Canadian clubs chose to join the Northern States Ski Association until February 28, 1920, when the Montreal Ski Club, the Quebec Ski Club, the Ottawa Ski Club and Cliffsides joined together in a Canadian umbrella organization called the Canadian Amateur Ski Association. Today, this organization is known as the Canadian Ski Association.

The next major growth impetus came when cross-country skiing was allowed into the 1924 Winter Olympics in Chamonix, France. Canada didn't send anyone that year but prepared to send a four-person team to St. Moritz, Switzerland in 1928 instead. In the end, only three people went—by boat. It took a week to get

there. The team included one member from Ontario—Merritt Putnam, from Toronto—who placed 40th in the 18km (11mi) race. Members of the Toronto Ski Club were thrilled with their representative's success. Then it was the Ottawa Ski Club's turn for glory. Four members of the club qualified for the 1932 Lake Placid, United States winter Olympics, including William "Bud" Clark, who also qualified for the 1936 winter Olympics in Garmish-Parenkirchen, Germany.

At about this time, the Toronto Ski Club began looking for good ski hills that would test and challenge their skills. They eventually found what they were looking for on the Niagara Escarpment (see p 44) north of Barrie near Collingwood. Although the Escarpment ridge runs all the way from the Niagara peninsula to Tobermory and can be found within a short drive of Toronto, most of the ridge in the southern region is covered with good farming soil. Only in the Collingwood area does it take on mountainous proportions in a 541m-high (1,774ft) outcrop known as the Blue Mountains.

The area was already well used by the Collingwood Ski Club, which had opened in 1935 and introduced the area's first tow lift in 1938. The property that the Toronto Ski Club bought in 1940 was located right next to the Collingwood Ski Club, so people were already beginning to recognize the area as a ski haven. The development really began to take off a year later, however, when the Toronto Ski Club hired enthusiastic skier and promoter Jozo Weider. Toronto skiers started flocking to the area, and locals took up cross-country skiing as a favoured winter activity. Beaver Valley Ski Resort opened in 1948, and the Osler Bluff Ski Club opened in 1950.

Canada's first snowmaking equipment appeared in Don Mills, Ontario in 1956. Camp Fortune got snowmaking equipment a year later.

Although the 1960s were a time of increased ski development in Ontario, cross-country skiing suffered due to the introduction of a "super diagonal" binding that held the heel of a ski boot tightly to a ski and enabled a skier to take a hill faster than any previous design. While members of the earlier clubs oscillated between what they called ski jumping and ski running, the new equipment kept members close to the tow lifts, and they almost abandoned the Nordic trails that lead away from the slopes. Eventually, skiers became defined as alpine skiers or cross-country skiers. The trend was established when the Alpine Ski Club opened in 1960, along with Georgian Peaks and then Devil's Glen Ski Club in 1962. Cross-country skiing became the cheaper, less-trendy sport.

Cross-country skiing enjoyed its second heyday when ski manufacturers began replacing planks of wood with composite structures that included aluminium, carbon, engineering plastics, fibreglass, Kevlar, metals and other synthetic materials in the early 1970s. In fact, North Bay native Dave Rees, who competed for Canada in the 1968 winter Olympics in Grenoble, France, was the last Canadian racer who competed on wooden skis. The change sped cross-country skiing up considerably and led to an incredible growth in the industry that lasted for more than 10 years and helped attract younger men and more women to the sport.

The trend of more woman joining the sport enabled Canada to send its first woman's Nordic team to the 1972 winter Olympics in Sapporo, Japan. Although many women athletes have competed since then, Sue Holloway, from Ottawa, stands out as Ontario's most successful. Holloway—who also competed as part of Canada's woman's canoeing team in the summer games later that same year, as well as for the next two Olympic games—participated in the four-person 5km (3mi) Nordic relay team that took 7th place at the 1976 Olympics in Innsbruck, Austria. The feat still stands as Canada's best accomplishment in cross-country skiing.

A third growth spurt for cross-country skiing began when freestyle came into vogue. Although the skating techniques had been used in Norway since 1907, they only got wide recognition when the half skate (also known as the marathon skate) technique (see p 70) was used by Bill Koch to win the 1983 World Cup title.

Loon

Since then, both freestyle and classic competitions have been important parts of the cross-country ski scene in Ontario. The sport's reputation also increased favourably when two Ontario-based cross-country ski athletes achieved notable success for Canada in international competition. Al Pilcher,

from Orangeville, was part of the four-person 10km (6.2mi) relay team that came in 9th in the 1988 Olympics. A year later in Lahti, Switzerland, he achieved Canada's best-ever result in the Nordic World Championships by coming in 7th in the 50km (31mi) race. Angela Schmidt-Foster, from Midland, came in third at the 1987 World Cup in Canmore, qualified for the Olympics four times, and then achieved one of Canada's best Olympic finishes by coming in 29th in 1992. These successes have led more people to try out the sport, thereby creating more cross-country venues throughout the province.

Ontario's participation as host of several important international cross-country skiing events—including World Cups at Hardwood Hills (see p 222) and Thunder Bay and the 1995 Nordic World Ski Championships in Thunder Bay— has led to the development of a wide variety of impressive ski centres that benefit recreational skiers, tourists and racers alike.

Today, of three training centres for Canada's national cross-country skiing team, one is located in Thunder Bay, Ontario. This National Team Development Centre provides more than 750hrs of training per year to 12 to 15 premier athletes. The athletes compete at the regional, national and international levels between November and April.

Further Information

Canadian Ski Museum
1960 Scott St.
Ottawa, ON K1Z 8L8
☎ *(613) 722-3584*
www.skimuseum.ca

Canadian Olympic Association
85 Albert St., suite 1400
Ottawa, ON K1P 6A4
☎ *(613) 244-2020*
www.coa.ca

National Team Development Centre
www.ntdc-tbay.on.ca

Clubs and Organizations

Today, the club system for cross-country skiing has grown to the extent that it covers the entire province and now connects skiers in Ontario to similar entities around the world. The primary organizations exist to achieve recreational, competitive, safety, instructional, lobbying and marketing goals.

Recreational Clubs

Almost every community in Ontario has a recreational club that provides cross-country ski and snowshoe touring throughout the winter. Many of these clubs arose in the late 1970s. The Trakkers, for example, have been providing Sunday and weekend ski trips for Toronto residents in highway coaches to Southern Ontario ski resorts since 1978. They often combine trips with the North Toronto Ski Club. Newer clubs are also still being created in communities, particularly as they grow. One of the newer of these, for example, is the Silver Fox Nordic that was created in 1996 to serve the central community of Deep River.

All the members of these clubs are among an estimated 50,000 people from more than 400 cross-country skiing clubs across the country who jointly run Cross Country Canada, an organization that offers lessons for children, operates the National Ski Team, and runs competitive events for both strong athletes and average skiers.

Further Information

Cross Country Canada
Bill Warren Training Centre
1995 Olympic Way, Suite 100
Canmore, AB T1W 2T6
☎ *(403) 678-6791*
📠 *(403) 678-3644*
canada.x-c.com

Racing Authorities

Cross-country ski racing in Canada is controlled by Cross Country Canada through a group of provincial divisions. The Ontario division, known as Cross Country Ontario, works closely with the Ontario Federation of School Athletic Associations (OFSAA), a group that combines student-athletes, teacher-coaches, teachers, principals, and sport administrators.

Further Information

Cross Country Ontario
120 Roxborough Dr.
Sudbury, ON P3E 1J7
☎*(705) 674-4741*
www.xco.org

Ontario Federation of School Athletic Associations (OFSAA)
7880 Keele St., Suite 206
Concord, ON L4K 4G7
☎*(905) 761-5540*
⇌*(905) 761-5542*
www.ofsaa.on.ca

Instructional Organizations

Cross-country ski instructors can be trained and certified by a non-profit organization called the Canadian Association of Nordic Ski Instructors (CANSI). CANSI certifies instructors to teach four classic technique levels (numbered one through four) and three telemark technique levels (numbered one through three). A group of CANSI-certified instructors has also started the Ski Telemark school to teach telemark skiing at a variety of resorts throughout Ontario. In the United States, the Professional Ski Instructors of America includes members that teach Nordic and alpine skiing, as well as snowboarding.

Further Information

CANSI National Office
PO Box 819
Chesterville, ON K0C 1H0
☎*(613) 448-2888*
⇌*(613) 448-2820*
www.cansi.ca

Ski Telemark
R.R. #1, 1691 Oak Hill Rd.
Campbellcroft, ON L0A 1B0
☎*(905) 797-1074*
⇌*(905) 797-1072*
members.home.net/markkino/tele mark/ski-tele

Professional Ski Instructors of America
133 South Van Gordon St., Suite 101
Lakewood, Colorado 80228
☎*(303) 987-9390*
⇌*800-222-I-SKI*
www.psia.org

Masters Skiers

Skiers who are 30-years-old and older have their own international association, the World Masters Ski Association, which has divisions in many countries throughout the world. Master Skiers in Canada rely on the Canadian Masters Cross Country Association and those in the United States have the American Cross Country Skiers (AXCS). All three associations promote skiing among adults with competitions and races, with each country running its own masters' competitions.

Further Information

Canadian Masters XC
PO #503, Port-au-Port, NF A0N 1T0
x-c.com/clubs/masters
☎*(709) 648-9425*

RR#2, Kaministiquia, ON P0T 1X0
☎*(807) 933-4716*

American Cross Country Skiers (AXCS)
PO Box 604
Bend, Oregon 97709
☎*(541) 317-0217*
axcs@xcskiworld.com

Safety Volunteers

More than 5,300 volunteers serve on the Canadian Ski Patrol System (CSPS), a national organization that was created by Dr. Douglas Firth in 1940 to provide emergency assistance to skiers throughout Canada. Members of the Nordic team, which make up about 10% of the total, patrol trails in eight zones in Ontario by sweeping the trails for obstructions, looking for injured skiers and encouraging safe skiing that prevents accidents. They are well trained in first aid, cardiopulmonary resuscitation, search and rescue, evacuation, survival, emergency shelter and accident-prevention techniques. CSPS provides each member with a 40hr beginners' course that must be refreshed every year.

Further Information

Canadian Ski Patrol System (CSPS)
4531 Southclark Place
Ottawa, ON K1T 3V2
☎*(613) 822-2245*
⇋*(613) 822-1088*
www.csps.ca

Lobbying and Marketing Entities

All organizations representing skiers in Ontario are members of a national umbrella collective called the Canadian Ski Council and their provincial division— the Ontario Ski Council. The same groups have also joined with some ski centres and manufacturers, CANSI, and Tourism Ontario to promote cross-country skiing in southern Ontario. All three organizations include Biathlon Ontario, CANSI, Canadian Association for Disabled Skiing, CSPS and Cross-Country Ontario.

Cross-Country Skiing and Snowshoeing

Further Information

Canadian Ski Council
2800 Skymark Ave., Suite 32
Mississauga, ON L4W 5A6
☎ *(905) 212-9040*
⊨ *(905) 212-9041*
www.skicanada.org

Ontario Ski Council
www.snowontario.com

**The Ontario Nordic Ski
Committee**
http://www.xcontario.com

Annual Events

Over the years, cross-country ski clubs in Ontario have learned to mimic the tradition started by organizers of the American Birkebeiner in 1973. At this event, more than 9,000 skiers of every level, from the most competitive racer to the newest amateur, meet in the Cable Hayward area on the last weekend of February every year to trek across the woodlands of Wisconsin. The result is a friendly 51km (32mi) race that qualifies as North America's largest cross-country ski tournament. Although none of the Ontario races have grown to the same extent, the Keskinada Loppet near Ottawa has joined the Birkebeiner on the Worldloppet list, which includes only 14 world-class cross-country ski races.

There are lots of other great races in Ontario too, including a 24hr extravaganza called the Nordic Lappe in Thunder Bay, the Sibley Ski Tour at Sleeping Giant Provincial Park, the Porcupine Ski Loppet in Timmins, and the Wabos Wilderness Tour north of Sault Ste. Marie. All these, and more, are described below.

December

Haliburton Sprint, Glebe Park, Haliburton

The Haliburton sprint offers a short race early in the season to get skiers primed.

Further Information

Haliburton Highlands Cross-Country Ski Club
c/o Blake Paton, RR#2
Haliburton, ON K0M 1S0
☎ *(705) 457-5177 or 447-2202*
www3.sympatico.ca/bpaton/nordic/hsc.html

January

Triangle Cross-Country Ski Club Annual Loppet and Ski Tour, Brockville

This annual event offers 5km (3mi), 10km (6mi), and 15km (9mi) races for adults and seniors and a 2km (1.2mi) race for children.

Further Information

The Triangle Cross-Country Ski Club of Brockville

PO Box 127
Brockville, ON K6Y 5W2
communities.msn.com/TriangleCr ossCountrySkiClubofBrockville

Haliburton Invitational, Glebe Park, Haliburton

The Haliburton Invitational offers a full weekend of competition, for classic skiers on Saturday and freestyle competitors on Sunday. Races range from 1.5km (.9mi) for children to 15km (9mi) for adults. For further information, contact the Haliburton Highlands Cross-Country Ski Club, as listed above.

Hiawatha Invitational

This traditional weekend of classic and free-style races has been held annually for the past 45 years. Races are set up for children, elite racers, recreational skiers and skiers with disabilities.

Further Information

Soo Finnish Nordic Ski Club

c/o Bob Fadock, Race Secretary
139 East Champagne Dr.
Sault Ste. Marie, ON P6A 6S7
☎ *(705) 945-7577*
www.hiawatha.net/community/ soofinnish

Kamview Classic and Kamview Tour, Thunder Bay

The Kamview Classic and the Kamview Tour offers a weekend full of races for everyone. Classic skiers can choose the 8km (5mi) or 15km (9mi) race on Saturday, while freestyle competitors can choose either 15km (9mi) or 30km (19mi) on Sunday.

Further Information

Thunder Bay Nordic Trails

Kamview Nordic Centre
R.R.#3, Site 2, Box 9
Thunder Bay, ON P7C 4V2
☎ *(807) 475-7081*
⇒ *(807) 577-9772*
www.nordictrails- tb.on.ca/sibleytour.htm

Nakkerloppet, Ottawa

This casual backcountry tour attracts intermediate and expert skiers who travel together for 25km (15.5mi) along a rough, narrow trail. The event lasts from 4 to 6hrs.

Further Information

Nakkertok Ski Club

PO Box 4476, Postal Station "E"
Ottawa, ON K1S 5B4
www.nakkertok.ca

North Bay Invitational

The annual North Bay Invitational takes place on the

last weekend in January. Classic skiers compete on Saturday; freestylers compete on Sunday. Distances range from 7.5km (5mi) to 15km (9mi). Children ski for 1.2km (.7mi) to 3.2km (2mi), depending on their age.

Further Information

North Bay Nordic Ski Club
630 Northshore Rd.
North Bay, ON P1B 8G4
☎*(705) 495-0332*
www.onlink.net/nbmsc

February

Keskinada Loppet, Gatineau Park, Ottawa

Although the Keskinada Loppet is actually located in Québec, it's included on this list for three reasons: almost 3,000 skiers participate every year, making it Canada's largest cross-country ski race; it's only 10min from Ottawa; and it's Canada's only officially designated Worldloppet race, a ranking that puts it with the American Birkebeiner among the world's top 14 races. Classic-style racers can choose the 5km (3mi), 25km (15.5mi) or 50km (31mi) competitions on Saturday, while freestyle racers compete in 10km (6mi), 25km (15.5mi) or 50km (31mi) races on Sunday. There's also a 2km

(1.2mi) mini-Keski for children on Sunday.

Further Information

Keskinada Loppet
PO Box 554. Succ. B
Hull, QC J8Y 6P3
☎*(819) 595-0114*
⇆*(819) 595-5210*
www.keskinada.com

Laurentian Nordic Invitational
and **Sudbury Fitness Challenge Nickel Loppet**

Race distances are 15km (9mi) and 5km (3mi) for women, 30km (19mi) and 8km (5mi) for men, 1km (.6mi) and 3km (1.9mi) for children

Further Information

Darlene Klein, Race Secretary
822 Grandview Blvd.
Sudbury, ON P3A 4Z9
☎*(705) 560-0365*
⇆*(705) 560-0365*
www.vianet.ca/~rlucas/nod

Silver Spoon Classic, Deep River

This annual challenge for classic skiers includes races of 1.5km (.9mi), 3km (1.9mi) and 6km (3.7mi) distances for children, 10km (.6mi) and 15km (9mi) distances for adults, 6km (3.7mi), 10km (6.2mi) and 15km (9.3mi) distances for masters aged 51 and over, and 3.5km (2.2mi) and 8km

(5mi) distances for skiers with disabilities.

Further Information

Silver Spoon Ski Fest
c/o Ann Serdula, Race Secretary
PO Box 2126
236 Thomas St.
Deep River, ON K0J 1P0
bright-ideas-software.com/Silverspoon

Sounder Ski Tour, Parry Sound

This two-day series of competitions features both freestyle and classic races at 3km (1.9mi), 7km (4.3mi), 12km (7.4mi), and 24km (15mi).

Further Information

Georgian Nordic Ski and Canoe Club
PO Box 42
Parry Sound, ON P2A 2X2
☎(705) 746-5067 or 342-9397, Peter Wiltmann
☎(705) 746-9482, Bill Martin
☎(705) 746-4936, Tim Dyer
www.georgiannordic.com

Temiskaming Nordic Ski Loppet, New Liskeard

Participants in this one-day event can choose to ski 5km (3mi), 10km (6mi) or 20km (12mi), although only the 5km (3mi) is open to skaters.

Further Information

Temiskaming Nordic Ski Club
PO Box 2019
New Liskeard, ON P0J 1P0
☎(705) 679-5106
www.nt.net/tnsc

March

Hardwood Hundred, Barrie

Cross-country skiers try to complete 100km (62mi), 50km (31mi) or 25km (15.5mi) in one day. Awards go to a male and female 100km (62mi) finisher, to the four-person team with the best results and to the group with the best results.

Further Information

Hardwood Hills Cross Country Ski and Mountain Bike Centre
RR#1
Oro Station, ON L0L 2E0
☎(705) 487-3775
☎800-387-3775
=(705) 487-2153
www.hardwoodhills.on.ca

Highlands Loppet, Duntroon

This annual loppet attracts about 75 recreational and competitive skiers who compete for a distance of either 12.5km (7.75mi) or 25km (15.5mi). There's also a three-person 2km (1.2mi) relay for kids.

Cross-Country Skiing and Snowshoeing

Further Information

Highlands Nordic
PO Box 110
Duntroon, ON L0M 1H0
☎*(705) 444-5017*
☎*800-263-5017*
www.highlandsnordic.on.ca

Lappe Nordic

This annual 24hr relay has
attracted a few wacky individuals, although teams can
consist of up to a dozen
people. The March 31/April
1, 2001 race was particu-
larly memorable because
Werner Schwar skied
315.6km (195.7mi) in just
23hrs, beating the Canadian
record of 305km (189mi)
and the North American
record of 310km (192mi).

Further Information

Lappe Nordic Ski Club
c/o Lappe Ski Centre
Thunder Bay, ON
flash.lakeheadu.ca/~lnordic

Mabel Lake Tour

Classic skiers compete to
finish a 19km (12mi)
backcountry tour.

Further Information

Soo Finnish Nordic Ski Club
c/o Paul and Margaret Pothier
69 Ontario Ave.
Sault Ste Marie, ON P6B 1E2
☎*(705) 945-8375 (after 5:30pm)*
*www.hiawatha.net/community/
soofinnish*

Porcupine Loppet, Timmins

This annual event has taken
place every year since 1981
(except in 2000 when snow
conditions forced the Porcupine Ski Runners Club to
cancel it). The race is open
to individuals and teams.
Classic or freestyle skiers
can choose to race 10km
(6mi), 17km (10.5mi) or
25km (15.5mi).

Further Information

Porcupine Ski Runners Club
Ski Runners Rd., PO Box 250
Schumacher, ON P0N 1G0
☎*(705) 360-1444*
www.porcupineskirunners.com

Sibley Ski Tour

The year 2002 will mark the
25th anniversary of this
fabulous race. Recreational
skiers can choose to com-
plete the 10km (6mi) family
fun tour, while more ath-
letic types will want to pick
either the 20km (12mi) or
50km (31mi) challenges

Further Information

Thunder Bay Nordic Trails
Kamview Nordic Centre
RR 3, Site 2, Box 9
Thunder Bay, ON P7C 4V2
☎*(807) 475-7081*
⮱*(807) 577-9772*
*www.nordictrails-tb.on.ca/
sibleytour.htm*

Wabos Wilderness Loppet

This ski tour includes an hour-long ride on the Algoma Central Snow Trail, a 27km (16.7mi) back-country ski tour and a barbecue at Stokely Creek Lodge.

Further Information

Stokely Creek Lodge & Ski Touring Center
RR 1, Goulais River, ON POS 1EO or
PO Box 507
Sault Ste. Marie, MI 49783
☎ *(705) 649-3421*
⇌ *(705) 649-3429*
www.stokelycreek.com

Snowshoeing

Snowshoeing refers to walking along the top layer of snow by attaching flat, meshed, oval-shaped contraptions to a boot or shoe with bindings. The sport enables one to explore narrow, untracked paths that are beyond the reach of dogsleds, snowmobiles or even skis.

The sport has been enjoying a renaissance over the past couple of years, as people realize how easy and convenient it is to learn and practice. Anyone who wants to wander outside during the winter, whether for exercise, bird-watching, star-gazing, viewing the aurora borealis, or just enjoying the forests and meadows will find snowshoeing pleasurable and satisfying.

Types of Trails

In Ontario, snowshoers have access to two types of cleared and marked trails: ungroomed and groomed. Ungroomed trails are suitable for backcountry snowshoers with sturdy equipment that can be used to blaze a track or follow in the track of previous snowshoers. Groomed trails are single-track, flat, wide, smooth surfaces, which are often open to snowshoers and cross-country skiers. (Please stay off of any trail that's trackset for cross-country skiing.)

Styles

At one time, all snowshoes were made of large wooden frames that were wide enough to hold the weight of a person on many types of snow, rawhide lace decking (this is the meshed portion), and leather bindings, but today's modern versions are made of aluminum, plastic and other synthetics. While these newer materials make snowshoes smaller and lighter than they once were, it's still their shape that determines whether a snowshoe is used for recre-

Cross-Country Skiing and Snowshoeing

ational, sportive or mountaineering purposes.

Recreational

Recreational, or touring, snowshoes have large oval frames with a long tail at the back for balance.

Sport

Racing or athletic snowshoes are very small ovals that are almost round, without tails.

Mountaineering

Mountaineering snowshoes have large oval frames, without a tail, and with toe and/or heal claws that enable the shoe to grip icy services. This type of snowshoe is meant to be used with snow poles.

History

Modern myth suggests that snowshoes were developed in northern Asia about 4,000 to 6,000 years ago. They were then brought to North America and Finland by a group of wanderers, some of whom crossed the Bering Strait, and others who walked to Karelia, Finland, where they memorialized the activity with thousands of rock carvings that date back 3,500 to 5,000 years.

It's just as likely, however, that North American Aboriginal groups learned how to construct snowshoes by watching animals walking easily on the snow. They could have designed snowshoes to enable their own feet to do the same thing.

It is known that Aboriginal groups have been using snowshoes for hunting and checking traplines in the winter for thousands of years.

Clubs and Organizations

Snowshoeing hasn't yet developed beyond a means of transportation or light recreation in Ontario yet, although many ski clubs, hiking clubs, running clubs, ski resorts and parks are beginning to offer the activity as a complementary sideline to their cross-country skiing events. The sport is particularly appealing for older Canadians who can't move as fast as they once did, and for families who want to take their time introducing young children to the winter outdoors in a safe, non-crowded environment. Enthusiastic bird-watchers and hikers who want to explore their favourite wilderness trails will also find snowshoes an ideal way to get into areas that can't be groomed, such as to the tops of rock formations or into deeply forested regions.

Anyone interested in the sport should look for a local hiking or cross-country ski club to join and influence.

Profile of Ontario

When it comes to winter scenery, Ontario benefits from its immense size, extreme climate, diverse topography, major glacial landforms, numerous lakes, stunning waterfalls and scenic canals. The region also provides winter habitat for many birds and mammals, ensuring that skiers and snowshoers will enjoy incredibly diverse experiences.

Size

Ontario is so large and oddly shaped that it covers both Eastern and Central time zones. It covers 1,068,580km^2 (412,579 sq mi), 10.7% of Canada's total landmass. Land makes up 83% of its total area, while water makes up the remaining 17%. The territory encompasses cities and countryside, 807,000km^2 (31,158 sq mi) of

vast forests and 17,610km^2 (6,799 sq mi) of rocky tundra beyond the tree line.

The province borders on five U.S. states (Minnesota, Michigan, Ohio, Pennsylvania and New York), two Canadian provinces (Manitoba and Québec), four of the five Great Lakes (Superior, Huron, Erie, and Ontario), and two bays (Hudson and James).

Climate and Its Effect on Temperature

Because of its large size, the number of climatic zones in Ontario ranges from a minimum of three to at least 14, depending on which variables are considered. Wladimir Köppen's system, for instance, divides Ontario into three distinct regions based on a comparison with worldwide precipitation, temperature and vegetation. When the U.S. Department of Agriculture published a map of climatic zones for North America, however, it chose to consider only one variable: minimum winter temperature. That map divides Ontario into five zones. When Agriculture Canada performed the same exercise in

Canada goose

the 1960s, the department compared low winter temperatures, frost-free period, summer and winter precipitation, summer high temperatures, snow depth, wind speed and the hardiness of 174 shrubs at 108 stations throughout Canada. Its map divides Ontario into 14 zones.

All this is to say that the more you know about Ontario, the more local variations in climate you find. Thanks to the effects of latitude, summers are generally hot in the south, and cooler as you move north but there are many variations to the rule because of the effect of local landforms, prevailing winds and proximity to water. Winter temperatures vary to an even greater degree. While winter is cold across the province, it is frigid in the north. Average winter temperatures vary from −18.5°C (-1.3°F) in Kapuskasing to 6.7°C (44.1°F) in Toronto. Local wind speeds exacerbate the effects. Thunder Bay also wins the superlatives in this category, because it holds Ontario's record for the coldest day according to wind chill. On January 10, 1982, the local temperature in Thunder Bay dropped to −36°C (-32.8°F) with a wind speed of 54km/hr (33mph) for a windchill temperature that reached -70°C (94°F).

Humidity exacerbates the effect of cold temperatures on skiers. The level of humidity in a region depends on its proximity to large bodies of water and the prevailing winds. Prevailing winds have a role because they carry moisture as they move from west to east. Perhaps not surprisingly, humidity is very high in the south and on coastal areas and lower in the northwest.

Despite all these variations, for the most part, Ontario's weather is quite predictable, although frequently changing. When preparing for your trip, call ahead to the region you want to visit and ask locals what the weather's like. Then prepare for anything to happen, from a wild snowstorm to unseasonably-warm temperatures.

The Unbearable Importance of Snow

For skiers and snowshoers, the presence of snow and the effects of the temperature on it are the most important factors for a successful day of skiing or snowshoeing.

For the most part, Ontario receives plenty of snow of all types. Annual precipitation, which includes snow, is highest in southwestern Ontario (London), with

909.4mm (36in) and lowest in the northwest (Thunder Bay) with 711.2mm (28in). Average annual snowfall ranges from a low of 131.2cm (51in) in Toronto to a high of 319.9cm (125in) in Kapuskasing. Most places average about 200cm (78in) a year.

Yet precipitation amounts don't tell the whole story. High temperatures affect the snow cover and the type of snow received to such a great degree that there's often no snow at all in southern Ontario, while the snowbelt region—an arc that leads east from Georgian Bay between Owen Sound and Orangeville through to Orillia and Bracebridge—suffers snow storm after snow storm.

Not surprisingly, many of the developed ski resorts in Ontario are within a snow belt where deep snow-cover is almost guaranteed for most of the winter. Yet ski clubs in this region still rely heavily on snowmaking equipment to extend and improve the season. That's because it isn't the presence of snow alone that ensures a great day of skiing or snowshoeing; the type and consistency of snow crystals, how they combine, and what happens to them on the ground also matters.

A system devised by the 1951 International Commis-

sion on Snow and Ice classifies snow crystals into seven basic forms and three non-snow forms. These snowflake types include:

- common snowflakes (irregular crystals)
- star snowflakes (stellar crystals or spatial dendrites)
- smooth, drifting flakes (needle crystals)
- smooth flakes that have been shaved almost straight on the edges (column crystals)
- moist, large wet flakes (plate crystals)
- jagged chunks (asymetrical crystals)
- dry, non-packing flakes (powder crystals)
- ice pellets (graupel)
- frost (hoarfrost) and
- granular ice tufts (rime)

Some of these snowflakes combine as they fall from the sky in a process known as precipitated snow. Snow that changes as it travels to or lies on the ground is called metamorphosed snow. Snowshoers and cross-country skiers rely on a good base of airy metamorphosed snow for a deep snow base that has enough air to stay friable, yet is still packed enough to provide glide.

Many experts have decided to borrow words from Alaskan Aboriginal, Russian and Japanese languages to describe the types of snow that exist. Some of the types that skiers and snowshoers need to take into account include:

- falling or precipitated snow (*anniu* or *aniu* from Inupiat)
- ground snow (*api* from Inupiat)
- fresh snow or powder (*nutaryuk* from Yup'ik)
- bottom snow layer, depth hoar or corn (*pukak* from Inupiat)
- snow drift (*kimoaqtruk* from Inupiat)
- drifting snow or sugar (*siqoq* from Inupiat)
- sun crust, breakable crust or cement snow (*siqoqtoaq* from Yup'ik and Inupiat)
- wind packed snow or crud (*upsik* from Inupiat)
- windblown drifts that look like waves of water or windslab (*sastrugi* from Russian)
- smooth fine snow surface (*salumaroaq* from Inupiat)
- deep snow requiring snowshoes or fluff (*det-thlo(k)* from Athabaskan)
- rough large-flaked snow surface (*natatgonaq* from Inupiat)

There doesn't seem to be any term for the slang word "glop," however, which means wet snow lying on the ground and spells disaster for both snowshoers and cross-country skiers. (Since glop frequently occurs in some parts of Ontario, I recommend that you pack a pair of waterproof hiking boots along with your ski or snowshoe equipment.)

Trails covered with wind-packed snow are ideal conditions for recreational touring, while those with snow drifts or drifting snow might require heavier backcountry equipment. Trails covered in a hard icy shell of snow require equipment that is as light as possible for floatation while being as wide as possible for even weight distribution. It should also have a strong gripping mechanism, whether of wax, scales or clamps.

Skiers and snowshoers need to recognize the type of snow they're likely to confront on a trip to decide if they require equipment with good gripping action, as they might need for graupel, or equipment with a tendency to glide easily over moist wet snow, which is often sticky.

Since the possibilities for different combinations of snow cover and snow consistency are almost endless, a skier or snowshoer usually compromises in choosing equipment of the appropriate size, weight and required grip ability for the snow conditions that exist. Powder crystals—which sometimes fall from the sky or, as is more often the case, are created by snow guns—are the ideal snow-flake type, since they don't stick or pack. Any skier or snowshoer can travel on powder with just about any equipment. So just keep wishing for more powder!

Topography

Ontario includes four major topographic regions: the Canadian Shield (also known as the Precambrian Shield), the Hudson Bay Lowland, the St. Lawrence Lowland and the Great Lakes Lowland.

The largest of these is the Canadian Shield, which covers about two-thirds of the province in an arc around Hudson Bay. This ancient plateau once held towering mountains of hardened volcano magma and tough bedrock hardened by heat or a combination of heat, water and pressure. Known as the La Cloche range, the mountains were thrust up by volcanoes 3.8 million years ago. Since then, the tops of the mountains have disappeared, as a result of erosion by four glaciers, wind and water. The result is a layer of rock that lies very close to the surface and slopes gently toward the north. A southeastern extension of the Canadian Shield, which is known as the Frontenac Axis, separates

the St. Lawrence and Great Lakes lowlands. The Frontenac Axis forms the Thousand Islands in the St. Lawrence River and ends as the Adirondack Mountains of New York. Skiers in the southern portion of the Canadian Shield and along the Frontenac Axis can see jagged outcrops of some of the oldest rock on the planet. Skiing and snow-shoeing in this region is primarily a backcountry experience, along rocky, slippery trails.

The Hudson Bay Lowland is a subarctic area of flat bogs and small trees that circles Hudson Bay. There are no roads through the region and much of it is inaccessible to skiers. This is the kind of region that can only be discovered on long snowshoe treks that involve backcountry camping and preferably skijoring.

The St. Lawrence Lowland is a flat—less than 91m-high (300ft)—plain of sand and clay that extends along the St. Lawrence River into Québec. Much of the region has been developed, although there are many lakes alongside the nature trails and throughout the backcountry areas. The region is bordered on the west by the Ottawa-Bonnechere Graben, a fault in the earth's crust that has created a series of giant rippling pink boulder ridges

Cross-Country Skiing and Snowshoeing

that provide great back-drops for snowshoeing and cross-country skiing.

The Great Lakes Lowland region is that portion of Ontario that lies south of the Niagara Escarpment. The area is mostly flat, al-though some rivers have dug deep gorges and val-leys that collect and keep the snow longer than sur-rounding regions, making them prime ski and snow-shoe destinations.

Major Glacial Landforms

Ontario has several major landforms left behind by the glaciers. Some of the most significant, including the Niagara Escarpment, the Oak Ridges Moraine and the Sleeping Giant, offer magnificent scenery to skiers and snowshoers.

The Niagara Escarpment

Glaciers left a 736km-long (442mi) horseshoe-shaped ridge between Queenston and Tobermory called the Niagara Escarpment. The northern 80km (50mi) por-tion of the escarpment juts out into Lake Huron and is known as the Bruce Penin-sula. Ontario's oldest trail, the Bruce Trail runs for 800km (496mi) across the landmark. Much of the trail is perfect for snowshoeing or backcountry skiing.

The Oak Ridges Moraine

Another ridge, the Oak Ridges Moraine, runs for about 200km (124mi) from the Niagara Escarpment in the west to the Trent River in the east. Some of this trail can be used for snow-shoeing or skiing.

The Sleeping Giant

Glaciers and erosion have helped create a giant rock formation that looks exactly like Gulliver in the land of the Lilliputians. The forma-tion is now protected within Sleeping Giant Provincial Park (see p 343). The park grooms several trails for cross-country skiing.

Lakes and Rivers

Snowshoers and skiers will appreciate the views along the many trails that navigate beside and over water. The many fast-flowing rivers and open bodies of warm water that don't freeze attract a great many birds looking for winter food, while the many more frozen lakes and rivers are used by wolves and other wildlife as easy travel corri-dors. Such opportunities for bird and wildlife viewing are endless. Freshwater covers 17% of Ontario, although—thanks to the 1,094km (680mi) shoreline along James and Hudson bays—some residents also have access to saltwater. Much of that water comes from Lake of the Woods and four of the five Great Lakes, which are jointly controlled by Canada and the United States. Together, the five Great Lakes make up the world's biggest continuous body of fresh water. The province also lays claim to 250,000 other lakes, many of which are located in the west. Big lakes include Lake Nipigon, Lac Seul, Lake Abitibi (shared with Québec), Lake Nipissing, Lake Simcoe, Rainy Lake, and Big Trout Lake.

Lake Huron and Lake Superior are also known for their frosty ice formations that are created as the fast-moving ice floes freeze into solid waves. Only parts of Lake Ontario freeze over during the winter, but skiers passing those spots along the Waterfront Trail (see p 372) can watch locals ice fishing in tiny huts that dot the wide span of solid, flat ice.

Waterfalls

Ontario's waterfalls look like fairy ice castles in the winter as the sun shines on ice sculptures that have frozen in a halo around a stream of fast-moving water in the centre of a pink or grey mound of rock.

The Niagara River flows between Lake Erie and Lake Ontario, creating the scenic Niagara Falls as it goes. Niagara Falls is Ontario's most popular falls, but it certainly isn't the only one. Balls Falls on the Niagara Peninsula is also located nearby, with two different falls.

Other towns also have waterfalls that make them proud. Kakabeka Falls (see p 334) near Thunder Bay are the northern version of Niagara. Owen Sound is home to three scenic waterfalls—Inglis Falls (see p 230), Jones Falls and Indian Falls. The town of Elora has its own falls that tumbles over the tooth of time.

There's also Recollet Falls on the French River, Healey Falls in Campbellford, and Hilton Falls, in a conservation area of the same name near Milton.

Cross-Country Skiing and Snowshoeing

Canals

Three canals have been dug in Ontario: the Welland Canal, the Rideau Canal and the Trent-Severn Waterway, all of which provide good travel corridors for wildlife and interesting historical viewing for winter visitors. Skiing and snowshoeing opportunities exist along and beside each route.

The **Welland Canal** bypasses Niagara Falls to link Lake Erie with Lake Ontario, which—thanks to the Niagara Escarpment—sits 100m (326.5ft) above. The existing canal runs 42km (26mi) from Lock 1 in St. Catharines to Lock 8 at Port Colborne, but three older versions also exist.

The **Trent-Severn Waterway** runs for 386km (240mi) from Trenton to Port Severn. A system of 44 locks connects Lakes Rice, Lovesick, Buckhorn, Pigeon, Sturgeon, Stony, Balsam, Simcoe and Couchiching.

Originally built to serve as a protected supply route after the War of 1812, the **Rideau Canal** connects Ottawa and Kingston. The Rideau Trail (see p 282) follows part of the 202km (126mi) route of 47 locks and 24 dams that allows ships to climb the Canadian Shield.

Winter Bird-Watching

There at least 86 varieties of bird species that spend the winter in various parts of Ontario. The shores of the Great Lakes are ideal spots for winter birdwatching, in particular for canvasbacks, common crows, common flickers, common loons, common mergansers, common scoters, Glaucous gulls, gray partridges, great black-backed gulls, horned larks, red-breasted mergansers and surf-scoters. Thanks to the shelter of the Niagara Escarpment, the southern part of the province, along with Toronto and Niagara hosts a great number of birds that wouldn't normally be found at such a high latitude, including American kestrels, American goldfinches, American robins, blue birds, Canada geese, Coopers hawks, and white-breasted nuthatches. In northern and central Ontario, look for Bohemian waxwings, boreal chickadees, boreal owls, golden eagles and gray jays. For a complete list of the birds that winter in Ontario, refer to Appendix 1.

Where to Ski and Snowshoe in Ontario

Public Lands

Ontario has many types of publicly held lands accessible to skiers and snowshoers.

National Parks

There are 18 national parks and historic sites in Ontario. The parks, which have the best skiing and snowshoeing opportunities are: Bruce Peninsula National Park (see p 155); Fathom Five National Marine Park; Georgian Bay Islands National Park; Point Pelee National Park (see p 181), Pukaskwa National Park. The Fort St. Joseph, Rideau Canal and Sault Ste. Marie Canal national historic sites also have trails suitable for snowshoeing and cross-country skiing.

Further Information

Parks Canada National Headquarters
25 Eddy St.
Hull QC K1A 0M5
☎(819) 997- 0797
☏(819) 953-8770
parkscanada.pch.gc.ca

Provincial Parks

There are more than 270 provincial parks in Ontario, and many offer groomed cross-country trails and snowshoeing trails. Some of the most interesting have been mentioned throughout this portrait. The ones with the best trails are covered in the regional chapters of this guide.

Further Information

The Ontario Ministry of Natural Resources Information Centre
900 Bay St., room M1-73
Toronto, ON M7A 2C1
☎*(416) 314-2000 (English)*
☎*800-667-1940 (English)*
☎*800-667-1840 (French)*
(Note: attendants at these numbers can also transfer you directly to the parks.)

Ontario Parks
300 Water St.
Peterborough, ON K9J 8M5
☎*888-668-7275 reservations*
www.OntarioParks.com

Ontario Tourism
☎*(416) 314-6557 TDD*
☎*800-ONTARIO (668-2746, English)*
☎*800-268-3736 (French)*

Conservation Areas

Conservation authorities are partners with the provincial government, member municipalities and local water

Cross-Country Skiing and Snowshoeing

1. Ausable Bayfield	14. Kettle Creek	27. Otonabee
2. Cataraqui Region	15. Lake Simcoe Region	28. Quinte
3. Catfish Creek	16. Lakehead Region	29. Raisin Region
4. Central Lake Ontario	17. Long Point Region	30. Rideau Valley
5. Conservation Halton	18. Lower Thames Valley	31. Saugeen
6. Credit Valley	19. Lower Trent	32. Sault Ste. Marie
7. Crowe Valley	20. Maitland Valley	Region
8. Essex Region	21. Mattagami Region	33. South Nation
9. Ganaraska Region	22. Mississippi Valley	34. St. Clair Region
10. Grand River	23. Niagara Peninsula	35. Toronto and Region
11. Grey-Sauble	24. Nickel District	36. Upper Thames River
12. Hamilton Region	25. North Bay - Mattawa	
13. Kawartha	26. Nottawasaga Valley	

Conservation Authorities

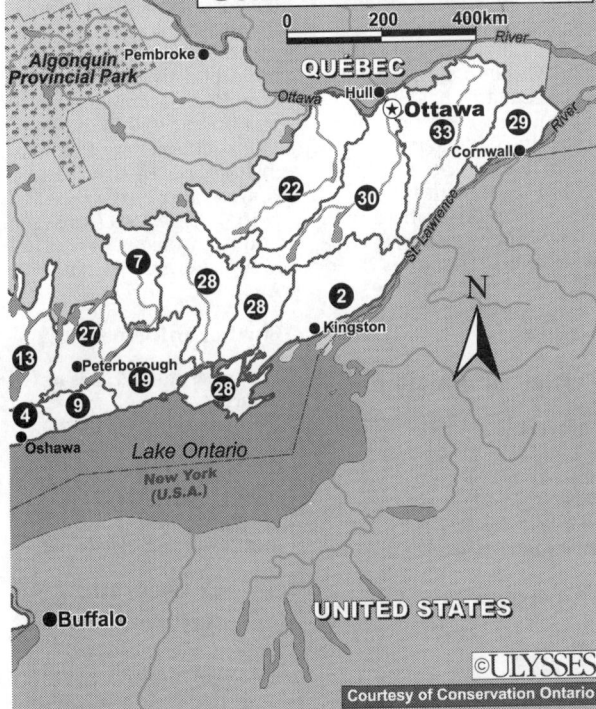

0   200   400km

QUÉBEC

Algonquin Provincial Park
Pembroke

Ottawa River

Hull
★ Ottawa
33
29
Cornwall

22
30

7
28
28
2
Kingston

27
13
Peterborough
19
28
9
4
Oshawa

Lake Ontario

New York (U.S.A.)

Buffalo

UNITED STATES

©ULYSSES
Courtesy of Conservation Ontario

Northern Ontario

Lake Nipigon
Hearst
QUÉBEC

Marathon
Chapleau Crown Game Preserve
Timmins
Rouyn-Noranda

16
Thunder Bay
Lake Superior
Wawa
21
Réserve faunique de La Vérendrye

Lake Superior Provincial Park
Chapleau

24

UNITED STATES
Sault St.Mary
32
Sudbury
North Bay
25
Mattawa

Lake Michigan
Manitoulin Island
Killarney Prov. Park
Parry Sound
Algonquin Provincial Park
Huntsville

Lake Huron
Georgian Bay
Wasaga Beach

Owen Sound
Peterborough

0   300   600km

experts in organizations that are mandated to protect and maintain all the public land within a single watershed. Ontario has 36 such authorities. Each one owns a group of conservation areas that has been established to prevent flood, erosion and the prime natural resources within each watershed. The areas offer a variety of opportunities to skiing and snowshoeing enthusiasts.

Further Information

Conservation Ontario
Box 11, 120 Bayview Parkway
Newmarket, ON L3Y 4W3
☎(905) 895-0716
⇌(905) 895-0751
www.conservation-ontario.on.ca

Conservation Lands of Ontario

Five conservation authorities have joined together in a unique marketing entity called The Conservation Lands of Ontario (CLO). Since it was created in 1997, CLO has tried many different ways to increase shoulder and off-season business. It has been successful with three projects so far: offering adventure packages to major corporations like Canada Life and Nortel, publishing trail books and selling bottled water. The organization is still receiving seed money from the conservation authorities, but has already generated funds for several special environmental projects deemed important by the conservation areas. Members that are mentioned within the regional chapters in this guide include: Backus Heritage Conservation Area (see p 153), Crawford Conservation Area (see p 94) and Mountsberg Conservation Area (see p 107).

Further Information

The Conservation Lands of Ontario
400 Clyde Rd., PO Box 729
Cambridge, ON N1R 5W6
☎(519) 621-2761
☎888-376-2212
⇌(519) 621-4844
www.conservationlands.com

Conservation Nature Tours

The Saugeen Valley and Grey Sauble Conservation Authorities have teamed up to offer nature vacations and courses within their conservation areas. They haven't started offering cross-country skiing and snowshoeing yet, but plan to do so soon.

Further Information

Conservation Nature Tours
c/o Saugeen Valley Conservation Authority
RR 1 Hanover, ON N4N 3B8
☎888-301-4CNT (268)
⇌(519) 364-6990
svca.on.ca/naturetours

Botanical Gardens and Arboretums

Thanks to dedicated organizations and individuals, Ontario has 17 botanical gardens, many of which include large plant collections and arboretums that make good skiing and snowshoeing destinations. The larger ones include the Ottawa Arboretum, the Centennial Botanical Conservatory in Thunder Bay, the Claude E. Garton Herbarium and the Arboretum at Lakehead University in Thunder Bay, the Humber Arboretum in Rexdale, the Royal Botanical Gardens in Hamilton and the University of Guelph Arboretum.

Further Information

The Canadian Botanical Conservation Network
c/o The Royal Botanical Gardens
PO Box 399
Hamilton, ON L8N 3H8
www.rbg.ca/cbcn

The Humber Arboretum has been open seven days a week, year-round since it opened in 1982. The 96,237ha (237,705-acre) park contains 3km (2mi) of self-guided trails, a Nature Orientation Centre, a circular wooden viewing deck and the Dunington Grubb Gardens. The 10ha (25-acre) Woodlot and Meadow Garden contains Carolinian hardwood forest of ash, maple, beech and ironwood encircling a naturalized meadow of more than 5,000 plants, and makes for a prime skiing or snowshoeing area.

Further Information

The Humber Arboretum
☎ *(416) 675-5009*
www.metrotor.on.ca/services/parks/parks/humar.html

The Federation of Ontario Naturalists

The Federation of Ontario Naturalists started what has become Ontario's largest non-governmental nature reserve system in 1961. So far, the program has preserved 18 properties with a total of 1,488ha (3,676 acres) of imperiled and vulnerable habitat. Within these properties are countless rare and endangered species, including the spotted turtle, the blue racer snake, the ram's head lady slipper orchid and the bald eagle.

Although the lands are primarily biological reserves, Bruce Alvar Nature Reserve, Kinghurst Forest Nature Reserve, Petrel Point Nature Reserve and Stone Road Alvar Nature Reserve have short interpretive trails suitable for skiing and snowshoeing. These areas are very sensitive, and care must be taken to stay on the trails.

Cross-Country Skiing and Snowshoeing

Further Information

The Federation of Ontario Naturalists
355 Lesmill Rd.
Don Mills, ON M3B 2W8
☎ *(416) 444-8419*
☎ *800-440-2366 (within Ontario)*
⟿ *(416) 444-9866*
www.ontarionature.org

Private Lands

Many private land owners who specialize in cross-country skiing, including Dagmar (see p 96), Haliburton Nordic Trails (see p 225), Hardwood Hills (see p 222), Fern (see p 217), Horseshoe Valley (see p 228), Sherwood Inn (see p 247), and Wigamog (see p 254) belong to a marketing organization known as "Ski Ontario," which is officially registered under the name "Ontario Snow Resorts Association."

Further Information

Ontario Snow Resorts Association
125 Napier St., PO Box 575
Collingwood, ON L9Y 4E8
☎ *(705) 443-5450*
⟿ *(705) 443-5460*
www.skiontario.on.ca

Tour Operators and Wilderness Educators

Many private companies in Ontario offer trips and courses that include snow-shoeing and cross-country skiing. They include:

Alba Wilderness School and Nature Experiences
RR. #4,
Lanark, ON K0G 1K0
☎ *(613) 259-3236*
☎ *800-477-0423*
www.magma.ca/~alba

Algonquin Outfitters
RR 1
Dwight, ON P0A 1H0
☎ *(705) 635-2243*
⟿ *(705) 635-1834*
www.algonquinoutfitters.com

Muskoka Outfitters
40 Manitoba St.
Bracebridge, ON P1L 1S1
☎ *(705) 646-0492*
⟿ *(705) 646-0493*
www.muskokaoutfitters.com
www.snowshoeing.ca

Tracks and Trails
RR 2
Creemore, ON L0M 1G0
☎ *(705) 446-1444*
www.tracksandtrails.com

Trips & Trails Nordic Ski and Cycle
258 Hastings St. N., PO Box 1650
Bancroft, ON L0L 1C0
☎ *(613) 332-1969*
☎ *800-481-2925*
⟿ *(613) 339-2807*
www.mwdesign.net/tipstrail

YMCA Wanakita
RR 2
Haliburton, ON K0M 1S0
☎ *(705) 457-2132*
☎ *800-387-5081*
⟿ *(705) 457-1597*

Practical Information

This chapter includes all the information you'll need to prepare for a cross-country skiing or snowshoeing trip.

This includes: off-season training; what to wear; the equipment you'll require and how to care for it; warming up and cooling down; a basic description of skiing and snowshoeing techniques; trail etiquette and safety; racing rules and regulations; a brief guide to the potential illnesses, such as hypothermia, that could affect you while on the trail; and checklists for day trip necessities, overnight necessities and handy items.

Off-Season Training

If you want to avoid sore muscles, frustration, or injury in the first month of a season that starts in late November at the earliest, you'll want to do some training before the winter snow hits. It doesn't have to be the kind of training that elite athletes do, though. The trick to having a good cross-country skiing or snowshoeing season is to have a good season doing whatever else you like to do off-season, whether it's aerobics, baseball, cycling, hiking, in-line skating, running, soccer or tennis. In-line skating will probably help cross-country skiing the most, particularly if you choose to roller ski instead, while hiking will probably improve your snowshoeing season. Whatever off-season sports you prefer, the idea is to build and keep a habit of exercising your arms and legs all year round.

If you haven't kept the exercise habit throughout the year, you can begin preparing about a month before you want to ski or snowshoe. Plan to exercise for about an hour every second day. Alternate between three types of exercise: a cardiovascular workout that builds endurance, such as running, biking, swimming or rowing at comfortable speeds; general strength building exercises that emphasizes multiple repetitions of small leg and arm weights; and a specific strength-building exercise, such as roller skiing or hiking that will test the muscles (both legs and arms) that you're planning to stress. You'll also want to take in a sauna, massage or whirlpool session at least once a week, to break up all the tension building up in your muscles. If you plan to race during the season, include some speed training in the mix, such as interval or pace training, and gradually increase the regimen to more than an hour a day.

If you can't train before the season starts, and can't wait to get on the trails anyway, spend the first two weeks of the season doing short runs on flat trails. Increase your time and effort progressively over the third

week and you will avoid the muscle pain altogether.

If you haven't done anything all year and you want to get out onto the snow anyway, just take it easy and expect some muscle soreness for a couple of days after your initial efforts.

What to Wear

It's always shocking how quickly weather conditions can change while you're out on the trail. If it seems quite cold when you start out, you'll probably start sweating as soon as the visitor centre is beyond easy reach. Even if it's pleasantly warm and sunny, a snowstorm just may hit the area by lunchtime. The only way to stay comfortable all day is to wear many layers so that you can add and remove items as temperatures and humidity change. Plan on bringing four different layers—undergarments, main clothing, warm clothing, and waterproof (or snow proof) clothing.

Undergarments

Begin with **loose, breathable underwear** of whatever type you prefer. Whether you choose panties, jockey shorts, briefs or undershirts, consider those made of a polyester Lycra blend that bends easily and dries quickly. (The drying factor will make all the difference in keeping you warm.) Women should consider wearing a quick-drying **sports bra** that is designed both for comfortable movement as well as breast support. Snowshoers might want to consider **long johns**, although cross-country skiers rarely need such warmth. Next comes a pair of **liner socks**, preferably a brand new quick-drying synthetic type, although cranky old-timers still prefer cotton.

Main Clothing

The old-timers know what they're talking about in the pants department. You'll easily exchange style for comfort with a pair of old-fashioned **knee-length jodhpurs** made of corduroy or heavy cotton. Failing those, simply wear a pair of **loose-fitting comfortable pants** that enable your legs to move easily. If you're racing or training heavily, you might want to consider **tight Lycra nylon tights** that breath well without getting in your way. Next comes a **light, loose-fitting long-sleeved shirt**, preferably a **turtleneck** to protect your neck from wind, although many skiers choose to wear a regular shirt and a **scarf** or **dickie** (the neck-only portion of a turtleneck). Just be sure that the scarf is tied well so that it can't get caught in a branch along the trail.

Warm Clothing

Consider wearing long **cross-country ski socks** that protect your feet and your lower legs, or a pair of new warmth-enhancing **thermal socks**. (These new socks are made of combinations of nylon, wool, spandex, cotton, acrylic and polyester fleece, so you can choose the most comfortable type for you. They cost a fortune, but they're worth it.) A warm breathable **fleece jacket**, of whichever thickness you need for adequate warmth comes next. (Fleeces come in light, medium and heavy thicknesses, so that you can choose the right combination of warmth and weight for the conditions you will likely face.) Snowshoers might also want some lighter **fleece pants**, but they are rarely necessary for cross-country skiers. Last but not least, don warm comfortable **gloves** (or **gloves and liners**) that bend easily to grip poles. Always wear a **hat**, preferably one that covers the ears, to prevent 80% of your body's warmth from escaping into the cold. If you tend to get a cold face, or when conditions are very cold, consider wearing a **balaclava** that combines a hat with a facemask.

Waterproof/ Snowproof Layer

Top with a **waterproof windbreaker**, made of Gore-Tex, Entrant or other such material. You may also want to bring some **waterproof overpants** in case of a storm, or in case you want to sit down at lunch. Good **boots** are important, too. Invest in a warm waterproof pair that protects your ankles while enabling easy heel lifting, and your feet will thank you. If you're an expert planning lots of backcountry trips, you may want to wear climbing boots that will still grip the snow and ice when you choose to remove your skis or snowshoes. Snowshoers and backcountry skiers will want to wear **gaiters** to keep the snow out of their boots.

Other Important Items

Wear a **watch**. You'll want to keep track of the time, especially if planning a trip on a long or circuitous trail.

Consider wearing a **fanny or travel pack** close to your body to carry money and identification.

You now have enough layers to face just about any weather or circumstances. Don't be too concerned if you feel a bit like frosty the snowman all bundled up; you'll rarely wear all the layers at one time, and when you do, you'll appreciate every synthetic warmth-capturing waterwhisking fibre in the ensemble.

Cross-Country Skiing Equipment Basics

The type of cross-country skiing you plan to do will determine how you want to equip yourself. Most beginning and intermediate skiers will be well served by the racing and touring packages—many of which are waxless—set up by each manufacturer every year. Each package includes skis, boots and bindings for either racing or touring for an approximate cost ranging from a couple of hundred dollars up to just under a thousand dollars. Second-hand equipment is also available, particularly from rental shops at the end of the season.

Avid skiers will prefer to select skis, boots and bindings that meet individual specifications, depending on which activities one chooses most often.

The selection of proper **skis**, for example, means combining the ideal width, with the proper stiffness and bend, the right length and a waxable or waxless grip zone. **Ski width** can be either narrow or wide; narrow skis are better for track-set conditions, while wider skis make trailblazing in deep snow a joy. The **stiffness and bend of a ski's arch** is represented in "ski jargon" as single or double cambered. Single cambered skis are designed to work best on flat or rolling terrain, while double cambered skis allow for more precise turning and easier ski management on a downhill grade. **Length** usually depends on your weight, height and whether you want to ski in the classic form, which requires longer skis (usually above a person's head by one arm-length); the free-style skating form, with shorter skis; the telemark form with shorter skis that have metal edges and a narrow middle; or a hybrid length that allows for more than one activity (not the best choice). While skating skis don't have a **grip zone**, all the other types of cross-country skis require wax or scales to create a grip zone. The multiple possible combinations of all these different properties are usually represented in a multitude of models based on six different levels of activity: classic cross-country racing, classic cross-country touring (many of which are waxless), skating racing, skating touring, backcountry and telemark.

Parts of the Ski

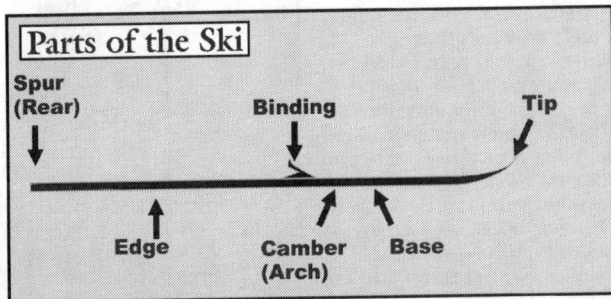

Spur (Rear)   Binding   Tip

Edge   Camber (Arch)   Base

The biggest decision for classic skiers is between **waxless and waxable skis**. Purists claim that the waxless skis don't perform as well as their wax-needing cousins, but others claim that the time saved makes up for the inconvenience. If you're a beginner or intermediate skier, waxless skis are probably fine, although you will notice that they sometimes slip on very cold days, especially if the trails get too icy. In very icy conditions, you can klister the scales, but removing the wax can get very messy and can take some time. More experienced skiers will find that properly waxed skis grip better than waxless skis in almost all conditions. A skier with waxed skis can move faster, make tighter turns and stop more easily than waxless skis allow.

Boots come in racing, touring or climbing models, with either toe or cable bindings that vary in strength, depending on the style of skiing you plan to use (skating bindings limit heel movement) and whether you plan to ski on groomed trails or along steeper backcountry locations. The classic styles are cut just above the ankle and have a soft sole that enables a skier to raise a heel easily. Skating boots are higher, so as to better support the ankles, with a stiffer sole to limit heel movement.

When it comes to **bindings**, the type is not as important as is your ability to release them easily. Modern toe and cable bindings that can be released with a pole are ideal, although try them out in the store before buying to make sure you like them. If you're purchasing used skis, you might face the option of buying boots and skis with three-pointed toe bindings, which are difficult to use, clog easily with snow and wear out over time. Make sure the price is low enough to make the inconvenience worth the trouble.

There isn't much selection in terms of **poles** for classic skiers or skaters—in fact, shorter skiers often find themselves cutting poles to the required length, which is 85% of a person's height for classic skiing or 90% for skating. Beginning or purely recreational classic

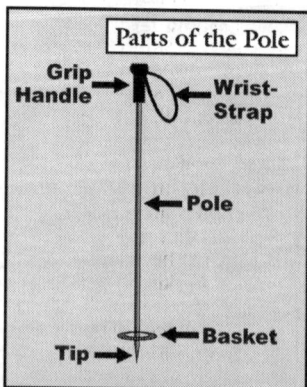

Parts of the Pole

Grip Handle → ← Wrist-Strap

← Pole

← Basket

Tip →

poles are usually a bit shorter, and should reach to about a person's arm pits. **Backcountry** poles are much thicker and sturdier, with larger baskets at the end.

Backcountry, telemark and biathlon skiers will also require **synthetic mohair skins** for climbing steep ungroomed trails and **gaiters** to prevent the snow from getting into their boots.

Other potential equipment includes: a **biathlon rifle**, **carrying harness**, **snow cover** and **"speed sling"** for biathletes; a **pulka** (see p 60) for pulling small children; and a **dog harness**, **lead** and **belt** for skijoring.

Snowshoeing Equipment Basics

Besides snowshoes and harnesses, no additional equipment is required for snowshoeing. If you like, you can use ski poles to give your arms a workout or to provide support when climbing a hill.

A snowshoe has three parts: a frame, decking and a harness. **Frames** are made of wood, plastic, rubber, aluminum or other synthetic material. **Decking** (the mesh between the frame) is made of rawhide lace, plastic, rubber, aluminum or other synthetic material; the best choice depends on the weight and expectations of the wearer. (Newer synthetic materials enable heavier individuals to wear smaller snowshoes.) **Bindings** are leather, plastic, rubber or other synthetic material. Fixed bindings, which are shaped like either the letter *H* or the letter *A*, keep your heel closer to the shoe, and enable snowshoes to stay attached to your feet. Newer, expensive models offer hinged bindings (free rotation bindings) that enable you to move the entire foot, except the toes.

Snowshoes come in three basic styles: recreational (elongated oval with a tail), sportive (oval), and mountaineering (scrunched oval with toe or heal claws).

Recreational snowshoes are used for touring and backcountry snowshoeing. They are usually designed to be asymmetrical so that each foot can be attached towards the inner edge of the shoe. Also, the toes are often pointed or turned up slightly to make travelling through deep snow easier.

Sport snowshoes, which are used for running and training, are symmetrical ovals so that each foot can be attached to the very centre of the shoe. They typically come in three sizes: 20cm by 64cm (8" x 25"), 23cm

Practical Information

by 75cm (9" x 30"), and 25cm by 91cm (10" x 36").

Mountaineering snowshoes have a crampon or claw attached to the back of them to enable better climbing. They often have serrated teeth all along the sides of the frame to make it possible to grip on ice.

Children's Special Needs

Children of all ages enjoy both cross-country skiing and snowshoeing, although in the early years, they may well be introduced to the sports from the vantage point of a pulka. A pulka is an enclosed sleigh that enables a skier or snowshoer to pull infants and toddlers, even on track set trails. That way, adults can get their exercise while children remain comfortably ensconced in a warm, dry environment. (Many kids sleep through the entire trip.) The most popular brand of pulka in Canada is the Baby Glider, which is manufactured in Québec by cross-country ski Olympic champion Pierre Harvey, although many other brands exist.

As children begin to walk, of course, you'll want to introduce them to the sport. They usually pick up snowshoeing soon after they learn how to walk, although they'll enjoy the challenge of cross-country skiing more the following year. Either way, introduce them to skiing without poles so that they can learn the balance that will make the sport easier later on.

Although all children under the age of 12 fall into the "jackrabbit" racing category, Cross Country Canada further divides them into seven groups that are based on a child's age and the likely level of skill that a child can attain by that age. They are: ski bunnies, green, yellow, orange, red, blue and purple. The same categories work for snowshoeing, too.

These categories provide a convenient framework for determining when children need new equipment. Note that it's always better for a child to use equipment that's slightly too small, rather than too large. If you want or need to limit purchases or swaps, delay them as long as possible and then get the right size for your child. Don't buy larger sizes with the hopes of having a child grow into the equipment. If a child is in a growth spurt, it might be better to rent equipment for one season.

Ski Bunnies

(3 to 5yrs)

Children between the ages of three and five years are just learning the basics, something that can be easily accomplished on cheap plastic equipment, whether skis or snowshoes. Skis should strap onto a child's own boot and should be about the same height as the child. The poles should reach a child's underarms. Most of the cheaper models come in only one size, but it doesn't matter. Just don't force the child to use them. They'll do so when they're ready. Rely on your pulka for skiing entertainment.

Green

(6yrs)

At six years of age, children need decent touring equipment that enables them to keep up with their parents and/or older siblings. For skis, you can stick with the waxless classic type that are the same height as the child's outreached arm and poles that reach the child's underarm. You'll need decent boots that attach with bindings. For snowshoes, choose a pair of sport shoes that are small enough to manoeuvre easily.

Yellow

(7yrs)

At seven years of age, children will start deciding their own fate. If you're lucky, you'll be able to make them use last year's snowshoes, skis and poles for another year. If not, get them waxable hybrid skis and teach them how to remove the grip wax for skating. Hybrid skis are taller than the child but not so tall that they reach the child's outstretched arm. Stick to classic length poles that reach the child's underarm. Also, make sure that the ski bindings don't rub the track when the child edges the ski.

Orange

(8yrs)

Your eight-year-old needs new snowshoes and a pair of waxable hybrid skis, possibly the ones you bought last year (unless you delayed until this year). Make sure the poles are the right size for the activity the child prefers—skating poles reach the child's chin, while classic poles reach the child's underarm. Poles also must have adjustable straps.

Practical
Information

You may also want to introduce your child to poling while snowshoeing.

Red

(9yrs)

A nine-year-old will probably complain about removing the grip wax for skating all the time, but don't give in. New skis are on the agenda for next year. Lessons at this age concentrate on technique. The snowshoes from last year should still be okay, unless your child's size has changed substantially.

Blue

(10yrs)

At 10 years of age, children want the equipment they prefer, whether classic and/or skating or hybrid and whether waxless or waxable. At this point, they should have the knowledge and skills to select their own equipment, especially if they are competing in races. Get them what they want, not what they need. (They'll be keeping it for at least two seasons, anyway.) If you must buy new snowshoes, this is a good time to introduce a child to the backcountry.

Purple

(11yrs)

The typical 11-year-old doesn't need new equipment, unless you stalled last year's purchase.

Equipment Care

Caring for your equipment is easy. All it takes is storing and cleaning, and in the case of cross-country skis, waxing.

Storage

Storing snowshoeing and skiing equipment is easy, but important, particularly with skis to avoid scratching. Most importantly, find a spot to hang your skis and snowshoes on a wall or from a ceiling, so that they don't get damaged with rough handling. Poles and clamps should also be hung, if possible. Mohair skins can be folded and placed in a drawer, and boots can be stored just about anywhere until the following season.

Waxing Cross-Country Skis

The only other care required for skis is waxing

Waxing Your Classic Skis

1 = Rear Glide Zone
2 = Grip Zone
3 = Front Glide Zone

A = Glide Wax
B = Base Binder,
     Grip Wax and Klister
C = Glide Wax

and cleaning them. All skis, whether waxless or waxable, require at least one coating of glide wax every year to stay in optimal condition and to function properly. Beginner and occasional intermediate classic skiers can be less scrupulous about waxing practices, but if you're a skater, a racer, an avid skier looking to improve, someone who wants to keep a pair of expensive waxless skis for a lifetime, or if you are planning long touring trips lasting anywhere from 8hrs to several days, you'll need to learn how to properly apply wax.

To do this, you need to know that a skating ski has one waxing zone, known as the glide zone, while a classic ski has three waxing zones: a grip zone (also known as the grip region, kick zone or kick region) and two glide zones on either side of the grip zone.

The many varieties of each wax type exist to satisfy individual skier preferences for application, colour and results. Some waxes can be ironed or rubbed on to a base while others are applied with spray applicators. Colours range from those that visually indicate temperature to those designed to match ski equipment.

Don't be daunted by the bewildering range of waxing products available. Although there are 10 different manufacturers (Fast Wax, Maxiglide, Rex, Rode, Ski-Go, Solda, Star, Start, Swix and Toko), they all offer only four basic types of wax: glide wax, base binder, grip wax and klister. Glide wax protects skis from drying out; base binder enables grip wax to stick to synthetic or wood skis, grip wax enables skis to stick to the snow so that a skier can push forward, and klister enables skis to stick to ice or melting snow.

Swix Wax Lines

Each wax manufacturer has different bracket temperatures and colours, depending on what materials are used and how the wax is prepared. To give you an idea of the possibilities, consider the number of options provided by Swix, a Norwegian wax company that has been distributing its products since 1909. Swix offers three different hard wax lines: "Original Three" for those skiers who want the basics, the V-line for intermediate and expert skiers; and the Crystal line for racers. They also offer two lines of klisters—a basic line that includes red, blue, silver and white klisters and the Crystal line for racers.

"Original Three" Hard Waxes

Green wax
-10°C (14°F) to -30°C (-22°F)

Blue wax
0°C (32°F) to -15°C (5°F)

Red wax
freshly fallen snow
0°C (32°F) and up

"V-line" Hard Waxes

White polar wax
-15°C (5°F) to - 30°C (-22°F)

Green special
-10°C (14°F) to -15°C (5°F)

Green
-7°C (19°F) to -13°C (8.6°F)

Blue special
-5°C (23°F) to -9°C (16°F)

Blue
-3°C (27°F) to -8°C (18°F)

Blue special (Canada's best-selling wax)
-1°C (30°F) to -7°C (19°F)

Violet special
0°C (32°F) to -1°C (30°F)

Violet
0°C (32°F)

Violet extra
0°C (32°F) to 1°C (34°F)

Red special
-1°C (30°F) to 2°C (36°F)

Red
0°C (32°F) to 3°C (37°F)

Red extra
mix of red and yellow klister
1°C (34°F) to 3°C (37°F)

"Crystal" Hard Wax Line for Racers

Waxes for racers have to cover two different snow temperature ranges, one for new fallen snow and the other for transformed snow that has been packed down by crowds or compacted by time and weather changes. They also contain additives that prevent the wax from wearing off too quickly, because racers tend to travel longer distances in shorter times than the rest of us.

Light blue
newly fallen snow
-7°C (19°F) to -20°C (-4°F)
transformed snow
-10°C (14°F) to -30°C (-22°F)

Blue wax
newly fallen snow
-2°C (28°F) to -8°C (18°F)
transformed snow
-4°C (25°F) to -12°C (10°F)

Flexi-light violet
newly fallen snow
0°C (32°F) to -2°C (28°F)
transformed snow
-2°C (28°F) to -8°C (18°F)

Violet
newly fallen snow
1°C (30°F) to 0°C (32°F)
transformed snow
0°C (32°F) to -4°C (25°F)

Silver
newly fallen snow
2°C (36°F) to 0°C (32°F)
transformed snow
1°C (34°F) to -2°C (28°F)

Klisters (for icy conditions)

Original Red klister
cold transformed ice

Blue (used to be Original Purple)
cold transformed ice

Silver Universal
transformed ice

White Universal
snow that's changed to ice

Red Crystal
newly fallen snow
1°C (30°F) to 3°C (37°F)
transformed snow
0°C (32°F) to 2°C (36°F)

Yellow Crystal
newly fallen snow
2°C (36°F) to 5°C (41°F)

In addition to these, four new lines of Crystal klisters with additives to keep them from wearing out, are now available.

Glide Wax

Glide wax prevents the base from drying out. If you have waxless skis, it's the only one you really need, although base binder (see below) is also recommended. It should be applied to the entire base of skating skis and to the glide regions of classic skis at least once a year, more often if you notice a white coating on your synthetic base that indicates a dried out surface.

These days, glide wax comes in the original iron-on cake formats (although it's now available in a variety of new colours as well as in the original white) or in several spray-on applications, including pump and aerosol sprays or gel.

If you choose an iron-on cake format glide wax, you can use any old iron, although make sure that it doesn't get too hot. (If the wax smokes, the iron is too hot.) You might also purchase a special wax mouse that is designed to stay at the proper temperature. If you choose one of the new sprays or gels and you have classic skis, it's easier to apply the wax to the entire base and remove it from the grip zone after it dries. These should also be applied to waxless skis.

Base Binder

Synthetic classic skis require a base binder on the grip zone, particularly when the snow is very hard and abrasive. Waxless skis need something to protect the scales from drying out, although they only require a spray base binder that must be wiped off before it dries, so that it doesn't fill in the scales. Waxable skis need a base binder for protection and to enable the grip wax to stick well to the base. This base binder can either be sprayed or ironed onto the grip zone. Old-fashioned classic skis made of wood use pine tar as a base binder.

Grip Wax (also known as kick wax) and Klisters

All classic skis require grip waxes and klisters on the grip zone. Grip waxes are hard waxes in lipstick-like applicators, while klisters are soft waxes with a glue-like consistency in steel toothpaste-like applicators. The appropriate grip wax or klister matches the snow condition, temperature and humidity on the track you want to travel to ensure that the grip zone of your cross-country ski sticks to the snow enough to enable you to push forward without slipping sideways. If you are planning a long tour, you'll usually need to add grip wax layers every couple of hours or so, as conditions change.

Racers and avid enthusiasts own gages that measure snow temperature to determine which grip wax to use, but beginner and intermediate skiers who don't require precise grip action often choose their grip wax based on air temperature, a trick that works well enough because snow temperature is slightly warmer than air. As skiers' skills improve, however, they begin noticing relatively small variations in how well skis grip and that leads them to seek waxes that closely match precise snow temperatures.

Waxless skis do not usually require grip wax, although some skiers choose to put wax on their scales in particularly cold conditions. Maxiglide is a gel that can be applied to the scales with a finger, and is specially formulated for waxless skis.

You should apply three separate coats of hard wax (grip wax). Ideally, the first layer of grip wax should be ironed on to the grip zone to provide coverage that's thin and even. The first layer should also be the hardest (or coldest) choice

for the day, since softer (warmer) wax works when applied on top of harder (colder) wax, but not the other way around. The second, third and additional layers can be applied to the grip zone by taking the small lipstick-like applicator and drawing several small *V*s onto the grip zone. (Applying many small *V*s rather than a few thick *V*s will prevent the wax from forming wads.) Use a synthetic cork to rub the hard wax evenly along the zone.

Klisters are soft enough to go on top of any other wax, and only one coat is required. They usually smooth onto the zone with a finger, although manufacturers also sell little "klister paddles."

Note: Make sure that the middle groove is clear of wax and klister when you're finished.

If you apply the wrong grip wax, you will either slip on your skis or they'll stick so that it will be difficult for you to push forward. If you're slipping, you simply apply a stickier wax on top of the wax you've already applied. If you're sticking, you'll have to remove the wax you've applied with a citrus wax remover and start again. To avoid this happening too often, you might consider taking one of the many waxing clinics offered by clubs and sports stores throughout the ski season.

Beginner's Wax Kit

Beginners are often daunted by the wide selection of waxes available, but any skier can achieve results with a limited collection of only seven waxes that can be purchased as needed throughout the first skiing season. Before the season begins, you'll need a glide wax spray to protect your skis, and perhaps a base binder. Then, as the season starts, you'll need three grip waxes that cover "warm," "cold" and "colder" snow temperatures (the exact temperatures covered by each formula depends on the manufacturer). When it gets extremely cold and the trails start icing over, you may need a cold klister. Then, if you plan to ski in the spring, you'll need another klister for snow that's so warm that it melts as you ski over it. Learning to use these seven waxes properly will ensure many years of cross-country skiing happiness for some, while others will gain the confidence and knowledge to expand their wax collections for more precise needs.

Cleaning

Only grip wax needs to be removed on a regular basis,

preferably right after every tour. After spending so much time waxing your grip zone, it seems like a shame to remove the wax, but it's a rare day when snow temperatures match those of the previous day. There are wax solvents, base removers and newer biodegradable citrus solvents in spray, pump or liquid form. All three require you to apply the solvent to the skis, wait for a while (longer with the citrus solvents), and then remove the wax with a small spatula scraper and a cotton rag.

Whatever you do, don't use paintbrush cleaner or Varsol to remove the wax from your skis. Although the wax will come off, the petroleum in these products leaves an oily film that soaks into the skis permanently, preventing them from ever being cleaned properly again. Besides ensuring that wax will not stick to your skis, the film also voids your equipment warranty.

Warm-up and Cool-down

Before heading out onto the trails, be sure to get your muscles warmed up with a brisk walk or some quick stretches.

You should also start your day slowly, whether snowshoeing or skiing, on a flat easy trail that enables you to hone your skills a bit before heading towards the trails you prefer or the backcountry. Many of the centres in Ontario are designed with warming up in mind, and you'll see that the more intermediate and advanced trails often lead off easier trails.

When you get back, take a bit of time to stretch out your leg, shoulder and arm muscles and relax, before stopping altogether. Your muscles will thank you the day after!

Cross-Country Skiing Techniques

There are 18 cross-country skiing techniques designed to keep you continually moving across flat and rolling terrain, up and down hills and turning. The best way to improve your technique is to take a course offered by one of the many teachers certified by the Canadian Association of Nordic Ski Instructors (CANSI), Ski Telemark or the Professional Ski Instructors of America (see p 30). Most Ontario ski centres offer courses for individuals or groups.

Diagonal Stride

The first technique a new cross-country skier should learn is the "diagonal stride." Although the diagonal stride is a classic skiing technique, perfecting it also enables freestyle skiers (skaters) to build the skills they need to learn skating techniques.

The diagonal stride is just like a gliding walk. It consists of pushing forward off with one ski, and pushing back with the opposite pole and then repeating the action with the opposite ski and pole, while alternately balancing your body over each ski as you move forward. At first, try to glide as far as you can, as a payoff for all the work. Then start again.

Free Skate (V Skating in the United States)

The "free skate" uses the gliding and balancing skills of a classic diagonal stride, although instead of pushing forward and pulling back, shorter skis and a wider track enable you to move widely from side to side instead of forward and back. It takes practice to transfer your weight from ski to ski while turning your head and body to face the direction of travel from side

Practical Information

to side, unless you already have some power skating or inline skating skills. All the weight goes from one ski to push and then to the other ski to glide. No poles are used.

Double Poling

When you get gliding fast along relatively flat terrain, "double poling" can increase your speed. "Double poling" is used in both classic and freestyle (skating) skiing. It consists of extending both poles forward at once, leaning forward with the body so that you feel like you're bent over and standing on your toes, and then pushing both poles against the snow at the same time and pushing back to increase your speed.

In classic skiing, a skier can also increase speed on only one ski using the one-step double poling (kick double poling) method, by pushing back with one ski and transferring all weight onto an opposite ski before double poling.

Offset Skate
(also known as the V1 Skate)

Freestyle skiers (skaters) who transfer weight from ski to ski, turn from side to

side in advance of each diagonal stride, and pole on only one side of the free skate, are successfully using the "offset skate" technique. The technique should only be used on uphill terrain, but is apparently easy for beginners to learn. Both poles and one ski touch the ground at the same time.

One Skate
(also known as V2)

Advanced freestyle skiers have the balance to combine the leg action of the free skate with double poling on both sides of every skate to conduct the "two skate" technique.

Two Skate
(also known as the V2 Alternate or the Open Field Skate)

Freestyle skiers can combine the free skate and double poling actions into a "one skate." The trick is to push, double pole while gliding on one foot, then switch to the other side and push and glide again, without double poling.

Half Skate
(Marathon Skating)

Freestyle skiers can combine the free skate and

double poling into a "half skate" or "marathon skate" by transferring weight onto only the left or right ski, which is placed outside of the track on an angle to the gliding ski in the track. You then use the ski outside of the track to push the gliding ski inside the track, while double poling for speed. While this technique allows a skater to use a classic track, since one ski can remain within the track, it can also be practiced on the regular skating trail.

The Side Step

Skiers can climb very steep grades by turning sideways and stepping up the grade, ski by ski, as though on a staircase. This method is not recommended on groomed trails.

The Herringbone

The "herringbone" is the classic technique for climbing steep grades and obtains its name from the herringbone pattern left on the trail. Skiers step out of the track at roughly a 45° angle and then place their skis one after the other in a *V* pattern, all the while leaning on the inside edge of their skis to grip the hill. The width of the *V* and the amount of edging you use to maintain traction de-

pends on the steepness of the grade.

Uphill Climbing (or Uphill Diagonal Stride)

Strong skiers speed up and shorten their diagonal stride to climb grades.

The Snowplow (Snowplow Wedge or Double Stemming)

The snowplow enables a skier to descend a grade in control. A skier simply points his tips together to form an *A* with his skis. (Note: classic skiers have to get out of the track, if one exists, to snowplow.)

The snowplow

Diagonal Skate (Diagonal V Skate)

The diagonal skate, which combines the diagonal

Practical Information

stride with the free skate, is usually used to climb stiff grades. While free skating with your legs, use a traditional poling and arm action by matching an opposite arm with an opposite leg. You'll use the edge of your skis to grip and the *V* between your legs widens as the grade steepens.

Downhill Running

Although short boots and a loose heel add challenge, cross-country skiers can travel downhill using alpine techniques, such as keeping ankles and knees together and flexed while doing small, quick turns or bending the knees and skiing in a straight direction.

The Snowplow Turn (Basic Turning)

A skier can turn on a grade while doing the snowplow, simply by turning both feet together in the desired direction and by leaning the outside ski onto its inside edge.

The Half Stem (Half Wedge in the Track)

A classic skier who knows how to snowplow can adapt the technique to stop while keeping one ski in the track. Slowly remove one ski from the track and place it at an angle to the one that remains in the track. Apply gentle pressure to the diagonal ski until you stop. This system can also be used to turn without a track, as long as one ski is straight and the other is angled.

Basic Christie Turn (Basic Star Turn)

Skiers can turn on a downhill grade by steering the skis into a *V* in the direction they want to go and sliding the uphill ski so that it's parallel to the downhill ski.

The Moving Step (Skating Turn)

Skiers can turn on a downhill grade with a moving step. They begin with skis parallel. The inside ski is then picked up and turned into the new direction. They then put all their weight on the inside ski while the outside ski is stepped parallel. The process can be repeated as many times as you want to turn.

The Change-Up (The Kick Turn)

Although frequently used by alpine skiers, the change-up is the most difficult turn to learn on cross-country skis. It consists of almost jumping sideways onto the ski edges to stop or turn quickly midway along a downhill slope.

Snowshoeing Techniques

Snowshoeing techniques are not as complicated as skiing techniques, primarily because the sport still represents basic transportation rather than leisure. You need only 10 easy techniques to keep you continually moving across flat and rolling terrain, up and down hills and turning. Whatever you do, though, don't try to walk backwards. Snowshoes are not designed for walking backwards and you're likely to fall.

Not many centres offer courses in snowshoeing yet, but a few tour operators (see p 52) offer trips and courses that will enable you to improve your technique.

Walking and/or Running

After strapping on a pair of snowshoes, you only need to walk or run to get moving. In some cases, you'll have to learn to widen your gait a bit to make up for the wider snowshoes, but this poses no difficulty.

Poling

Since there is no glide, matching the motion of opposite arms and legs is the best way to use poles when snowshoeing.

Straight Climb

The easiest way to climb a steep slope, particularly if it's narrow, is to face up the hill and climb. You'll find that the snowshoes grip best if you place the decking firmly on the snow without leaning on any edge.

Angled Climb (Traversing)

If you have the space, you may prefer to climb the hill at about a 45° angle and then turn and climb again at the same angle. Avoid turning your shoe com-

(see p 52)

Practical Information

pletely sideways on the hill, since snowshoe edges do not grip.

The Side Step

Like skiers, snowshoers can climb very steep grades by turning sideways and stepping up the grade, shoe by shoe, as though on a staircase. This method is not recommended on groomed trails, however, and can be quite time consuming.

The Herringbone

Also like skiers, snowshoers can climb using a herringbone pattern, by spreading their shoes in a *V* pattern as they climb a hill. The only difference is that snowshoers do not need to lean on their edges, which don't grip anyway, because snowshoes don't usually slide on hills unless they are very icy. Mountaineering snowshoers have an advantage in climbing, since they can rely on the claws attached to their shoes. Like skiing, the width of the *V* and the amount of edging you use to maintain traction depends on the steepness of the grade.

Long Step Descending

Snowshoeing down a hill can be accomplished by taking longer steps. It can be quite a lot of fun, especially if the trail allows you to slide (glissade) part of the way.

Angled Descent (Traversing)

If you have the space, you can traverse the hill by placing your shoes at about a 45° angle and then turning and climbing again at the same angle. Avoid turning your shoe completely sideways on the hill, since snowshoe edges do not grip.

Slow V Turn

Make wide turns by gradually moving your shoes in a wide *V* pattern.

Step Turn

If a path is very narrow, it may be necessary to pick up one foot and move it in a 90° angle from the other foot. Then you can pick up the second foot and put it next to the first.

Trail Etiquette and Safety

For the most part, skiers and snowshoers who are considerate of others will naturally follow most of the trail etiquette and safety guidelines.

The 12 steps to good trail behaviour are:

1. Remain in control so that you can stop or avoid other people or objects.

2. Those descending always have right of way.

3. Do not stop if you are obstructing the trail or if you are not visible from above or from around a corner.

4. Yield to others when entering a trail or starting a downhill slope.

5. Remain at the scene of an accident or collision to inform the ski patrol.

6. At outdoor centres, ski or snowshoe only on marked trails designed for the purpose, and in the proper direction indicated by markers. (Normally, skiers stay to the right, but not everywhere.) Also, choose trails that match your abilities and requirements. (Not all trails allow skijoring, polkas or snowshoeing.)

7. Stay off closed trails.

8. Observe all warning signs.

9. Leave wilderness areas clean and undamaged.

10. Don't litter—carry garbage off the trail to dispose of it.

11. Ski to the right when skiing a double track. Stay on the snowshoe trail when it exists.

12. Step to the right off the track when faster skiers or snowshoers approach yelling, "track."

Some skiers and snowshoers, particularly young children, seem to find rule 12, the requirement to move out of the way, a difficult one to follow. They seem to think that calling "track" is a demand for them to move faster. Everyone's tempers will remain calm if slower travellers learn to step out, or move to the right side, of the track so that faster travellers can pass without stopping. Misunderstandings will also be avoided if faster travellers learn to call out track in time to allow slower people to move out of the way, and recognize that some situations—pulling a pulka

A Summary of the Cross Country Canada Racing Rules and Regulations that Apply to Loppets

There is no official limit to the distance or format of loppets, which are officially known as "popular cross-country races." To be certified, however, loppets must offer at least one distance of 30km or greater, perhaps as two 15km loops. Canadian race directors must also offer 1 to 10km distances for children under the age of 12yrs, 5 to 15km distances for skiers aged 13 to 16yrs and 10 to 30km distances for skiers aged 17 to 20yrs. They are also encouraged to offer shorter distances to adults, to encourage participation from novice loppet racers.

Race Information

You'll probably hear about a race through an official "race notification" that includes all the information you'll need to compete, including the date, place, technical data, conditions for entry, names of race officials, and the time and place for a team captain's meeting, the time and place for the draw that determines competitor order, start time, location of official notice board, time and place of prize allocation, final date and registration procedures.

Participants register by sending in an entry form by mail, e-mail or fax, accompanied by the appropriate early-bird, regular or late fee.

Start Times

Elite racers will often have a separate start time, and some races also have different start times for each age category, for women, for men or for groups that represent the time that race entries were received.

Course Design

Most popular cross-country races in Canada are designed with flat or nearly flat start and finish areas, although the remainder of the course will be varied, with a variety of hills and turns. Ideally, a course will include an equal number of uphill climbs, rolling terrain and descents.

The width of the course will be at least 3.5m (11.5ft). Ideally, skiers will pass the same loops twice, at the most. If there are road or highway crossings on the course, they will be straight, well-marked and covered with snow. Trail intersections will also be marked, and the course will have enough markers to prevent racers from getting lost.

Along the course you can expect water stations about every 10km (6mi), although the distance changes on easy or difficult courses. Distance markers identify every 5km (3mi) section.

There will also be a heated first-aid station at the start and/or finish area. Every race has a chief medical officer, who is often a medical doctor, in charge of an emergency first aid, evacuation and notification plan for injuries, accidents and death.

Disqualification of Racers

The chief medical officer has the right to remove any competitor who doesn't seem capable of finishing the race safely.

Competitors can also be disqualified for trying to skip parts of the course, for taking outside assistance to complete a course, for interfering with other competitors, or for refusing to allow other competitors to pass. (Most popular cross-country ski races have at least two tracks so that slower skiers can stick to the right.)

Permitted Actions

When competing, racers can change poles or a single ski, although only if the ski or binding is damaged. No waxing or cleaning is allowed during a race, although exceptions are made for classic competitors who need to add wax or remove snow or ice from their skis.

Prizes

If you win, prizes might consist of mementos or money. If you tie with someone, both competitors receive the exact same prize because race directors are prohibited from using draws or further competitions to distribute prizes.

Practical Information

for instance—make it more difficult for slower skiers or snowshoers to move out of the way. The problem is not too difficult in Ontario, however, since many centres have double tracks to provide slower skiers with their own space and lots of the snowshoe trails are wide enough to accommodate everyone.

Racing Rules and Regulations

Although many cross-country skiers will ski for years without ever entering a race, Ontario offers many opportunities to compete at so many levels that you may well consider entering a competition occasionally to test your prowess, improve your technique and have fun with other skiers.

In Ontario, there are several types of races including cross-country, roller skiing, Nordic combined and ski jumping for women, men, mixed groups, children, masters and competitors with disabilities.

Age Group Breakdown

Races in Canada are usually divided into the following age classifications:

Jackrabbits aged 12yrs and under;

Challengers aged 13yrs to 16yrs;

Juniors aged 17yrs to 20yrs;

Males aged 21 to 61yrs (subdivided into 10-year age brackets),

Females aged 21 to 61yrs (subdivided into 10-year age brackets).

Ages are based on a competition year, which runs from January 1 to December 31, although the season in Canada starts in November. That means that a person turning 17 years old on January 3 would compete in the junior class in November and December.

Most cross-country ski races in Ontario are sanctioned by Cross Country Canada (see below), a federal regulating body for the sport, which has come up with a 59-page guide to the rules and regulations for holding races in Canada. Since most new racers will sign up for "popular cross-country races" (also known as loppets), we've summarized the Cross Country Canada guidelines that apply to loppets in a sidebar (see box "A Summary of the Cross Country Canada Racing Rules and Regulations that Apply to Loppets,"). Coaches, race coordinators and elite competitors should contact Cross Country Canada to see what rules apply to the races they plan to enter or run.

Further Information

Cross Country Canada
Bill Warren Training Centre
1995 Olympic Way, Suite 100
Canmore, AB T1W 2T6
☎*(403) 678-6791*
(403) 678-3644
http://canada.x-c.com

Potential Illnesses on the Trail

Although careful preparation should prevent any illness on the trail, accidents sometimes happen. That's why Nordic volunteers with the Canadian Ski Patrol System (see p 31) cover most of the skiing and hiking trails in Ontario. If something happens to you out on the trail, or you find someone else who is hurt, the Canadian Ski Patrol is trained to help.

Dehydration

A lot of sweating, without replenishing fluids, can cause skiers and snowshoers to get dehydrated. Initial symptoms include becoming thirsty, followed by feelings of light-headedness and fainting. If it continues, dehydration can lead to a dangerous drop in blood pressure. The only cure is to replace water and

electrolytes by drinking a sports drink, an electrolyte drink or salted water.

Falls and Collisions

If a skier or snowshoer suffers a serious fall or collision, make sure that other skiers or snowshoers block the path behind or above the victim until the person has moved off the trail, if possible. Send someone else to get the ski patrol, if possible. Otherwise, wait until the ski patrol arrives. If you suspect a head, neck or spinal injury, do not move the victims in any way, but simply cover them with clothes or blankets to treat for shock. If there is bleeding, cover with a gauze and apply pressure, until the ski patrol arrives to take over. Although broken bones that occur in open fractures are evident when a piece of the bone is sticking out, you might also suspect broken bones when a victim's limb is in an odd position or can't be moved properly. Any broken bones should be splinted with whatever soft straight item can be found. (If necessary, wrap a stick in a piece of clothing to make a splint).

Frostbite

Very cold temperatures can prevent blood from circulat-

Practical Information

SIGNS AND SYMPTOMS
OF HYPOTHERMIA

37°

N.B. *Signs and symptoms can vary from one person to the next; they are therefore not reliable indicators of the body's internal temperature. A rectal thermometer is the only precise way to determine the body's internal temperature; an oral thermometer is not reliable since the mouth cools down very quickly. The more the core temperature falls, the more marked the symptoms become.*

36°

Precursory signs of hypothermia
(core temperature 36°C)
- The person tries to move about to warm up.
- Pale, swollen and smooth skin.
- Muscles contract, but moving can compensate for the shivering.
- Fatigue and signs of weakness begin.

35°

Signs of mild hypothermia
(core temperature 35°C to 34°C)
- Intense and uncontrollable shivering begins.
- The victim's movements become less and less coordinated.
- The victim remains conscious and is able to help themselves.
- The cold will cause the victim pain and discomfort.

33°

Signs of moderate hypothermia
(core temperature 33°C to 32°C)
- Shivering decreases and the muscles become stiff.
- Victim becomes confused, apathetic.
- Drowsiness and strange behaviour may begin.
- Speech becomes slurred, vague and inarticulate.
- Breathing is slow and shallow.

31°

Signs of serious hypothermia
(core temperature 31°C to 29°C)
- Shivering decreases or stops.
- Weakness and lack of coordination are marked; the victim appears exhausted.
- The victim becomes clumsy, and lacks coordination; the person appears drunk, will not admit there is a problem and may even refuse your help. Victim gradually loses consciousness.

29°

Critical stage of hypothermia
(core temperature less than 29°C)
- Victim is unconscious, appears dead.
- Breathing is very faint or not apparent.
- Skin is grey and may take on a blueish-grey tint.
- Pupils are dilated.
- The victim's body is rigid.

BODY TEMPERATURE

From the brochure *Survivre à l'hypothermie* from the Société canadienne de la Croix-Rouge, Division du Québec.

TREATMENT OF HYPOTHERMIA

If you have not succeeded in preventing hypothermia despite being well prepared, or if you come upon someone suffering from hypothermia, the first rule is to begin treating them as soon as possible. The lower the body temperature drops the more difficult it is to warm up the victim.

Initial steps

- Protect the victim from the cold, wind and rain.
- Find or built a dry shelter; and find a way to keep it warm.
- Avoid other dangers, even if this means setting up camp immediately and abandoning the rest of your excursion.
- Light a fire quickly or turn on your campstove.
- Give the victim a warm drink; **avoid alcohol.**
- Make sure no one else in your group is showing any signs of hypothermia.

Mild case

- Replace wet clothes with dry ones.
- Give the victim a warm and sweetened drink and some high energy food.
- Cover the victim with blankets or a sleeping bag; isolate them from the cold, cover the head and neck. Avoid further heat loss and allow the body to warm itself up.
- Light exercises may help warm the victim up, though they will quickly use up all their energy.

Moderate case

- Apply warm and moist cloths to the victim's head, neck, chest and groin. **Heat should be moderate** (comfortable on your elbow).
- Arrange to keep the victim warm for several hours.
- If the victim is conscious, begins to warm up and is **capable of swallowing**, give them a **few sips** of a warm and sweet drink.
- The victim should be examined by a doctor.

Serious case

- Get medical assistance as soon as possible.
- Place the victim in a prewarmed sleeping bag with another person, or better still place them between two people. Contact with the skin, especially around the neck and chest is very effective.
- Try to keep the victim awake. Breathe out hot air near their nose and mouth. Try to make steam in the room.
- Ignore the victim's statements that they are fine. The situation is serious. Pay close and constant attention.
- Apply moderate heat to the head, neck, chest and groin; prevent the temperature from falling any further while at the same time ensuring it does not rise too quickly

Critical case

- Medical help is essential, hospitalization is obligatory.
- The victim has lost consciousness, so treatment must be given very carefully. Rough handling could cause the heart to stop.
- Maintain the belief that the victim can be revived; do not give up.
- If there is breathing or a pulse, **no matter how weak or slow, do not do cardiopulmonary resuscitation,** rather pay attention to any changes in vital signs.
- Keep the surrounding temperature stable with sources of moderate external heat.
- If there is no breathing or pulse for one or two minutes, administer cardio-pulmonary resuscitation (by a trained individual).

ing to any exposed skin, such as cheeks, ears and nose, or through tissues that are farthest from the heart, such as those in the fingers and toes. When this happens, the skin or tissue suffers permanent damage called frostbite. Early warning signs include redness, cold, tingling, numbness and swelling. After that, blisters can appear, followed by a paleness and hardening of the skin or tissue. If the frostbite occurs over a large part of the body, the skin may appear purple instead of white. Pain can lessen and even disappear as the frostbite gets worse. If you believe you are suffering from frostbite, do not rub the skin or apply snow. You can attempt to warm the body part by gently placing it under an armpit, behind a knee, or by wrapping it in blankets, but don't attempt this warming if you must stop the effort while you rush to the hospital. Frostbitten limbs that have been thawed can become damaged more easily than while still in their frostbite state. Medical authorities will probably use a warm water bath to reheat the area, but the treatment can be quite painful, and severe frostbite can lead to amputation or a permanent burning sensitivity to cold called chilblains or pernio. Better to prevent frostbite in the first place by stopping and returning to the trail centre as soon as coldness or numbness begins.

Frostnip

Very cold temperatures can also cause exposed skin to be chilled, but not damaged, a condition called frostnip. Frostnip causes the skin to become pale, harden, swell and throb. Eventually the skin may peel and remain sensitive to cold for months, although no permanent damage is obvious.

Heat Exhaustion

A lack of water and salt can cause heat exhaustion, even in the winter. Early signs include red cheeks, muscle weakness, mild confusion, headache and nausea. Children feel dizzy and faint. Vomiting is common. Drinking enough water should prevent heat exhaustion from occurring, but if you begin to feel dizzy or light headed, stop moving. If possible, lie flat and raise your feet. Sprinkle yourself with cool water. Drink a high-energy drink or as much water as possible. Eat something salty. Stop until you feel better, and even then, ski or snowshoe only as long as necessary to get off the trail and back home.

Hypothermia

Any prolonged exposure to cold air can cause your body temperature to drop below a normal level, a condition known as hypothermia. Tired, hungry children easily suffer this condition. Symptoms include a persistent chill, uncontrollable shivering, skin numbness and a change in muscle coordination. Confusion, lethargy and frequent falls follow. Treatment includes wearing warm clothes, consuming warm beverages, and application of an external source of warmth. One of the best recommendations for treatment on the trail involves having another person share a sleeping bag with the victim, to share body heat.

Immersion Foot

If feet are cold and moist over several days (as could happen on longer skiing or snowshoeing excursions), they can become pale, clammy and cold with very limited blood circulation. Unless feet are warmed, dried, cleaned and elevated frequently, an infection called Immersion Foot can develop. The condition is treated with antibiotics.

Rabies

Bats, coyotes, foxes, skunks and raccoons are all potential rabies carriers. Skiers and snowshoers should avoid any animal that easily approaches them, especially if it seems to be moving erratically or salivating. If you are bitten, clean the wound with antiseptic and get to a hospital immediately.

Sprains and Strains

Skiers and snowshoers can strain muscles and tendons or sprain or tear ligaments while on the trail, particularly on difficult trails. Symptoms of minor strains and sprains include mild pain and swelling, while bruising or instability and a sensitivity to touch indicate more serious strains. Severe pain, swelling and an inability to move indicate the most extreme cases. Applying cold snow or ice to the area can help relieve the pain and reduce the swelling until a doctor can be seen.

Day Trip Necessities

Even if you're planning a short day trip, you'll need several essentials to ensure

Practical Information

comfort and be prepared for unforeseen circumstances. They include:

- Baby pulka with diaper bag (if applicable)
- Baby wipes or antiseptic towelettes (if applicable)
- Backpack or daypack that fits well, contains lots of extra space for clothing layers and has at least one outside tie for carrying garbage bags
- Duct tape (for emergency equipment repair)
- Extra clothes for children (if applicable)
- Extra socks and hats
- Facial tissue or toilet paper
- First-aid kit (acetaminophen, adhesive bandages, alcohol, antiseptic towelettes, baby or child acetaminophen (if applicable) candle, first-aid cream, gauze, matches, sting relief, scissors, tensor bandage)
- Flashlight or headlamp
- Gloves (capilene liners and Gore-Tex covers)
- High energy sports drink, fruit juice
- Matches (waterproof)
- Nylon rope (to build a carry-all out of snowshoes, or a sleigh out of skis for transporting an injured person off the trail in an emergency)
- Plastic bags to carry garbage
- Rain gear
- Snacks (dried fruit, nuts, cookies, chocolate, salted crackers)
- Sunscreen
- Sweater
- Waxes
- Water (at least one litre per person)
- Whistle

Other Handy Items

While most of the items on this list have obvious uses, the hiking boots may seem out of place. In much of Ontario, however, snow cover is not guaranteed, especially in the spring. If you get in the habit of bringing your hiking boots along on any trip, the weather won't cause any inconveniences.

- Binoculars
- Cash
- Camera
- Compass
- Field guides (plants, birds, butterflies, spiders, reptiles, amphibians)

- Hiking boots (in case there's no snow)
- Lip balm
- Maps
- Noise-maker for pack (bell, pots, windchimes)
- Notebook and pencil
- Swiss Army knife
- Whistle
- Wands for marking a backcountry trail

Overnight Necessities

All items previously listed, plus:

- Butane or gas campstove, with appropriate fuel

- Candles (to replace the intimacy of a campfire)
- Clothing
- Cooking pot and bowl
- Food and drink (no cans or bottles)
- Insulating mattress
- Muscle cream
- Sleeping bag
- Sleepwear
- Soap
- Utensils
- Tent (unless you're planning to build an igloo or quinzhee)
- Toothbrush and toothpaste
- Towel

Greater Toronto

N

9
27 400
Aurora
Bolton
1
Caledon East 50
10 7
Brampton
11
401
QEW
12 25
3
Campbellville
15
Oakville
Burlington
Hamilton
©ULYSSES

11
21 18 6 404 4 12
20
Markham Pickering Ajax
22
Scarborough
13 8 2
19
17
Toronto
23
Mississauga

7
2 9
Newcastle
10 14
401 5 16
Oshawa

Lake Ontario

1. Albion Hills Conservation Area
2. Bunting Trail
3. Crawford Lake Conservation Area and Iroquoian Village
4. Dagmar Resort
5. Darlington Provincial Park
6. Durham Regional Forest Main Tract
7. Enniskillen Conservation Area
8. Five Winds Ski Touring Club
9. Ganaraska Forest
10. Heber Down Conservation Area
11. High Park
12. Hilton Falls Conservation Area
13. Kortright Centre for Conservation
14. Long Sault Conservation Area
15. Mountsberg Conservation Area
16. Northumberland County Forest
17. Petticoat Creek Conservation Area
18. Pleasure Valley
19. Seaton Hiking Trail
20. Seneca College King Campus
21. Skyloft Ski and Country Club
22. Toronto Zoo
23. Trakkers Cross Country Ski Club

0   50   100km

Greater Toronto

The Toronto area doesn't get enough snow to be a cross-country skiing and snowshoeing mecca, but there are several areas in the region that have a reputation for decent trails when snow cover is good and others that benefit from sheltered locations that hold the snow well.

The most famous of these is **High Park** (see p 102), a 161ha (398-acre) west-end Toronto park. High Park has become known for cross-country skiing since 1887 when a newspaper reporter photographed Ontario's first cross-country skier plying his new craft in the area. The impressive stand of black oak savanna and conifer forest that existed at that time was almost destroyed over the past century, although volunteers and city officials are working together now to restore the natural ecosystem. Cross-country skiers and snowshoers will enjoy exploring the frequently changing landscape that's slowly coming back into its own. The area is especially beautiful after a recent snowfall.

The park also gives its name to a local club, known as the High Park Ski Club, that organizes bus tours to regional cross-country ski destinations throughout the December to March season. Toronto area outdoor enthusiasts who want to travel a bit farther afield can also join excursions set up by the **Five Winds Ski Touring Club** (see p 100) and the **Trakkers Cross Country Ski Club** (see p 116). Destinations depend on the weather and club planning circumstances. Five Winds Ski Touring Club maintains its own backcountry trail system on Gibson River in the Muskokas, while High Park and Trakkers go to whichever groomed, trackset trails are likely to have the best conditions each weekend.

If they're lucky, the groups travel to **Pleasure Valley** (see p 111), an admirable trail system that's less than an hour away. They also like **Albion Hills Conservation Area** (see p 91), which is farther, but has a better track record for snow cover. Its 26km (14.9mi) of trails are also groomed and trackset for both classic and skating techniques and the park offers warm-up facilities, heated bathrooms and a snack bar. **Dagmar Resort** (see p 96) also gets top marks with frequent skiers, for all the same reasons,

plus the fact that it uses snowmaking equipment on 3km (2mi) of its 22km (14mi) trail system. This ensures that skiers get a good run even when snow conditions aren't ideal.

Groups don't usually travel to trails that aren't groomed, so they miss out on lots of good trail systems that other skiers will want to check out. Best bets include three major forest tracts that are situated on different parts of the Oak Ridges Moraine. The **Ganaraska Forest** (see p 101), northeast of Kendal, is the largest continuous forest in southern Ontario, thanks to a successful reforestation project begun in the 1930s. The forest covers a total of 4,200ha (10,374 acres) and offers 100km (62mi) of trails that crisscross the entire area. The **Durham Regional Forest Main Tract** (see p 99), near Uxbridge, is only a tenth of Ganaraska's size, but also contains at least 100km (62mi) of cross-country and snowshoeing trails. The 2,673ha (6,602-acre) **Northumberland County Forest** (see p 109), north of Cobourg, offers 26km (16mi) of trails for both cross-country skiers and snowshoers.

The **Long Sault Conservation Area** (see p 106) maintains a 25.3km (16mi) trail system on the Oak Ridges Moraine as well, and part of it is a white cedar and eastern hemlock swamp that attracts a wide variety of wintering birds.

Individual skiers who don't mind ungroomed trails have the opportunity to explore some incredibly beautiful sights, such as Hilton Falls, a 10m-high (33ft) waterfall with the ruins of a mill sitting beside it. With 16km (10mi) of groomed trails that are not trackset, **Hilton Falls Conservation Area** (see p 104) has prepared for an influx of skiers and snowshoers.

The **Bunting Trail** (see p 93) in Pickering also offers up plenty of beautiful scenery in its 25km (15.5mi) of woodland trails named in honour of former forestry superintendent Bill Bunting. There's another 10km (6mi) of groomed trails at the picturesque Devil's Den Valley at **Heber Down Conservation Area** (see p 102). The **Seaton Hiking Trail** (see p 112), a picturesque site on West Duffins Creek, consists of three different trails for a total of 9.7km (6mi).

The Greater Toronto Region also contains several small, but impressive-looking forest regions that are worth visiting if you happen to be in the area. They include **Enniskillen Conservation Area** (see p 99), which has 3km (2mi) of trails around two lakes and through a wet cedar forest, and **Petticoat Creek Conservation Area** (see p 110), which has a 1km (.6mi) trail in an area with bluffs and a cattail marsh. The bluffs and marsh create a microclimate that keeps American robins

and brown creepers in the park all winter.

If you enjoy historical interpretation backed by stunning scenery, you'll be delighted by a visit to **Crawford Lake Conservation Area and Iroquoian Village** (see p 94). Crawford Lake maintains 14km (9mi) of groomed trails through the Niagara Escarpment next to a replicated Iroquoian village. Intermediate and advanced skiers can continue from the Crawford Lake trails over the Niagara Escarpment to another 5km (3mi) of trails at **Rattlesnake Point Conservation Area**.

Birders can also use skis or snowshoes to explore one of the many marshes that attract ducks, herons, gulls and other unusual birds to the Toronto area in the winter. One of the most significant such areas begins at **Darlington Provincial Park** (see p 97). A trail connects Darlington with McLaughlin Bay Wildlife Reserve and the Second Marsh Wildlife Area.

A number of locations cater to families with small children who can only ski for short periods of time and need additional fun activities. **Kortright Centre for Conservation** (see p 104), for instance, tracksets 6.5km (3.7mi) of trails for classic skiing, and also offers visitors the chance to learn how to play snow snakes or kick-sledding, among other activities. The **Toronto Zoo** (see p 115) allows skiers to use a 10km (6mi) system of trails that leads past polar bears, moose, wolves, cougars, elephants, lions and reindeer as well as other fascinating animals. The 16km (9.9mi) trail system at **Mountsberg Conservation Area** (see p 107) satisfies everyone in the family with an opportunity to see elk, bison and raptors, explore a sugar bush, guess at kid's trivia and admire all the birds that overwinter in an impressive marsh.

The Toronto region only offers one location that enables skiers or snowshoers to stay overnight so they can hit the trails at the crack of dawn. The **Seneca College King Campus** (see p 112), which has 15km (9mi) of trails on its property, also operates an inn known as Eaton Hall. This option isn't open to many people, however, since the inn has limited space for individual bed and breakfast guests.

Individual skiers who want impeccably groomed trails, yet prefer to avoid groups, might also want to check out **Skyloft Ski and Country Club** (see p 113). Skyloft is only open to members on weekends but caters to anyone during the week. The club maintains 10km (6mi) of beautiful cross-country ski trails that lead away from the alpine hills and through three different forest tracts.

Tourist Information

Tourism Toronto
207 Queens Quay W.
PO Box 126
Toronto, ON M5J 1A7
☎*(416) 203-2500*
☎*800-363-1990*
⇒*(416) 203-6753*
www.torontotourism.com

Albion Hills Conservation Area (♥)

Location:	Hwy. 50, between Hwy. 9 and Bolton
Number of trails:	5
Total distance:	26km (16mi)
Level of difficulty:	● ■ ◆
Groomed:	100%
Trackset:	100%, 19km (12mi) classic, 7km (4.3mi) skating
Interesting features:	Oak Ridges Moraine, woodlands, swamp, Bruce Trail

Greater Toronto

Albion Hills Conservation Area. Courtesy of Conservation Toronto and Region.

Fee:	$10/day; $8/half-day adults or whole day seniors; $6/half day seniors; $5/day, $3/half-day children 5-14yrs; infants and toddlers free; $90/season $130/family
Other activities:	Ice skating, tobogganing
Services:	**(R)** *($13/day)*
Amenities and other services:	Parking, heated lodge, waxing centre, proshop, toilets, telephones, snack bar (weekends)

Albion Hills was created in 1954, which makes it the oldest conservation area in Ontario. Its location on the Caledon Hills, which form part of the Oak Ridges Moraine, means that you can expect to encounter hilly terrain. Five cross-country ski trails begin behind the chalet. The **Green Trail**, which is a 2km (1.2mi) loop, leads through a flat field and then into a cedar forest. The **Yellow Trail** loops for 2.5km (1.6mi) through a maple, beech and hemlock forest directly behind the chalet. It also leads through part of a swamp. The **Blue Trail** leads moderate-level skiers on a 6km (3.7mi) loop through the centre of Albion Hills, crossing Centre-ville Creek, which flows into the Humber River and past Lake Albion. The **Red Trail**, a 9km (5.6mi) loop for advanced skiers, joins the Yellow trail for a short portion, then continues past the sugar shack and into a coniferous forest of pine, spruce and hemlock, crosses Centreville Creek twice, once over a wooden bridge that was built as an Armed Forces exercise a few years ago. Skaters will enjoy the **Black Trail**, which begins at the Red Trail, crosses the Humber River and then loops for a total of 7km (4.3mi).

Getting There

Take Highway 50 north from Bolton or south from Highway 9.

Further Information

Toronto and Region Conservation Authority
5 Shoreham Dr.
Downsview, ON M3N 1S4
☎(905) 880-0227or 880-4855
☎(416) 667-6299
☎800-838-9921
www.trca.on.ca

Bunting Trail

Location:	North of Bowmanville
Number of trails:	5
Total distance:	25km (15.5mi)
Level of difficulty:	●
Groomed:	No
Trackset:	No
Interesting features:	Woodlands, Wilmot Creek
Fee:	No
Amenities and other services:	Parking

Greater Toronto

Getting There

Access the trails from either Ochonsky Road or Station Street in the town of Orono.

Further Information

Municipality of Clarington
40 Temperance St.
Bowmanville, ON L1C 2A6
☎ *(905) 624-3379*
⇆ *(905) 623-0830*

Crawford Lake Conservation Area and Iroquoian Village

Location:	South of Campbellville
Number of trails:	5
Total distance:	14km (8.7mi)
Level of difficulty:	● ■ ◆
Groomed:	100%
Trackset:	100% classic
Interesting features:	Reconstructed Iroquoian Village, Niagara Escarpment,
Fee:	$7/adult, $4/child (less than 14yrs)
Other activities:	Snow snakes Aboriginal game (a long, flexible spear is thrown down a packed trough in a hill)
Amenities and other services:	Parking, toilets, telephones, heated lodge, soft drinks

Visitors to Crawford Lake will probably begin on snowshoes with a short tour through the reconstructed Iroquoian Village. A palisade wall encircles four longhouses—two of which are complete and two others which are only exterior frames—burial platforms, a grinding stone, a central firepit, a sacred plant garden, a three-sisters (corn, beans and squash) garden and a games field.

Cross-country skiers have several connecting trails to explore from the "start of trails" behind the heated lodge. Begin with the 1.4km (.9mi) **Crawford Lake Trail** that loops around a meromictic lake that was either created when an underground cavern collapsed or by hydraulic mining. Look for the two corkscrew cedars that mark the front porch site of Lloyd Crawford's family cottage. From there, take the 1.5km (.9mi) **Woodland Trail** to reach the **Pine Ridge Trail**. The 3.6km (2.2mi) path loops through deciduous and pine forests and open meadows to the edge of the Niagara Escarpment. From there, you'll take the 2.4km (1.5mi) **Escarpment Trail** across a limestone plain to a lookout at the edge of the Nassagaweya Canyon. (There are several benches along the way, one of which honours Professor J. Percy-Smith, a Crawford Lake researcher who died in 1999.) If you want to continue skiing, take the 7.2km (4.5mi) **Nassagaweya Trail** through the Nassagaweya Canyon and along a footbridge across Limestone Creek to join up with the Bruce Trail. The Bruce Trail leads up and along the other side of the escarpment to Rattlesnake Point Conservation Area. You'll pass several lookouts over the canyon.

Getting There

Take Highway 1, also known as Guelph Line, south from Campbellville or north from Lowville.

Further Information

Crawford Lake Conservation Area
☎ *(905) 854-0234*
⇌ *(905) 854-2448*

Conservation Halton
2596 Britannia Rd. W., RR 2
Milton, ON L9T 2X6
☎ *(905) 847-7430 or 336-1158*
⇌ *(905) 336-7014*
www.hrca.on.ca

Dagmar Resort (♥)

Location:	Lakeridge Rd., in Ashburn, north of Ajax
Number of trails:	7
Total distance:	22km (14mi)
Level of difficulty:	● ■ ◆
Groomed:	100%, 3km (2mi) covered by snowmaking equipment
Trackset:	100% classic and skate
Interesting features:	Pine forest, scenic lookouts
Fee:	$10/adult; $8/senior or junior; $100/season
Other activities:	Alpine skiing, races, mountain biking
Services:	**(R)** *($12 or $14)*, **(L)** *($25/hr)*, **(A)** *(although not widely available)*
Amenities and other services:	Parking, toilets, telephones, heated lodge with snack bar and waxing centre

Dagmar Resort prides itself for its great trail grooming and the fact that it's one of the few ski resorts in Ontario to use snowmaking equipment on its cross-country trails. The results speak for themselves, and you can expect a wonderfully varied cross-country ski experience here.

There are seven trails in two areas. The 3.5km (3mi) **Meadowview Trail** for beginning skiers and the .3km (.2mi) **Evergreen Alley**, a loop for moderate skiers, both travel in open fields west of the lodge. Advanced skiers can warm up on the west trails and then take the difficult .7km (.4mi) **Olympia** extension to travel back to the easy 3.5km (2mi) **Express Loop**, the main trail located in the northern wooded section of the property.

Beginning skiers, or those who just want to relax on an easy trail, can continue from the Express Loop onto the easy portion of the **Deer Loop**. Confident intermediate skiers can extend the ski to a total of 4.7km (3mi) by skiing north on a short, unnamed intermediate section of the Deer Loop. Confident intermediate skiers can also extend their ski on the Express Loop by choosing the 3km (2mi) **Pine Valley Loop**.

Despite its name, the 7.5km (5mi) **Jackrabbit** course is designed for experts, not children aged 12yrs and under. In
fact, it is the most difficult trail on the course and leads
along a hilly, curving track with a great lookout on one
side.

Note: Watch the signs that indicate direction. At this course
skiers are always directed to the left of the trail, rather than
the right. Luckily much of the course is double trackset so
that slower skiers can move to the right track.

Getting There

From Ajax, go north on Harwood to Highway 2. Turn right
(east) and travel 3km (1.9mi) to Lakeridge Road. Turn left
(north). Dagmar is 18km (11mi) away.

Further Information

Dagmar Resort Limited
1220 Lakeridge Rd.
Ashburn, ON L0B 1A0
☎ *(905) 649-2002 or 686-3207*
www.skidagmar.com

Darlington Provincial Park

Location:	Oshawa
Number of trails:	4
Total distance:	7.8km (4.8mi)
Level of difficulty:	●
Groomed:	No
Trackset:	No
Interesting features:	McLaughlin Marsh, white birch forest, view over Lake Ontario, warm-up cabin dating from the 1830s (restored in 1967), McLaughlin Bay
Fee:	$6/vehicle/day
Other activities:	Winter camping, bird-watching
Amenities and other services:	Parking, toilets, telephones, lodge, snack bar, maps, gift shop

Greater Toronto

Don't let Darlington's location close to Highway 401 deter you from visiting. The park also sits on the shore of Lake Ontario, next to McLaughlin Bay, a warm marsh that protects ducks, herons, gulls and other bird populations from the winter chill. On years when snow cover is sufficient, which is rare, cross-country skiing is permitted on all four easy trails throughout the park.

The trails are: the 2.2km (1.4mi) Burk Trail loop, the 1.5km (.9mi) Robinson Creek Trail, the 1.5km (.9mi) McLaughlin Bay Trail, and the 2.6km (1.6mi) portion of the Waterfront Trail. The McLaughlin Bay Trail includes an impressive deck that looks out over Lake Ontario.

The McLaughlin Bay Trail and the Waterfront Trail continue past Darlington's borders into the McLaughlin Bay Wildlife Reserve, which is owned by General Motors of Canada Ltd., and the Second Marsh Wildlife Area, which is frequented by Oshawa birders. Together, the three marshes make up a significant watershed in Greater Toronto.

Getting There

Take Highway 401 to Courtice Road South at Exit 425. Drive west for 2km (1.2mi) to Darlington Park Road.

Further Information

Darlington Provincial Park
RR 2, 1600 Darlington Park Rd.
Bowmanville, ON L1C 3K3
☎ *(905) 436-2036*
= *(905) 436-3729*
www.cwise.com/darlpark.html

Durham Regional Forest Main Tract

Location:	Uxbridge
Number of trails:	10
Total distance:	100km (62mi)
Level of difficulty:	● ■ ◆
Groomed:	No
Trackset:	No
Interesting features:	Red and white pine plantation, Oak Ridges Moraine
Fee:	No
Amenities and other services:	Parking

Getting There

From Uxbridge, take County Road 1 south past Coppins Corners to the 7th Concession Road. Pass the Durham Forest Centre parking lot to the second driveway.

Further Information

Durham Forest Centre
400 Taunton Rd. E.
Whitby, ON L1R 2K6
☎ *(905) 852-3030*

Enniskillen Conservation Area

Location:	Enniskillen
Number of trails:	1
Total distance:	3km (2mi)
Level of difficulty:	●
Groomed:	No
Trackset:	No
Interesting features:	2 lakes, wet cedar forest
Fee:	$1/person

Greater Toronto

| Amenities and other services: | Parking, toilets |

Getting There

From Enniskillen, head west on Regional Road 3 to Holt Road. Turn right (south). The park entrance is on the right.

Further Information

Central Lake Ontario Conservation Area
100 Whiting Ave.
Oshawa, ON L1H 3T3
☎*(905) 579-0411*
(905) 579-0994
www.cloca.com

Five Winds Ski Touring Club

Location:	Downtown Toronto and Gibson River, between Georgian Bay and Gravenhurst
Total distance:	200km (124mi)
Level of difficulty:	◆
Groomed:	No
Trackset:	No
Interesting features:	Backcountry territory with marsh, rivers, lakes, and old growth hemlock trees
Fee:	Members only: $35/yr, $60/family
Other activities:	Trail clearing, training for wilderness travel
Amenities and other services:	Bus transportation from Yonge Street and the intersection of highways 400 and 7

This club is composed of about 150 experienced skiers who want to spend every Sunday of the winter skiing in uncivilized wilderness. Members have been working together to cut and mark trails on crown land in the Muskoka region of Ontario since 1971, and they now have more than 200km (124mi) of backcountry skiing trails established.

These aren't the typical groomed and trackset trails either. You'll need heavy skis, warm boots, a compass, a whistle and a pioneering attitude to join these trips. Most day trips involve about 6hrs of tromping through deep snow to enjoy thick hemlock forests, frosted marshes and pine and spruce woodlands. Pack a cold lunch and a warm beverage to sip along the trail.

Further Information

Five Winds Ski Touring Club
c/o membership secretary
18 Randolph Rd.
Toronto, ON M4G 3R7
www.outerimages.com/fivewinds

Ganaraska Forest

Location:	NE of Kendal
Number of trails:	10
Total distance:	100km (62mi)
Level of difficulty:	●
Groomed:	No
Trackset:	No
Interesting features:	Wild turkeys, red pine plantation
Fee:	$5/day
Amenities and other services:	Parking, toilets, telephones

Getting There

From Bowmanville, take Highway 115 north to County Road 9. Go east past Kendal, and follow the signs to Ganaraska Forest.

Further Information

Ganaraska Region Conservation Authority
PO Box 328
Port Hope, ON L1A 3W4
☎ *(905) 885-8173 or 797-2721*
⇥ *(905) 797-2545*
grca.on.ca

Greater Toronto

Heber Down Conservation Area

Location:	Whitby
Number of trails:	1
Total distance:	10km (6mi)
Level of difficulty:	●
Groomed:	No
Trackset:	No
Interesting features:	Devil's Den valley, former shoreline of glacial Lake Iroquois
Fee:	$1/person
Amenities and other services:	Parking

Getting There

From Brooklin, take Regional Road 3 west to Coronation Road. Turn right (south) past Macedonian Village and follow the signs to the entrance.

Further Information

Central Lake Ontario Conservation Area
100 Whiting Ave.
Oshawa, ON L1H 3T3
☎ *(905) 579-0411*
⇔ *(905) 579-0994*
www.cloca.com

High Park

Location:	Toronto
Number of trails:	Unspecified
Total distance:	10km (6mi)
Level of difficulty:	●
Groomed:	No

Trackset:	No
Interesting features:	Black oak savanna
Fee:	No
Other activities:	Hiking
Amenities and other services:	Parking, toilets, telephones, restaurant

High Park, a large wooded area on the west side of Toronto, can be a good practice location for cross-country skiing and snowshoeing when snow cover in Toronto is adequate. This park is ecologically significant because the stream was never buried and the valleys were never filled, making it one of the few natural ravines in the city. The area used to be full of open black oak savanna, which supports the wild lupines and prairies grasses needed for a vibrant butterfly and bird population. Authorities are restoring the few patches that remain. Some of the oldest oaks in the area may be 150 years old.

The High Park Ski Club began at the turn of the 20th century, when a group of cross-country enthusiasts started skiing in the park on the west side of Toronto. Since Toronto rarely has enough snow to ensure challenging skiing throughout the winter, the club evolved in the 1950s into a non-profit touring club that meets every second Thursday in Toronto and spends every weekend on bus trips to important ski destinations throughout Ontario. When there is good snowcover, however, often immediately after a storm, you'll probably see a member or two skiing in High Park.

Getting There

Take the 401 to the Keele Street Exit. Take Keele Street south to Bloor Street. Turn right. High Park is on the left.

Further Information

High Park Ski Club Inc.
1669 Bloor St. W.
Toronto, ON M6P 1A6
☎ *(416) 537-SNOW (7669)*
⇄ *(416) 537-3193*
www.highparkskiclub.on.ca

Greater Toronto

Hilton Falls Conservation Area

Location:	North of Campbellville
Number of trails:	7
Total distance:	16km (10mi)
Level of difficulty:	● ■ ◆
Groomed:	100%
Trackset:	No
Interesting features:	10m-high (33ft) waterfall, mill ruins
Fee:	$7/adult, $4/child (less than 14yrs)
Other activities:	Walking
Amenities and other services:	Parking, toilets, telephones, heated lodge, soft drinks

Getting There

Regional Road 9, north of Campbellville

Further Information

Hilton Falls
☎ *(905) 854-0262*

Conservation Halton
2596 Britannia Rd. W., RR 2
Milton, ON L9T 2X6
☎ *(905) 854-0234 or 336-1158*
⇍ *(905) 854-2448 or 336-7014*
www.hrca.on.ca

Kortright Centre for Conservation

Location:	South of Major Mackenzie Dr. and west of Hwy. 400
Number of trails:	2
Total distance:	6.5km (3.7mi)

Level of difficulty:	● ■
Groomed:	100%
Trackset:	100% classic
Interesting features:	Mature maple/beech forest
Fee:	$5/day, $3/day for students and seniors, $2 parking
Other activities:	Snow snakes, snowshoeing and kick-sled demonstrations, maple syrup festival, bird-feeder trail, nature walks
Amenities and other services:	Parking, toilets, telephones, visitor centre, snack bar, maps, gift shop, separate heated waxing centre

Kortright is an environment education centre that encourages people to appreciate and experience nature by demonstrating fun, healthy ways to enjoy winter without harming the environment. There are two cross-country ski trails: a beginner 1.5km (.9mi) loop that goes through hedgerows and old farming fields that are now meadows and a 5km (3m) perimeter trail for intermediate skiers that goes through a mature maple/beech forest.

Blue jay

The park also maintains a 2km (1mi) walking trail with 30 bird feeders so that visitors can view blue jays, cardinals, chickadees, downy woodpeckers, hairy woodpeckers, dark-eyed juncos, American tree sparrows and pine siskins, among others.

Kortright also operates a snow-bound winter activity hut, where organizers provide demonstrations and lessons on snowshoeing, kick-sleds, and an Aboriginal game called snow snakes, where you throw a long wooden rod with a large head (like a long flexible arrow) down a packed trough in a hill.

Getting There

From Toronto, take Highway 400 north to Rutherford Road. Drive west to Pine Valley Drive. The park entrance is 1km (.6mi) farther.

Greater Toronto

Further Information

Kortright Centre for Conservation
9550 Pine Valley Dr.
Woodbridge, ON L4L 1A6
☎*(905) 832-2289*
✉*(905) 832-8238*
www.kortright.org

Toronto and Region Conservation Authority
5 Shoreham Dr.
Downsview, ON M3N 1S4
☎*(905) 880-0227 or 880-4855*
☎*(416) 667-6299*
☎*800-838-9921*
www.trca.on.ca

Long Sault Conservation Area

Location:	Regional Rd. 20, Oshawa
Number of trails:	3
Total distance:	25km (16mi)
Level of difficulty:	● ■ ◆
Groomed:	No
Trackset:	No
Interesting features:	Oak Ridges Moraine, white cedar-eastern hemlock swamp, red and Scotch pine plantations
Fee:	$1/person
Amenities and other services:	Parking, toilets

Getting There

From Haydon, drive north on Grasshopper Park Road to Regional Road 20. Turn right (east) to get to the entrance. There's also an East Trail parking lot farther east.

Further Information

Central Lake Ontario Conservation Area
100 Whiting Ave.
Oshawa, ON L1H 3T3
☎*(905) 579-0411*
⇆*(905) 579-0994*
www.cloca.com

Mountsberg Conservation Area

Location:	Campbellville Rd., west of Campbellville
Number of trails:	5
Total distance:	16km (9.9mi)
Level of difficulty:	●
Groomed:	100%
Trackset:	No
Interesting features:	Raptor centre, elk, bison, sugar bush
Fee:	$7/day, $4/child (less than 14yrs)
Other activities:	Sleigh rides
Amenities and other services:	Parking, toilets, telephones, heated lodge

Mountsberg Conservation area is named after a 202ha (499-acre) water reservoir that was created when conservation officials dammed Bronte Creek to block some of its flow to Lake Ontario in 1966. The expanded wetlands have helped prevent flooding and filter sediments ever since, but they've also become very important for migrating waterfowl, bald eagles, tundra swans, osprey and blue herons.

All of the Mountsberg trails are flat and easy, which gives you a chance to look for the area's abundant birds and wildlife. Most of the trails lead along the edge of the Mountsberg reservoir, with the 5.6km (3.5mi) **Lakeshore Lookout Trail** providing the best lookouts over the water.

Families with young children might want to bring them on the **Nature Trivia Trail**, a 1.5km (.9mi) loop with posted nature facts, or the 1.5km (.9mi) **Sugar Bush Trail**. The sugar

Greater Toronto

Bald eagle

maples aren't tapped until March or April, but children will still appreciate seeing the stone house built by Duncan Cameron in 1880 and the sugar and candy houses along the trail.

The 6.5km (4mi) **Pioneer Creek Trail** leads away from Mountsberg Reservoir over several boardwalks past the marsh area, across several creeks and into some old homesteading fields. Notice the old hedgerows that used to divide the farmers fields and the cedar fences and stone walls that marked property boundaries.

With 472ha (1,166-acre), Mountsberg Conservation Area is more than just a water reservoir. It's also the home of the **Douglas G. Cockburn Raptor Centre**. Raptor Centre staff treat injured birds of prey, including hawks, kestrels, eagles, owls and turkey vultures. They also house and train birds that can't be released back into the wild because of human imprinting or permanent damage.

The permanently injured eagles, falcons, hawks, owls and turkey vultures live in enclosures that border the most popular trail at the park, the 1.6km (1mi) **Wildlife Walkway.** Most visitors just walk, rather than ski or snowshoe, past the enclosures to see relatively close-up views of the injured birds as well as some bison and elk.

Getting There

Take Campbellville Road west of Campbellville to Milburough Line. Turn north on Milburough Line to the park entrance and heated lodge.

Further Information

Conservation Halton
2596 Britannia Rd. W., RR 2
Milton, ON L9T 2X6
☎(905) 847-7430 or 336-1158
⊨(905) 336-7014
www.hrca.on.ca

Northumberland County Forest

Location:	North of Cobourg
Number of trails:	6
Total distance:	26km (16mi)
Level of difficulty:	● ■ ◆
Groomed:	No
Trackset:	No
Interesting features:	Pond
Fee:	No
Other activities:	Snowmobiling
Amenities and other services:	Parking

The Northumberland County Forest covers 2,673ha (6,602 acres) of the area north of Cobourg between Lake Ontario and Rice Lake. The mature red pine plantation was created to prevent sandstorms that occurred after the area was cleared for farming. Highway 45 runs through the centre of the area, and Burnley Creek crosses the very upper edge. All the snowshoeing and cross-country ski trails run to the west of Highway 45, while a 14km (9mi) snowmobile trail circles the forest on the east side of Highway 45.

There are six trails with coloured markings that indicate their level of difficulty. The two easy trails, the 1.6km (1mi)

Greater Toronto

Kiddy Loop and the 2.3km (1.4mi) **Orange Trail**, are marked with orange signs. The intermediate blue trail is 4km (2.5mi) long and links to the Green C Trail. There are four advanced trails, one **Red Trail** and three green loops (A, B, and C) that link together. The Red Trail continues for a 2.8km (1.7mi) loop between the ski parking lot and a pond. The **Green A Trail** is 9.8km (6mi); the **Green B Trail** is 4.4km and the **Green C Trail** is 5.2km.

As you ski or snowshoe the trails, watch for coyotes, white-tailed deer and wild turkeys.

Further Information

County of Northumberland
860 William St.
Cobourg, ON K9A 3A9
☎ *(905) 372-3329*
☎ *800-354-7050*
📠 *(905) 372-1696*

Petticoat Creek Conservation Area

Location:	Lake Ontario shore between the mouths of the Rouge River and Petticoat Creek
Number of trails:	1
Total distance:	1km (.6mi)
Level of difficulty:	●
Groomed:	No
Trackset:	No
Interesting features:	Bluffs, cattail marsh, overwintering American robins and brown creepers
Fee:	No
Amenities and other services:	Parking

Getting There

Access the conservation area from Whites Road, Rodd Avenue or Park Crescent in Pickering.

Further Information

Toronto and Region Conservation Authority
5 Shoreham Dr.
Downsview, ON M3N 1S4
☎ *(905) 880-0227 or 880-4855*
☎ *(416) 667-6299*
☎ *800-838-9921*
www.trca.on.ca

Pleasure Valley

Location:	Uxbridge
Number of trails:	3: green, blue and red
Total distance:	26km (16mi)
Level of difficulty:	● ■ ◆
Groomed:	100%
Trackset:	100% classic and skating
Interesting features:	Oak Ridges Moraine, natural woodlands
Fee:	$14/full day, $12/half day
Services:	**(R)**, **(L)**
Amenities and other services:	Parking, heated lodge with fireplace and snack bar, toilets, waxing and rental building

Getting There

Take Highway 401 to County Road 1, Brock Road in Pickering. Go north past Highway 7 and Claremont. The entrance is on the right-hand side.

Further Information

Pleasure Valley
2499 Brock Rd., RR 4
Uxbridge, ON L9P 1R4
☎ *(905) 649-3334*
www.pleasurevalley.on.ca

Greater Toronto

Seaton Hiking Trail

Location:	Follows West Duffins Creek from Hwy. 7 east of Green River to Sideline 24, north of Hwy. 2
Number of trails:	3 linear trails (Heritage, Wilderness, Walking)
Total distance:	9.7km (6mi)
Level of difficulty:	●
Groomed:	No
Trackset:	No
Interesting features:	West Duffin River Valley
Fee:	No
Other activities:	Mountain biking
Amenities and other services:	Parking

Getting There

From Pickering Village, take Regional Road 2 west to Regional Road 1. Turn right (north) and drive to the Third Concession. Turn left (west) and drive until the road ends at the parking lot and entrance on Rossland Road.

Further Information

Toronto and Region Conservation Authority
5 Shoreham Dr.
Downsview, ON M3N 1S4
☎ *(905) 880-0227or 880-4855*
☎ *(416) 667-6299*
☎ *800-838-9921*
www.trca.on.ca

Seneca College King Campus

Location:	King City
Number of trails:	3

Total distance:	15km (9mi)
Level of difficulty:	● ■
Groomed:	100%
Trackset:	100% classic
Interesting features:	Woodlands
Fee:	$6/day, $4/child or senior
Services:	**(L)** *(groups only)*, **(A)** *(Eaton Hall, modeled after a Norman château)*
Amenities and other services:	Parking, toilets, telephones, fireside warm-up area with snack bar

Getting There

Take Highway 11 north from Highway 7 or south from Highway 9 to side road 15. Turn west and drive to Dufferin Street. Turn north to the entrance of Seneca College's King Campus. Follow the signs to the cross-country ski centre.

Further Information

Seneca College, Recreation Services Department
13990 Dufferin St.
King City, ON L7B 1B3
☎*(416) 491-5050*
☎*(905) 833-3333*
www.seneca.on.ca/recreationservices/skicent

Skyloft Ski and Country Club (♥)

Location:	Chalk Lake Rd. W., Uxbridge
Number of trails:	6
Total distance:	10km (6mi)
Level of difficulty:	●
Groomed:	100%
Trackset:	100% classic and skating
Interesting features:	Quiet trails, wolf pen, pines, remains of a cabin that Margaret Atwood once used for writing retreats
Fee:	$8/day (weekdays)
Other activities:	Alpine skiing, snowboarding

Greater Toronto

Services: **(R)**
Amenities and
other services: Parking, toilets, telephones, heated
                           lodge, restaurant, and snowmaking
Other: Members only on weekends

Skyloft Ski and Country Club, which sits on the highest point of the Oak Ridges Moraine, combines prestige with beauty. The private club, which has welcomed Toronto and area residents since 1944, has a reputation as Prince Andrew's favourite weekend ski resort. Today, it attracts many young families and baby boomers that want to avoid the crowds at more popular alpine retreats.

Cross-country skiers and snowshoers will find even more tranquility on the almost-empty woodland trails that the owner developed for his daughter, who is a Nordic ski fan. Most skiers will appreciate the green **Big Foot Trail** which circles the edge of the entire Skyloft property in a 4km (2.5mi) loop, while the **Fox** and **Wolf** trails provide scenic short cuts. All three main trails begin with a steep drop off the alpine hills, and circle along rolling hills through woodland. While other trails wander through the pine bush and birch groves, the Big Foot Trail continues through a hardwood forest of beech and maple. Along the way, you'll see a dilapidated cabin that locals claim once housed a young Margaret Atwood on a writing retreat. Two or three of the trails lead past Sunvalley farm, which includes a pen housing two wolves. The owner has many stories about the changes in the area over the last few decades.

Getting There

Take Durham Road 21 from Goodwood east, past Coppins Corners to Concession Road 7. Turn right (south) to Chalk Lake Road. Turn left (east) and drive to the entrance of Skyloft.

Further Information

Skyloft Ski & Country Club
722 Chalk Lake Rd. W.
Uxbridge, ON L9P 1R4
☎ *(905) 471-2002 or 649-5160*
⇌ *(905) 649-6533*
www.skyloft.com

Toronto Zoo

Location:	North of Sheppard Ave.
Number of trails:	4
Total distance:	10km (6mi)
Level of difficulty:	●
Groomed:	100%
Trackset:	No
Interesting features:	5,000 animals contained without cages
Fee:	$15/person, $11/senior, $9/children 4-14yrs
Other activities:	Heated pavilions with plants and animals
Amenities and other services:	Parking, toilets, telephones, visitor centre, fast food

During the winter, skis are the perfect tools for exploring the Toronto Zoo's 287ha (710 acres) along four different trails.

The **Woodland Trail** winds through the Rouge Valley forest and alongside Weston Pond. Animals on display include American elks, moose, Arctic wolves, cougars, grizzly bears, musk oxen, northern bald eagles, raccoons, tundra swans and wood bison. Red fox and white-tailed deer also roam freely through the valley.

The **Kesho Park Trail** meanders through an African wild game reserve, with elephants, seals, lions, lynx, cheetahs, zebras, river hippopotamuses, gazelles and rhinos, among other animals.

The **Eurasia Trail** leads among animals from Europe and Asia, including reindeer, sheep, snow leopards and yaks.

The **Americas Trail** leads past the underwater polar bear exhibit, amongst other underground displays.

There are also four major tropical indoor pavilions, and several smaller indoor viewing areas so you can warm up after your ski.

Greater Toronto

Getting There

Take Highway 401 east from Toronto or west from Pickering to Exit 389, Meadowvale Road. Drive north to the zoo entrance.

Further Information

Toronto Zoo
361A Old Finch Ave.
Scarborough, ON M1B 5K7
☎ *(416) 392-5900*
⇌ *(416) 392-5963*
www.torontozoo.com

Trakkers Cross Country Ski Club

Location:	Toronto
Number of trails:	None
Fee:	Membership: $70/year
Services:	**(R)** *(not included)*, **(L)** *(included in membership)*
Amenities and other services:	Bus trips to ski resorts throughout Ontario

Trakkers is a recreational ski club that has been arranging group bus tours from downtown Toronto locations to cross-country ski resorts close to Toronto every Sunday during the winter since 1978. Ongoing learning is such a deep commitment for the club, that they include ongoing instruction as part of their membership fee.

Further Information

Trakkers Cross Country Ski Club
PO Box 84564
2336 Bloor St. W.
Toronto, ON M6S 4Z7
☎ *(416) 763-0173*
www.thetrakkers.com

The Niagara Peninsula

The snowshoeing and cross-country skiing season in the Niagara Peninsula is extremely short, primarily because the area is so well protected between two Great Lakes and the Niagara Escarpment. It rarely gets any significant snow cover and some years, there's no snow cover at all.

In fact, only two of the Niagara region sites— **Christie Lake Conservation Area** (see p 127) and **Valens Conservation Area** (see p 142)— groom their trails, and only in years when snow conditions warrant the effort. The rest of the sites prefer to let locals blaze trails whenever the snow flies. Still, it doesn't take long for the snow to be criss-crossed with trails, because locals recognize that cross-country skiing and snowshoeing are ideal ways to take in the scenic beauty, extraordinary bird-watching opportunities and historical landmarks that make the Niagara region famous.

Niagara Falls is, of course, the region's most famous landmark. Height is not what's significant about this waterfall, which is created as the Niagara River drops 55m (180ft) as it flows north from Lake Erie to Lake Ontario. What's really impressive is the incredible volume of water involved in the plunge. Prior to the 1950s, falling water was enough to erode the rock so that Niagara Falls moved 1m (3ft) upstream every year. Today, the volume has been significantly slowed to average about 155 million litres (34 million gallons) every minute so that the cascade moves about 36cm (1ft) every 10 years.

Cross-country skiers who want to explore Niagara Falls, and see the erosion that has occurred over the past several hundred years, will want to travel along the **Niagara River Recreation Trail** (see p 134). When there's enough snow to keep one gliding, the 57km (35mi) paved path that leads from Niagara-on-the-Lake to Fort Erie provides a smooth, level path for speedy touring. Consider stopping to visit several attractions along the way, including Queenston Heights Park, the Floral Clock, the Niagara Parks Butterfly Conservatory and Botanical Gardens, the Niagara Glen, the Spanish Aero Car, the Oakes Garden Theatre, Victoria Park and the Niagara Parks Greenhouse.

Snowshoers and cross-country skiers can also explore the shores of the two Great Lakes themselves. Very short trails lead along Lake Ontario at **Fifty Point Conservation Area** (see p 133) and along the shores of Lake Erie at **Long Beach** (see p 134).

While in the region, you may also want to explore the mountain-like ridge that creates the warm climate in this area and offers an ambiance that's worth travelling miles to experience. Known as the Niagara Escarpment, the protective ridge shields many forests in the region so that they are warm enough for unusual species that would normally grow thousands of miles further south. The resulting Carolinian forests include tulip trees, American chestnuts and white oak. Cross-country skiers and snowshoers can explore trails through

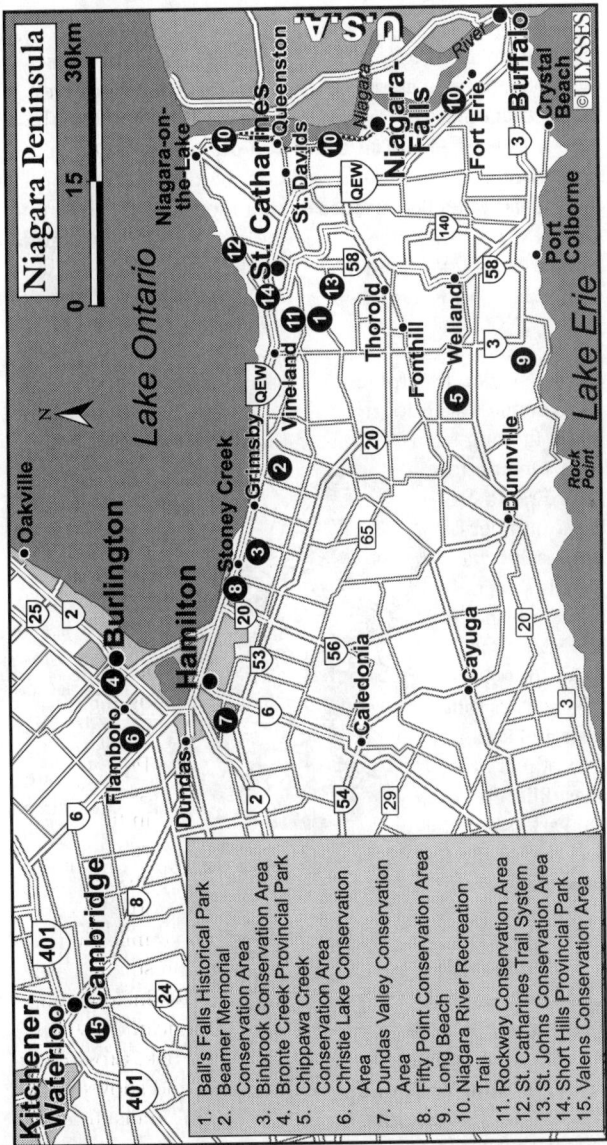

Niagara Peninsula

0   15   30km

N

Lake Ontario

Lake Erie

Niagara River

U.S.A.

Kitchener/ Waterloo
Cambridge
Burlington
Hamilton
Dundas
Flamboro
Oakville
Stoney Creek
Grimsby
Vineland
St. Catharines
Niagara-on-the-Lake
Queenston
St. Davids
Niagara Falls
Fort Erie
Buffalo
Crystal Beach
Thorold
Fonthill
Welland
Port Colborne
Dunnville
Cayuga
Caledonia
Rock Point

QEW
401
25
2
6
8
24
53
56
65
20
6
54
29
58
140
3
9
10
11
12
13
14
15

1. Ball's Falls Historical Park
2. Beamer Memorial Conservation Area
3. Binbrook Conservation Area
4. Bronte Creek Provincial Park
5. Chippawa Creek Conservation Area
6. Christie Lake Conservation Area
7. Dundas Valley Conservation Area
8. Fifty Point Conservation Area
9. Long Beach
10. Niagara River Recreation Trail
11. Rockway Conservation Area
12. St. Catharines Trail System
13. St. Johns Conservation Area
14. Short Hills Provincial Park
15. Valens Conservation Area

©ULYSSES

this Carolinian forest at many locations, including the **St. Catharines Trail System** (see p 139), **St. Johns Conservation Area** (see p 140) and the **Dundas Valley Conservation Area** (see p 128), which is surrounded by the limestone cliffs of the escarpment.

The Niagara Escarpment combines with local rivers flowing from Lake Ontario to Lake Erie to create a number of impressive waterfalls. Skiers and snowshoers can spot four different waterfalls at **Balls Falls Historical Park**, two others in **Short Hills Provincial Park** (see p 141) and two in the **Rockway Conservation Area** (see p 138).

Such free-flowing open water, combined with the limestone cavities in the Niagara Escarpment, attracts many birds throughout the winter and during spring migrations. Birders will want to check out **Beamer Memorial Conservation Area** (see p 123), which is a haven during the hawk migration, particularly when red-shouldered hawks return to the area in March. **Chippawa Creek Conservation Area** (see p 126) comes alive during the duck migration. **Binbrook Conservation Area** (see p 123) is known for its osprey population and the birds' huge nests can easily be identified during the winter. And the only time that children forget about the pigs and chickens that **Bronte Creek Provincial Park** (see p 124) officials use to help recreate life on a circa-1890 farm is when they spot one of the many long-eared owls that overwinter in the park. Bronte's location slightly north of the lakes also means that it often has enough snow for skiing when other locations in the region are bare.

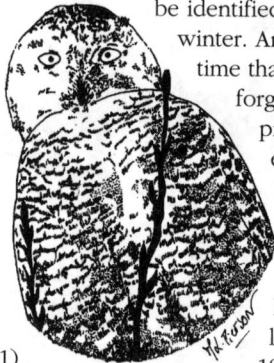

The Niagara Peninsula

Tourist Information

Tourism Toronto
207 Queens Quay W.
PO Box 126
Toronto, ON M5J 1A7
☎*(416) 203-2500*
☎*800-363-1990*
⇌*(416) 203-6753*
www.torontotourism.com

Southern Ontario Tourism Organization
180 Greenwich St.
Brantford, ON N3S 2X6
☎*800-267-3399*
⇌*(519) 756-3231*
www.soto.on.ca

Ball's Falls Historical Park

Location:	Regional Rd. 81 near Jordan
Number of trails:	3
Total distance:	7.6km (4.7mi)
Groomed:	No
Trackset:	No
Interesting features:	Historical village, circa 1810 gristmill, ruins of an old mill, four different waterfalls
Fee:	$3.50/vehicle
Amenities and other services:	Parking

Whether you like natural or cultural history, Ball's Falls Historical Park has a trail for you. You'll be able to travel by snowshoe to the gristmill that United Empire Loyalists John and George Ball built in 1810 to harness the energy of Twenty Mile Creek. The mill still stands at the edge of the Niagara Escarpment near High Falls, and still grinds flour just as it did during the War of 1812. The flow of water at the time was much stronger than it is now and was capable of supporting many different businesses over the years. The sawmill that once stood beside the mill is gone, but a home that the Bell family built in 1846 is still in place, as is a limekiln, an apple-drying shed and a barn. Conservation authorities restored an 1864 church, a carriage shed, an outdoor baking oven, two cabins and a blacksmith shop, which have all been placed together on the High Falls site so visitors can imagine what life in the village would have been like in the Victorian era.

Visitors who want to explore history on skis should take the 2.5km (1.6mi) **Cataract Trail** upriver to the 10.7m-high (35ft) Lower Falls. On the way, you'll see the ruins of a five-storey woollen mill and factory George Ball built in 1824. The woodlands on this trail are prime Carolinian forest and include black walnuts, butternut, eastern cottonwood, pignut hickory, sassafras, shagbark hickory, slippery elm, sycamore, tulip tree and white oak trees.

If you prefer natural history, slip on your snowshoes again to take the **Twenty Mile Creek Valley Trail**. The 2km (1.6mi) trail leads past the heritage buildings, through the Miller Arboretum and then directly onto the Niagara Escarpment beside Twenty Mile Creek. From here, the rocky, slippery path leads up and down the gorge, widening and thinning as the landscape allows. Views include a small waterfall and towering spruce and maple trees. The path ends on 21st Street (Glen Road) in Jordan.

A section of the **Bruce Trail** goes through the northern end of Ball's Falls Conservation Area, through the arboretum, along the Twenty Mile Creek Valley trail and then across the bridge to Fifth Avenue in the town of Louth.

Getting There

Take Regional Road 24 (Victoria Avenue) south from the Queen Elizabeth Way or north from Highway 3. You'll pass two intersections and the community of Vineland in the town of Lincoln. The entrance to Ball's Falls is on Regional Road 75, on the left side after the Vineland Quarry.

Further Information

Niagara Peninsula Conservation Authority
250 Thorold Rd. W., 3rd floor
Welland, ON L3C 3W2
☎ **(905) 788-3135**
⇆ **(905) 788-1121**
www.conservation-niagara.on.ca

Beamer Memorial Conservation Area

Location:	South of Grimsby
Number of trails:	1
Total distance:	1km (.6mi)
Level of difficulty:	●
Groomed:	No
Trackset:	No
Interesting features:	Niagara Escarpment cliffs, waterfall, red-shouldered hawk migration in March, three viewing platforms
Fee:	$3.25/adults, $2.25/seniors and students or $10/vehicle
Other activities:	Hawk watchtower
Amenities and other services:	Parking, toilets

Getting There

From the Queen Elizabeth Way, take Exit 71, and drive south on Christie Street, which becomes Mountain Road. Turn west on Ridge Road to Quarry Road. Turn north and continue to the park entrance.

Further Information

Niagara Peninsula Conservation Authority
250 Thorold Rd. W., 3rd floor
Welland, ON L3C 3W2
☎ *(905) 788-3135*
↔ *(905) 788-1121*
www.conservation-niagara.on.ca

Binbrook Conservation Area

Location:	South of Stoney Creek
Number of trails:	3
Total distance:	10km (6mi)

Level of difficulty:　● ■
Groomed:　No
Trackset:　No
Interesting features:　Lake Niapenco, mixed forest, osprey nest
Fee:　$3.50/vehicle
Other activities:　Hunting (Sep-Dec)
Amenities and other services:　Parking

Getting There

From the Queen Elizabeth Way, take Exit 88, and drive south on Highway 20 to Elfrida. Continue driving south on Highway 56 past Binbrook to Harrison Road. Follow the signs to the entrance.

Further Information

Niagara Peninsula Conservation Authority
250 Thorold Rd. W., 3rd floor
Welland, ON L3C 3W2
☎*(905) 788-3135*
⇌*(905) 788-1121*
www.conservation-niagara.on.ca

Bronte Creek Provincial Park

Location:　Between Burlington and Oakville
Number of trails:　1
Total distance:　5km (3mi)
Level of difficulty:　●
Groomed:　100%
Trackset:　100% classic (groups only)
Interesting features:　1890 farmhouse, ice house, woodshed, farm animals, playbarn, snowy owls, short-eared owls, wintering long-eared owls, red fox, coyote, ermine
Fee:　$4 adult, $2 children 4-17yrs and $2.25 senior or $12/vehicle; $40/season

Other activities: Skating, tobogganing, horse-drawn sleigh or wagon rides, maple syrup festival, children's playbarn

Services: **(R)** *(skis, snowshoes, skates)*

Amenities and other services: Parking, toilets, telephones, heated nature centre with snack bar, indoor skating rink

Bronte Creek Provincial Park offers a chance for families to experience the past and the present at the same time. They can visit an 1890s working Ontario farm, complete with a furnished Victorian farmhouse and a barn with sheep, pigs, chickens and other animals. Yet families can still count on the modern equipment and conveniences that make for a fun-filled day of recreation. The playbarn's loft, for example, includes tire swings and ropes right beside plastic jumping mats and slides. The nature centre rents both traditional snowshoes and modern ski equipment. The park's traditional activities, such as snowshoeing, cross-country skiing, a horse-drawn sleigh ride, tobogganing and iceskating are all done with modern equipment, including an indoor rink. Afterwards, you can enjoy hot chocolate or French fries in the snack bar.

Cross-country skiers should park in parking lot D, near the nature centre, where skis are available for rent. The groomed 5km (3mi) cross-country ski trail starts from just behind the barn. If a group has come through recently, classic grooves will be in place; otherwise the trails are groomed, but not trackset. The winter cross-country trail goes through an open field and then joins the Lookout Ravine Trail to run parallel to 12 Mile Creek, a stream that used to be known as Bronte Creek. Take your skis off to climb the lookout platform and see Lake Ontario's least disturbed river and ravine tributary. This is as close as we can get to seeing the same landscape Victorian settlers would have seen.

Snowshoers can park in lot F, which is closest to the 1km (.6mi) Trillium Trail and the 2km (1mi) Half Moon Valley Trail. The Trillium Trail leads through a

Trillium

wooded area that gets an abundance of spring flowers. The Half Moon Valley Trail explores the valley created by the former path of Bronte Creek. You may not even need your snowshoes to walk along the trail, which includes three stairways and a wooden deck path. If you want to explore the Half Moon Valley Trail, be sure to get the park trail guide. It explains how the area was set aside in 1800 as a First Nations Reserve for the Mississauga, but was sold in 1820. Legend has William Lyon McKenzie as the next inhabitant in the area; it is said that McKenzie used an underground cave in Half Moon Valley to hide from authorities after the Rebellion of 1837. In the years following, entrepreneurs established a brick kiln for local home-building and a sawmill that supplied white pine lumber to build the Welland Canal.

Getting There

Take the Burloak Drive exit off the Queen Elizabeth Way.

Further Information

Bronte Creek Provincial Park
1219 Burloak Dr.
Burlington, ON L7R 3X5
☎**(905) 827-6911**
www.OntarioParks.com

Chippawa Creek Conservation Area

Location:	Between Bismarck and Wellandport
Number of trails:	2
Total distance:	5km (3mi)
Level of difficulty:	●
Groomed:	No
Trackset:	No
Interesting features:	Wetlands, duck migration
Fee:	$3.50/vehicle
Other activities:	Hunting (Sep to Feb)
Amenities and other services:	Parking

Getting There

From the Queen Elizabeth Way, take Exit 57, and drive south to Highway 20. Turn right (west). When you reach Bismarck, turn south onto Regional Road 27. At Wellandport, turn west on Regional Road 45.

Further Information

Chippawa Creek Conservation Area
☎ *(905) 386-6387*

Niagara Peninsula Conservation Authority
250 Thorold Rd. W., 3rd floor
Welland, ON L3C 3W2
☎ *(905) 788-3135*
⇔ *(905) 788-1121*
www.conservation-niagara.on.ca

Christie Lake Conservation Area

Location:	West of Flamborough
Number of trails:	7
Total distance:	10km (6mi)
Level of difficulty:	●
Groomed:	100%
Trackset:	100% classic
Interesting features:	Christie Lake, Spencer Creek, Darnley Mill
Fee:	$5.25/vehicle
Other activities:	Christmas tree sales
Amenities and other services:	Parking, toilets, telephones, visitor centre with snack bar on weekends

Getting There

From Flamborough, take Highway 6 south to Clappison's Corners. Turn right (west) on Highway 5 and continue to the park entrance.

Further Information

Christie Conservation Area
☎*(905) 628-3060*

Hamilton Region Conservation Authority
PO Box 7099
838 Mineral Springs Rd.
Ancaster, ON L9G 3L3
☎*(905) 525-2181*
☎*888-319-HRCA (4722)*
⇌*(905) 648-4622*
www.hamrca.on.ca

Dundas Valley Conservation Area (♥)

Location:	On Hwy. 99 as it becomes Governor's Rd. in Dundas
Number of trails:	1 rail trail, 6 main trails and 12 side trails
Total distance:	84km (52mi)
Groomed:	No
Trackset:	No
Level of difficulty:	■ ◆
Interesting features:	Niagara Escarpment, sulphur springs, the Hermitage ruins, Griffin House, replica railway station trail centre
Fee:	$5.25/vehicle
Other activities:	Children's outdoor adventure courses on Saturdays
Amenities and other services:	Parking, toilets, telephones, visitor information centre with snack bar, gift shop and museum open on weekends

Cross-country skiing and snowshoeing are ideal at Dundas Valley Conservation Area, which includes 1,200ha (2,964 acres) of property surrounded by the Niagara Escarpment.

Intermediate skiers and snowshoers should stick to the 3.3km (2mi) Main Loop or to a portion of the 32km (20mi) Hamilton to Brantford Rail Trail, which leads east to Ewen

Road, near the north shore of Cootes Paradise, or west to Brantford.

More advanced cross-country skiers can access one or many of the five main spokes (Headwaters, Heritage, McCormack, Monarch and Spring Creek) that lead off the Main Loop. The Headwaters Trail passes the Griffin House towards the headwaters of Sulphur Creek to the west of the trail centre. The Heritage Trail leads up the Niagara Escarpment to Old Dundas Road. The McCormack Trail leads to overgrown farm fields and a pond area north of Governor's Road called Governor's Road Conservation Area. The Spring Creek Trail leads east of the trail centre to Sanctuary and Warren parks in Dundas.

Snowshoers should use the main loop and spokes to access a multitude of side trails, including several that are maintained by the Bruce Trail Association (see p 352).

Getting There

Take Governors Road, known as Regional Road 299, from Ancaster or Regional Road 399 from Dundas, to the entrance of the Dundas Valley Conservation Area.

Further Information

Hamilton Region Conservation Authority
PO Box 7099
838 Mineral Springs Rd.
Ancaster, ON L9G 3L3
☎ *(905) 627-1233, 648-4427 or 525-2181*
☎ *888-319-HRCA (4722)*
= *(905) 648-4622*
www.hamrca.on.ca

The Friends of Dundas Valley
PO Box 7099
838 Mineral Springs Rd.
Ancaster, ON L9G 3L3
☎ *(905) 627-1233*
communities.msn.com/friendsofthedundasvalley

Trails South of the Trail Centre

Hamilton-Brantford Rail Trail
This 32km (20mi) linear trail runs along the old Toronto, Hamilton and Buffalo Railway line. Head east towards Ewan Road near McMaster University in Hamilton or west towards Gordon Glaves Memorial Pathway in Brantford. The trail can also be used within the conservation area itself to form a loop with the Spring Creek Trail (see p 132).

Main Loop
This 3.3km (2mi) loop enables visitors to see the Hermitage, gatehouse and orchard, all in one short ski. A short detour part way along the trail leads to Sulphur Springs Road. Cross the road and ski a bit to the north to see the replica Victorian fountain. Then return south past your detour point to an entrance to the Headwaters Trail, which is on the same side. Griffin House is about 500m (1,640ft) along this trail. Retrace your path to the Main Loop to continue to the stone gatehouse. Be sure to take the short trail at the end of the small wall behind the gatehouse and gatehouse garage, which leads to a small frozen waterfall known as the Gatehouse Cascade. It is marked with posts with red arrows and begins south of the visitor centre, past the Hamilton to Brantford Rail Trail.

Orchard Side Trail
This 2km (1.2mi) trail loops around the old Merritt orchard, between the Main Loop and the Monarch Trail. A 150-year-old white oak marks the beginning of the orchard. A cider shack is located in the north corner.

Sulphur Creek Side Trail
This 1.5km (.9mi) trail leads from either the Main Loop or from the Monarch Trail along the north side of Sulphur Creek to Turnball Road.

Carolinian Woodlands Side Trail
This steep 1.4km (1.3mi) Bruce side trail (see p 351) climbs up the Niagara Escarpment from the Main Loop. It passes through prime Carolinian forest, where you can spot several American chestnut tree specimens. The trail ends on the Heritage Trail and you have to retrace your steps back to the Main Loop.

Heritage Trail

This 1.8km (1.1mi) trail leads from the Main Loop into a
mixed forest and up the escarpment, following the route of
nomadic Aboriginals. The trail comes out at the parking lot
of the historic Ancaster Old Mill, which is now a gourmet
restaurant.

Monarch Trail

This 7.1km (4.5mi) trail leads from the Main Loop north,
past the Resource Management Centre, a maple sugar
shack and then along the south side of Sulphur Creek to
Old Dundas Road. The trail proceeds past the parking lot
on Old Dundas Road into a loop to the west. A side extension enables you to climb Groundhog Hill for a panoramic
view of the valley.

Headwaters Trail

The Headwaters Trail begins on the Main Loop and continues for 10km (6mi) on the west side of Sulphur Springs
Road, just south of the fountain. It then leads past several
sulphur springs, and up and down many steep hills to the
headwaters of Sulphur Creek, where it loops around a
cattail marsh.

Homestead Side Trail

The Homestead Trail loops for 1km (.6mi) from the Headwaters Trail on Sulphur Springs Road.

Reforestation Side Trail

This 1km (.6mi) trail loops north from the Headwaters Trail
through a plantation next to a section of Martin's Road
that's closed to vehicles.

G. Donald Side Trail

This 1km (.6mi) trail loops north from the Headwaters Trail
through the Donald farm property to Woodend, an 1860s
home that was renovated in the 1980s to house the conservation authority's main offices.

Clear View Side Trail

This ironically named trail goes north from the Headwaters
Trail through a conifer plantation and then through a
mixed beech and maple forest for a total of .7km (.4mi).
You don't get a clear view of anything, other than trees.

Lookout Side Trail

This .5km (.3mi) trail leads south from the Headwaters Trail straight up the escarpment to the best lookout in the park.

Hilltop Side Trail

The Hilltop Side Trail leads south from the Headwaters Trail, up a hill next to the Ancaster Community Centre for a panoramic view of Dundas Valley. It then loops back for a total of 1km (.6mi).

Trails North of the Visitor Centre

Spring Creek Trail

This trail starts at the outdoor bird exhibit beside the Trail Centre. It then follows the south shore of Spring Creek up the Niagara Escarpment for a total of 3.3km. The trail crosses the creek several times until it reaches Sanctuary Park. It then follows the north shore of the creek to the top of the escarpment at Tallyho Road.

Exercise Side Trail

This .5km (.3mi) mini-loop enables trail users to take advantage of equipment that encourages stretching, sit-ups, chin-ups and other warm-up exercises before or after skiing or snowshoeing. It begins on the Spring Creek Trail, east of the bird exhibit.

John White Side Trail

This 5km (3mi) trail, which was named after a treasurer for the province of Ontario, leads north around the parking lots, beside a pond, then across Governor's Road to the McCormack Trail.

McCormack Trail

This 7.5km (4.7mi) trail loops north towards the Governor's Road Conservation Area and then joins the Bruce Trail (see p 351) at the north lookout. The Bruce Trail leads up the escarpment through old farm pastures and rolling hills. It begins on the John White Trail.

Sawmill Side Trail

This 3km (2mi) trail loops off of the McCormack and Spring Creek trails to continue north of the trail centre, past the parking lots, and around a pond.

Fifty Point Conservation Area

Location: Stoney Creek
Number of trails: 1
Total distance: 2km (1mi)
Level of difficulty: ●
Groomed: No
Trackset: No
Interesting features: Lake Ontario,
Fee: $5.25/vehicle
Other activities: Ice skating
**Amenities and
other services:** Parking, toilets, visitor centre with telephones and snack bar, restaurant

Getting There

Take the Queen Elizabeth Way from Toronto towards the Niagara region. Exit at Fifty Road in Stoney Creek and continue to North Service Road. Turn right and follow the signs to the conservation area.

Further Information

Fifty Point Conservation Area
☎*(905) 525-2187*

Hamilton Region Conservation Authority
PO Box 7099
838 Mineral Springs Rd.
Ancaster, ON L9G 3L3
☎*(905) 648-4427 or 525-2181*
☎*888-319-HRCA (4722)*
≈*(905) 648-4622*
www.hamrca.on.ca

Long Beach

Location:	Between Port Colborne and Rock Point
Number of trails:	1
Total distance:	3km (2mi)
Level of difficulty:	●
Groomed:	No
Trackset:	No
Interesting features:	Lake Erie, marsh
Fee:	$3.50/vehicle
Other activities:	Hunting
Amenities and other services:	Parking

Getting There

From the Queen Elizabeth Way, take Exit 57, and drive south to Chambers Corners at Highway 3. Turn south and drive to Regional Road 3. Turn west, and drive 5km (3mi) to the park entrance.

Further Information

Long Beach
☎*(905) 899-3462*

Niagara Peninsula Conservation Authority
250 Thorold Rd. W., 3rd floor
Welland, ON L3C 3W2
☎*(905) 788-3135*
⊷*(905) 788-1121*
www.conservation-niagara.on.ca

Niagara River Recreation Trail (♥)

Location:	Along the Niagara River from Niagara-on-the-Lake to Fort Erie

The Niagara Peninsula

ATTRACTIONS

1. McFarland House
2. Queenston Heights Park
3. Floral Clock
4. Botanical Gardens
5. Niagara Glen
6. Spanish Aero Car
7. Victoria Park
8. Canadian Horseshoe Falls
9. American Falls
10. Greenhouse
11. Oak Hall
12. Historic Fort Erie

Niagara River Recreation Trail

Queenston

Niagara Falls

Chippawa

Tonawanda Canal

River

Niagara

©ULYSSES

0   2.5   5km

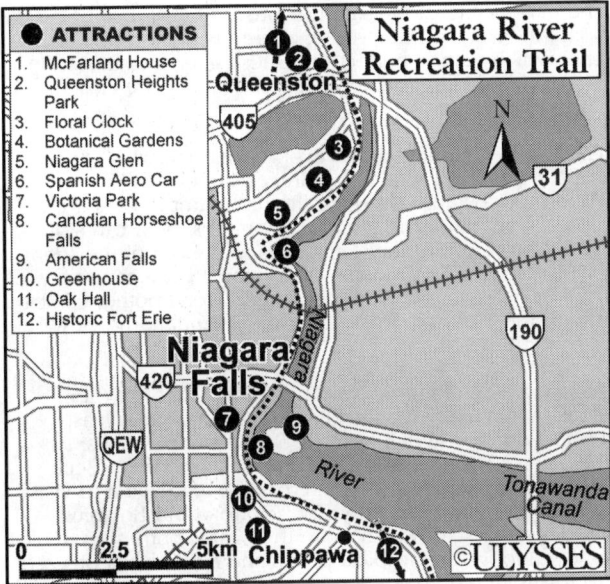

Number of trails:	1 linear
Total distance:	56km (35mi)
Level of difficulty:	●
Groomed:	No
Trackset:	No
Interesting features:	Niagara Falls, Dufferin Island, Millers Creek, Historic Fort Erie exterior, Niagara Parks Greenhouse, Niagara Glen, ducks, gull migration
Fee:	No
Other activities:	No
Amenities and other services:	No

Although the Niagara River Recreation Trail isn't groomed, local cross-country skiers use it the moment the snow flies, so visitors always have tracks to follow. The trail leads for 56km (35mi) from Niagara-on-the-Lake to Fort Erie. Although advanced skiers might try to ski the whole thing without stopping, there are several possible stops along the way that will tempt you to remove your skis and stay awhile.

The path begins at McFarland House, a circa 1800 brick home in Niagara-on-the-Lake, and ends at Historic Fort Erie, which helped protect the British garrison during the War of 1812. Unfortunately, both attractions are closed during the winter.

The first free attraction that is open year-round is Queenston Heights Park, where the Bruce Trail (see p 351) to Tobermory begins. Although the restaurant in the park is closed, you may want to cross the road so you can stop here. The climb up the stairs leads to the top of the 106m (350ft) Niagara Escarpment where you'll get a great view of the lower Niagara River and Toronto. Don't bother climbing up the Sir Isaac Brock monument though; the view is not worth the climb.

The next stop along the way is a 12m-wide (40ft) floral clock that actually works. Plan to rest here for at least 15min so that you can hear the Westminster chimes. Pass the Lewiston-Queenston Bridge and the Sir Adam Beck Generating Stations and then cross the road again to visit the Niagara Parks Butterfly Conservatory and Botanical Gardens. You can watch more than 2,000 butterflies fly freely amongst the tropical plants and feeding stations set up for them (admission fee). If you're hungry or thirsty, the year-round gift shop offers snacks.

If you prefer, you can hold your hunger until you get to the Niagara Glen, where a small nature shop offers cold drinks and light snacks. The Niagara Glen was once the site of Wintergreen Falls, which left behind a flat observation deck called Wintergreen Terrace and a jut of land 36m (118ft) down into the gorge beside the Niagara River that's known as the Wilson Terrace. If the weather is good and you have extra time, you may want to take your skis off to climb down the staircase to the trails on Wilson Terrace.

Continue past Thompson point and around the Niagara Whirlpool to the Spanish Aero Car, a cable car that takes visitors over the whirlpool rapids (admission fee). Continue towards the Great Gorge Adventure, in which an elevator takes you to a boardwalk next to the Whirlpool Rapids along the river at the bottom of the gorge (admission fee).

After passing the Whirlpool Rapids and Rainbow bridges, cross the road to visit the Oakes Garden Theatre, an art nouveau structure that was built as an outdoor stage in

1937. Today, the structure is filled with light displays during the winter.

Pass the Maid of the Mist Plaza, and you'll get to Queen Victoria Park and the star attraction, a view of Niagara Falls. This is when you find out that Niagara Falls is actually two cascades—the American Falls and the Canadian Horseshoe Falls. Both are approximately 55m (180ft) high, although 3m (10ft) of that distance is under water. Two islands—Goat Island and Grand Island—divide the Niagara River in two as it flows north from Lake Erie towards Lake Ontario. Goat Island is the landmass you see between the American Falls and the Canadian Horseshoe Falls

The Canadian Horseshoe and American Falls have been lit up since 1925, but it's only recently, thanks to the Niagara Falls Festival of Lights, that Queen Victoria Park also wears coloured lights throughout the winter. The show runs from dusk to either 10pm or midnight, depending on the time of year.

Stop for fast food at the Victoria Park Cafeteria Niagara River Recreation Trail or continue to the Table Rock Complex, next to the Canadian Horseshoe Falls. Table Rock also contains a fast food restaurant, toilets and a gift shop that are open year-round, as well as the Table Rock Restaurant, a full-service restaurant that's also open in the winter.

You'll want to cross the road briefly at the Niagara Power Station to visit the Niagara Parks Greenhouse, a wonderful stone facility that was built in 1894 and operates year-round. There's no admission fee to enter and take a look. You'll see lots of colour in the form of chrysanthemums, poinsettias, lilies or other seasonal flowers and you'll enjoy the singing of more than 70 tropical songbirds that fly freely throughout the greenhouse. There's also an impressive cactus collection to admire, along with turtles, tree frogs and toads.

Stay on the same side to ski past the golf course and Oak Hall to reach Dufferin Islands, a 11ha (28-acre) park made up of eleven islands. You can ski along a 2km (1mi) path that weaves over and past many little bridges. This is a prime bird-watching location.

The Niagara River Recreation Trail continues south towards King's Bridge Park, which offers a great view of the upper

Niagara River, and past the mouth of the Welland River and into Chippewa. At this point, the trail no longer runs directly beside the Niagara River. Instead, it winds along a tree-lined median between the Niagara Parkway and a residential street. You'll cross several bridges above Black Creek, Bakers Creek, Millers Creek and so on. During the month of December, you may want to stop at Mildred M. Mahoney's Dolls' House Gallery before reaching Mather Arch Park. The arch was built in 1940 as a memorial to Alonzo C. Mather, who used to own the land it sits on. The Town of Fort Erie moved its War Memorial to the park in 1970.

Getting There

Begin skiing at McFarland House in Niagara-on-the-Lake, at Historic Fort Erie in Fort Erie, or anywhere along the trail.

Further Information

The Niagara Parks Commission
PO Box 150
Niagara Falls, ON L2E 6T2
☎*(905) 371-0254*
☎*877-NIA-PARK (642-7275)*
⇔*(905) 356-8448*
www.niagaraparks.com

Rockway Conservation Area

Location:	East of Vineland
Number of trails:	1
Total distance:	2.6km (1.6mi)
Level of difficulty:	■
Groomed:	No
Trackset:	No
Interesting features:	Niagara Escarpment, Fifteen Mile Creek, two waterfalls, rapids, salt springs
Fee:	$3.50/vehicle
Other activities:	No
Amenities and other services:	Parking

Getting There

From the Queen Elizabeth Way, take Exit 57, and drive south on Highway 24 to Vineland. Turn left (east) on County Road 81 to 9th Avenue. Turn right (south) to County Road 69. Turn left (east) and travel about 5km (3mi) to the park entrance.

Further Information

Niagara Peninsula Conservation Authority
250 Thorold Rd. W., 3rd floor
Welland, ON L3C 3W2
☎ *(905) 788-3135*
⇌ *(905) 788-1121*
www.conservation-niagara.on.ca

St. Catharines Trail System

Location:	Lake Ontario to Short Hills Provincial Park in St. Catharines
Number of trails:	1 linear
Total distance:	22.5km (14mi)
Level of difficulty:	●
Groomed:	No
Trackset:	No
Interesting features:	Green Ribbon Trail, Twelve Mile Creek, Rodman Hall, Merritt Trail, Montebello Park, Walker Arboretum
Fee:	No
Other activities:	No
Amenities and other services:	Parking

Getting There

Access the trail from a parking lot on the west side of the harbour at Port Dalhousie, from east Port Weller, from Martindale Road, Bradley Street, Glendale Avenue, St. Paul Crescent or Short Hills Provincial Park (see p 141) in St. Catharines.

Further Information

**City of St. Catharines Recreation and Community
Service Department**
PO Box 3012
St. Catharines, ON L2R 7C2
☎ *(905) 937-7210*
⇌ *(905) 646-9262*

St. Johns Conservation Area

Location:	Fonthill
Number of trails:	2
Total distance:	3km (2mi)
Level of difficulty:	■
Groomed:	No
Trackset:	No
Interesting features:	Niagara Escarpment; Twelve Mile Creek; mature Carolinian forests, wetlands and ponds
Fee:	$3.50/vehicle
Other activities:	Fishing, birding
Amenities and other services:	Parking

Getting There

From the Queen Elizabeth Way, take Exit 57, and drive
south to Highway 20. Turn left (east), and continue to
Fonthill. Turn left (north) on Pelham Street in Fonthill,
which becomes Hollow Road. Continue 10km (6mi) past
Barron Road to the park entrance.

Further Information

Niagara Peninsula Conservation Authority
250 Thorold Rd. W., 3rd floor
Welland, ON L3C 3W2
☎ *(905) 788-3135*
⇌ *(905) 788-1121*
www.conservation-niagara.on.ca

Short Hills Provincial Park

The Niagara Peninsula

Location:	Rolland Rd., Wiley Rd., or Pelham Rd., St. Catharines
Number of trails:	10
Total distance:	23km (14.3mi)
Level of difficulty:	● ◆
Groomed:	No
Trackset:	No
Interesting features:	Niagara Escarpment hills, Carolinian forest, bluebirds, wild turkeys, exposed fossils in Dry Falls limestone, Twelve Mile Creek, Swayze Falls, Terrace Falls, Bruce Trail
Fee:	No
Other activities:	Horseback riding
Amenities and other services:	Parking

Short Hills Provincial Park sits at the foothills of the Niagara Escarpment, south of St. Catharines. Twelve Mile Creek, one of Niagara's few cold-water streams, flows through the park, creating a number of waterfalls as it flows over the limestone ridges. Two waterfalls, Swayze Falls and Terrace Falls, are accessed along trails of the same name.

The hills are full of Carolinian species, including black walnuts, cucumber trees and pawpaw. The park is also a winter haven for bluebirds, scarlet tanagers and wild turkeys.

The 10 trails in the park lead like spokes up and down the hills from a main paved trail. Cross-country skiers can take many of the flatter trails, while snowshoes are required for the trails up and down the short hills.

Getting There

Take Pelham Road south from St. Catherines to Gilligan Road, a gravel path that leads to the park entrance.

Further Information

Short Hills Provincial Park
c/o Rock Point Provincial Park
PO Box 158
Dunnville, ON N1A 2X5
☎ *(905) 774-6642*
⇌ *(905) 774-3264*
www.OntarioParks.com

Friends of Short Hills Park
PO Box 236
Fonthill, ON L0S 1E0
www.vaxxine.com/buzzworld

Valens Conservation Area

Location:	Regional Rd. 97 in Flamborough, between Cambridge and Freelton
Number of trails:	8
Total distance:	10km (6.2mi)
Level of difficulty:	●
Groomed:	100%
Trackset:	No
Interesting features:	Boardwalk over marsh, forests, pine plantations, deer
Fee:	$5/vehicle
Other activities:	Ice fishing (heated wood huts available), winter camping, winter hiking, skating
Amenities and other services:	Parking, heated lodge with heated toilets, telephones, soft drinks, heated showers, and hot chocolate (weekends only)

Valens is a very popular spot for ice fishing, but the primary hotspots for this activity are nestled around a water reservoir at a significant distance from the trails. Cross-country skiers and snowshoers who stick to the trails won't hear the crowds of people congregating on the fishing bridge and can enjoy a very quiet and peaceful experience.

Nine of the 10 different trails for cross-country skiers interconnect so that skiers can travel through the camping area,
across the boardwalk and in a loop around the wilderness
area without having to double back.

Getting There

Take County Road 97 east from Cambridge or west from
Freelton.

Further Information

Valens Conservation Area
☎(519) 621-6029

Hamilton Region Conservation Authority
PO Box 7099
838 Mineral Springs Rd.
Ancaster, ON L9G 3L3
☎(905) 627-1233, 648-4427, or 525-2183
☎888-319-HRCA (4722)
⇌(905) 648-4622
www.hamrca.on.ca

Southern Ontario

When travelling in southern Ontario during the winter, an adventurous attitude and hiking boots are just as necessary as your snowshoeing and ski equipment.

Snowfall varies widely from month to month and year to year. Some years, there's great snow cover in November, but it's gone before the end of February. Other years, the snow doesn't get deep until mid-January and then stays until mid-April.

Point Pelee National Park (see p 181), at the tip of the province, can count on only two months of snow cover, if that. Skiers and snowshoers who take advantage of the short season, however, will enjoy the wide variety of bird species that can be seen here. If they bring along their ice skates, they'll also have a unique opportunity to skate directly on the cattail marsh—a genuine Ontario winter experience.

Other areas with short, but impressive seasons include: **Fanshawe Conservation Area** (see p 161), **Laurel Creek Conservation Area** (see p 168), **Maple Keys Conservation Area** (see p 174), **Morrison Dam Conservation Area** (see p 176), **Pinehurst Lake** (see p 177), **Rondeau Provincial Park** (see p 183), the

Saugeen Rail Trail (see p 186) and the Wawanosh Conservation Area (see p 190).

Backcountry skiers and snowshoers will want to visit locations that don't have groomed trails, including the Allan Park Management Unit (see p 150), the Bannockburn Wildlife Management Area (see p 154), the Hay Swamp Management Area (see p 164), Hullett Wildlife Area (see p 165), and the Kinghurst Management Unit (see p 167).

You'll enjoy some of the best spring skiing around at locations that keep their snow longer than the surrounding regions, including Pinery Provincial Park (see p 178) and Longwoods Road Conservation Area (see p 169). The groomers at both parks pride themselves on providing good skiing throughout the season, no matter how long it lasts, and snowshoers also benefit from the deeper snow at these locations.

Southern Ontario

1. Allan Park Management Unit
2. Arboretum, University of Guelph
3. Avon Trail
4. Backus Heritage Conservation Area
5. Bannockburn Wildlife Management Area
6. Bruce Peninsula National Park
7. Colpoy's Ski Trail
8. Elora-Cataract Trail
9. Elora Gorge Conservation Area
10. Falls Reserve Conservation Area
11. Forks of the Credit Provincial Park
12. Fanshawe Conservation Area
13. Goderich to Auburn Rail Trail (GART)
14. Gordon Glaves Memorial Pathway
15. Hay Swamp Management Area
16. Hullett Wildlife Area
17. Inverhuron Provincial Park
18. Kinghurst Management Unit
19. Laurel Creek Conservation Area
20. Longwoods Road Conservation Area
21. Lynn Valley Trail
22. MacGregor Point Provincial Park
23. Maitland Trail and Menesetung Bridge
24. Maple Keys Conservation Area
25. Mono Nordic Ski Club
26. Morrison Dam Conservation Area
27. Naftel's Creek Conservation Area
28. Pinehurst Lake
29. Pinery Provincial Park
30. Point Pelee National Park
31. Rankin Ski Trail
32. Rondeau Provincial Park
33. Sauble Beach Cross Country Ski Trail
34. Saugeen Bluffs Conservation Area
35. Saugeen Rail Trail
36. Sawmill Cross Country Ski Trail
37. Shade's Mills Conservation Area
38. South Trail, Kincardine
39. Stoney Island Conservation Area
40. Wawanosh Conservation Area
41. Wildwood Conservation Area

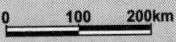

Southern Ontario

Parry Sound

Tobermory • **6**

Georgian Bay

6

Lake Huron

31 **7**
Wiarton •
33 **36**

26 Meaford

Owen Sound

Collingwood

Southampton • **22** **35** Chatsworth

17 **34** Flesherton

Tiverton • **10**

Kincardine • **39** Walkerton **18** Durham

38 Mount Forest

Shelburne

Amberley • **11** **25**

86 Harriston • Arthur • Grand Valley

Wingham **27** Elora • **9** 6

21 Listowel **8**

Goderich • **13** **40** Elmira • Conestogo **2**

23 **16** **24** **3** **Guelph**

10 Clinton **Kitchener-**

Bayfield • 8 Mitchell • **Waterloo** **19**

St. Joseph • **Stratford** **14**

Grand Bend • **Brantford**

29 **15** **5** St. Marys **41**

Parkhill **26** • Elginfield Woodstock

402 **London** Ingersol **21**

Sarnia **12** **28**

Port Huron Tillsonburg Simcoe **37**

Imlay City • Petrolia • **20** **4**

Courtright • St. Thomas • Aylmer Port Rowan

94 Glencoe • Port Stanley Port Bruce

Dresden • 3

Wallaceburg • Thamesville • Eagle •

Lake St. Clair Ridgetown •

Detroit Chatham • Blenheim

Windsor 401 Merlin • **32** *Lake Erie*

Tilbury •

Essex

Amherstburg • Leamington •

30

Lake Huron

Port Austin •

Harbor Beach •

Bad Axe •

UNITED STATES

UNITED STATES

0 100 200km

©ULYSSES

Snow conditions improve as you drive north along Lake Huron towards Georgian Bay and the Niagara Escarpment. The first hint of good snow cover usually begins upon reaching Goderich, a town that has been a cross-country skiing and hiking destination since the early 1990s when locals rescued an old 1.5km (.9mi) train bridge over the Maitland River that's now known as the **Menesetung Bridge** (see p 172). Use the Menesetung Bridge to access the **Maitland Trail** (see p 172), which travels beside the fast-flowing river of the same name, and the **Goderich to Auburn Rail Trail (GART)** (see p 162). On your way, be sure to visit the beach in Goderich. Lake Huron freezes so quickly that it turns its waves into ice and its sand beaches into hills, as though an active storm stands frozen in time for the benefit of visitors who can experience the astonishing beauty of constant wind movement without suffering the wind itself.

The rivers also provide some wonderfully scenic skiing near water. Just south of the town of Goderich, for example, is **Naftel's Creek Conservation Area** (see p 177), with one trail that follows the creek. The 25km (15.5mi) **Gordon Glaves Memorial Pathway** in Brantford also meanders along the banks of a river, providing skiers and snowshoers with prime waterfowl viewing along the way. Ditto for the **Lynn Valley Trail**, where a few brave tundra swans join the typical chickadees and mallards usually seen during Ontario winters. For a slightly different view of rushing water flowing and freezing over rock, visit the **Falls Reserve Conservation Area** (see p 159), just inland from Goderich.

Kincardine and Port Elgin both have good snow conditions most years, which benefit all the areas between them, including the **South Trail** (see p 189) and **Stoney Island Conservation Area** (see p 190) in Kincardine, and **Inverhuron** (see p 166) and **MacGregor Point** (see p 171) provincial parks, near Port Elgin. The snow cover also benefits another impressive rock formation at the **Saugeen Bluffs Conservation Area** (see p 185), just inland from Port Elgin, where skiers and snowshoers can enjoy the trails put down by snowmobilers.

The **Bruce Peninsula National Park** (see p 155), near the Lake Huron tip of the Niagara Escarpment, gets quite a bit of snow, but not as much as those areas to the south, east and west of the mountainous landform. The Wiarton area has no shortage of snow cover, which is why the **Colpoy's Ski Trail** (see p 156), the **Rankin Ski Trail** (see p 182), the **Sauble Beach Cross Country Ski Trail** (see p 184) and the **Sawmill Cross Country Ski Trail** (see p 186) are home to so many of the province's best cross-country ski racers.

Perhaps not surprisingly, the Orangeville skiers also have lots of snow in their region. They train at the **Mono Nordic Ski Club** (see p 174) in Monora Park near Orangeville, which, along with the **Forks of the Credit Provincial Park** (see p 160) near Alton, falls within Ontario's snowbelt. The snowbelt starts just north of the Caledon Mountain, a 427m (1,401ft) elevation along Highway 10 north of Brampton. The two locations are also linked scenically by the Credit River, which has its headwaters in the various springs in Monora Park and falls dramatically at the fork of the Credit's Cataract Falls, the site of an 1885 hydroelectric mill.

The **Elora-Cataract Trail** (see p 157) leads from the Cataract Falls to another equally dramatic site called the Elora Gorge. The Elora Gorge is a 2.4km-long (1.5mi) narrow canyon of solid rock that varies in depth from 18 to 24m (60 to 80ft). A portion of the Grand River runs along the centre of the gorge. Snowshoers who want to explore the area can do so at the **Elora Gorge Conservation Area** (see p 158).

Southern Ontario

In years of heavy snowfall, snowshoers and skiers will really enjoy the 104km-long (65mi) **Avon Trail**, which hooks up to 18km (11mi) of classic groomed trails in the **Wildwood Conservation Area** (see p 191).

If you're a history buff, you'll enjoy visiting the **Backus Heritage Conservation Area** (see p 153), the site of a 1798 wooden saw and gristmill that's still operational. Ski or snowshoe in the 283ha (700 acre) Backus woods, Canada's largest, most impressive stand of Carolinian forest.

Trees are also on display at **The Arboretum, University of Guelph** (see p 151) where you'll learn to identify all of Ontario's native tree species, and in **Shade's Mills Conservation Area** (see p 188), which has trails going through deep conifer stands.

Tourist Information

Southern Ontario Tourism Organization
180 Greenwich St.
Brantford, ON N3S 2X6
☎ *800-267-3399*
⇌ *(519) 756-3231*
www.soto.on.ca

Allan Park Management Unit

Location:	Between Hanover and Durham
Number of trails:	8
Total distance:	15km (9.3mi)
Level of difficulty:	● ■ ◆
Groomed:	100%
Trackset:	No
Interesting features:	Horseshoe moraine
Fee:	Donation
Other activities:	Snowmobiling

Amenities and **other services:**	Parking

Getting There

Take Highway 4 east from Hanover or west from Durham
to the hamlet of Allan Park. Turn south onto Concession 2
Side Road. The entrance will be on your left.

Further Information

Saugeen Valley Conservation Authority
RR 1
Hanover, ON N4N 3B8
☎ *(519) 364-1255*
⇌ *(519) 364-6990*
www.svca.on.ca

The Arboretum, University of Guelph

Location:	Arboretum Rd., Guelph
Number of trails:	5
Total distance:	10km (6.2mi)
Level of difficulty:	●
Groomed:	No
Trackset:	No
Interesting features:	Deer, mink, weasel, squirrel, fox and coyote trails
Fee:	No
Other activities:	Group walks, interpretive tours, self-guided tours
Amenities and **other services:**	Parking, toilets

Cross-country skiers and snowshoers will probably want to
start at the J.C. Taylor Nature Centre at the back of the
park. The best cross-country skiing trail is the 2km (1mi)
Trillium Trail, which loops through 10 different plant collections, including lilacs, maples and roses, and leads to the
Roy Hammond Rotary Tree Grove.

Southern Ontario

You may also want to go behind the nature centre to the **Victoria Woods Trail**, a 2km (1mi) loop through an old growth maple-beech forest that has never been clear-cut. From there, follow the .8km (.5mi) **Colonel John McCrae Trail** that leads through a hedgerow into the Gosling Wildlife Gardens, and further into **Wild Goose Woods**. Wild Goose Woods is a diverse ecosystem that attracts a wide variety of birds, as you'll find out if you ski along the 650m (1,232ft) Wild Goose Woods Trail. Although the path is short, it leads through marsh, forest and swamp and then into the **Hospice Lilac Garden**.

Other trails in the arboretum include the East Walk, the Native Trees of Ontario Trail, the World of Trees Trail and the Wall-Custance Memorial Forest Trail. They are all connected by the Ivey Trail, a 1.1km (.7mi) path that connects all of the trails with the arboretum and nature centre.

Getting There

Drive to Guelph and follow the signs to the university. Once on university grounds, turn east from East Ring Road onto Arboretum Road, which leads to parking lots on both sides of the arboretum, the OAC Centennial Arboretum Centre and the J.C. Taylor Nature Centre.

Further Information

The Arboretum, University of Guelph
Guelph, ON N1G 2W1
☎*(519) 824-4120, x2113*
www.uoguelph.ca/~arboretu

Avon Trail

Location:	Between St. Marys and Conestogo
Number of trails:	1 linear
Total distance:	104km (65mi)
Level of difficulty:	●
Groomed:	No
Trackset:	No

Interesting features: Avon River, Farmers Market, Waterloo
moraine, Wildwood Conservation Area
Fee: Donation
Other activities: Winter hiking

Getting There

Access the trail from Thames Road in the town of
St. Marys, at the intersection of Waterloo Regional Road 17
and Conestogo-Winterbourne Road in the town of Conestogo, from Wildwood Conservation Area (see p 191), or
from the Waterloo County Farmers Market on Weber Street
in Waterloo.

Further Information

The Avon Trail
PO Box 21148
Stratford, ON N5A 7V4
www.golden.net/~wlindsch/avon/avon.html

Southern Ontario

Backus Heritage Conservation Area

Location: North of Port Rowan and south of
Langton
Number of trails: 5
Total distance: 18.5km (11.5mi)
Level of difficulty: ● ■
Groomed: 65%
Trackset: No
Interesting features: Backus Woods Carolinian Forest
Fee: Donation
Other activities: John C. Backhouse Mill, Backus Home-
stead, 3 mills, 2 barns, 2 shops, play-
house and farm implements

**Amenities and
other services:** Parking, toilets, telephones and snack
bar in visitor centre

A visit to Backus Heritage Conservation Area means skiing
among Canada's best stand of untouched Carolinian forest.

Inspired by an interest in trees, original owner John C. Backhouse preserved the 283ha (700-acre) woodlot, and his ancestors respected his intentions. Now referred to as Backus Woods, the forest includes black gum, pawpaw, shagbark hickory, sweet chestnut, sycamore, swamp white oak and tulip trees among the maple, beech, yellow birch, red maple and red oak trees typical of an Ontario deciduous forest. The Charles Sauriol Carolinian Forest, a 60ha (148-acre) tract of regenerated farmland that was planted with red oak, sycamore and green ash in 1991, lies next to the property north of Concession 3.

Getting There

Take Regional Road 59 north from Long Point or south from Langton. Turn east on Regional Road 42 for the heritage village and Backus Woods or Highway 24 for Backus Woods only.

Further Information

Long Point Region Conservation Authority
RR 1
Port Rowan, ON N0E 1M0
☎*(519) 586-2201*
☎*877-990-9932*
(519) 428-1520
www.lprca.on.ca

Bannockburn Wildlife Management Area

Location:	East of Exeter
Number of trails:	1
Total distance:	1km (.6mi)
Level of difficulty:	●
Groomed:	No
Trackset:	No
Interesting features:	white cedar, deciduous forest, wetlands
Fee:	$2/day, $5/family/day, $20/year, $35/family/year
Amenities and other services:	Parking

Getting There

From Varna, take County Road 3 east to Concession 19.

Further Information

Ausable Bayfield Conservation Authority
RR 3
Exeter, ON N0M 1S5
☎ *(519) 235-2610*
⇌ *(519) 235-1963*
www.execulink.com/~abca

Bruce Peninsula National Park

Location:	East and west side of Hwy. 6
Number of trails:	7
Total distance:	26km (16mi)
Level of difficulty:	■ ◆
Groomed:	No
Trackset:	No
Interesting features:	Niagara Escarpment
Fee:	$2.25/person, $1.60/senior, $1.10/student, $5.35/family
Other activities:	Winter camping
Amenities and other services:	Parking, toilets, telephones and snack bar in visitor centre

Bruce Peninsula National Park is actually three parks in one. Those who like skiing or snowshoeing along sandy flat beaches will appreciate Dorcas Bay, on the shores of Lake Huron to the west of Highway 6. Those who prefer snowshoeing along limestone cliffs, through a mixed forest of aspen, birch, cedar, fir and spruce will enjoy Cyprus Lake on the shores of Georgian Bay, to the east of Highway 6. Those who prefer a more difficult backcountry experience will want to access the Bruce Trail via the Halfway Log Dump Trail.

Getting There

Take Highway 6 north from Wiarton or south from Tobermory.

Further Information

Bruce Peninsula National Park
PO Box 189
Tobermory, ON N0H 2R0
☎*(519) 596-2233*
www.parkscanada.gc.ca/parks/ontario/bruce_peninsula

Colpoy's Ski Trail

Location:	North of Wiarton, on Bruce Rd. 19
Number of trails:	5
Total distance:	22km (14mi)
Level of difficulty:	● ■
Groomed:	100%
Trackset:	No
Interesting features:	Beaver pond
Fee:	$4/day, $8/3-day weekend, $30/season; families: $12/day, $24/3-day weekend, $50/season
	Tickets available at Cliffside Resort
Amenities and other services:	Parking, barn serves as heated lodge

Getting There

Take Bruce Road 9 north from Wiarton.

Further Information

Bruce Ski Club
PO Box 205
Wiarton, ON N0H 2T0
☎*(519) 534-3476 (Joerg Leiss)*

Elora-Cataract Trail

Location: Between Elora and the Forks of the
                            Credit Provincial Park
Number of trails: 1
Total distance: 47km (29mi) linear
Level of difficulty: ●
Groomed: No
Trackset: No
Interesting features: Elora Quarry, the Cataract Falls at the
                            Forks of the Credit
Fee: No
Other activities: Snowmobiling

The Elora-Cataract Trail runs west from Cataract to the
Grand River, but the 8km (5mi) section between Black's pit
and the Forks of the Credit Provincial Park is located on
sideroads. To get from one end to the other consecutively,
you still have to walk for significant parts of the trip.

The areas that have been established, such as the part between Erin and Elora, make for beautiful skiing.

Getting There

Access the trail along County Road 18, behind the Elora
Public School in Elora or at the Forks of the Credit Provincial Park (see p 160).

Further Information

The Elora Information Centre
PO Box 814
152 Geddes St.
Elora, ON N0B 1S0
☎*(519) 846-9841*
☎*877-286-3058*
⇆*(519) 846-2058*
www.eic.elora.on.ca

Southern Ontario

Elora Gorge Conservation Area

Location:	On the Grand River, southwest of Fergus, northwest of Guelph
Number of trails:	1
Total distance:	12km (7mi)
Level of difficulty:	■
Groomed:	No
Trackset:	No
Interesting features:	Scenic river gorge with 18.3 to 24.4m (60 to 80ft) cliffs, the Grand River, the Irvine River, the Elora Mill Inn, the Tooth of Time, Lover's Leap, the Elora caves
Fee:	No
Amenities and other services:	Parking

Although the 142ha (351-acre) Elora Gorge Conservation Area is closed during the winter, you can still snowshoe or cross-country ski on the property, including on the trail that circles the deepest, narrowest gorges in southern Ontario.

There is a 5km (3mi) path that encircles the 18 to 24m-deep (60 to 80ft) gorge, although it's not groomed or even cleared during the winter, so you may not be able to follow the entire route.

Be sure to continue beyond the Conservation Area limits towards the town of Elora to see the Elora Mill, one of Ontario's oldest five-storey gristmills, which was built in 1859 after an earlier wooden mill burnt down. The exterior limestone walls are 1.6m (5ft) thick at the base and 30.5m (100ft) high. The mill still operates is own hydroelectric generating station, which produces 140 kilowatts of power for the mill's own use and for the use of the 3,000-person village of Elora.

Right next to the mill, in the middle of the Grand River, is an island that divides the river in two just as it drops down in a 60ft (24.3m) cascade. This island, which is commonly referred to as either "the tooth of time" or the "islet rock," symbolizes the town of Elora.

Getting There

Take Highway 6 north from Guelph and then turn onto County Road 18 to go southwest from Fergus to Elora. Drive over the bridge and turn west on County Road 21 to the park entrance.

Further Information

The Elora Gorge Conservation Area
PO Box 356
Elora, ON N0B 1S0
☎ *(519) 846-9742*
(519) 846-8781
www.grandriver.on.ca

Falls Reserve Conservation Area

Location:	West of Benmiller
Number of trails:	1
Total distance:	3km (2mi)
Level of difficulty:	■
Groomed:	No
Trackset:	No
Interesting features:	Benmiller Falls
Fee:	$2/person or $7/vehicle
Amenities and other services:	Parking, toilets

Getting There

Take Highway 8 east from Goderich for 6km (4mi) to County Road 1. Turn left to Benmiller, then follow the signs.

Further Information

Maitland Valley Conservation Authority
PO Box 127
93 Marietta St.
Wroxeter, ON N0G 2X0
☎ *(519) 335-3557*
⇌ *(519) 335-3516*
www.mvca.on.ca

Forks of the Credit Provincial Park

Location:	South of Alton
Number of trails:	4
Total distance:	8km (5mi)
Level of difficulty:	● ■
Groomed:	100%
Trackset:	100% classic
Interesting features:	Cataract Falls, mill ruins, farmstead foundations
Fee:	$6/vehicle
Amenities and other services:	Parking

Beginner cross-country skiers and snowshoers will love the Forks of the Credit Provincial Park, which has a wide range of mostly flat skiing and snowshoeing trails across its plains plus a good view of an almost-frozen waterfall and the ruins of a hydroelectric mill dating from 1885.

The name of the park comes from the fact that the north and south branches of the Credit River meet in the park and then travel together through a 4km (2.5mi) gorge in the park. Skiers will probably either take the Meadow Trail, which forms part of the Trans Canada Trail and the Caledon Trailway, or the Runs Trail, which roughly follows the north branch of the Credit River. The stone ruins you'll see along the way are the old foundations of 19th-century homesteads.

Use snowshoes or just walk west along the Falls Trail past the frozen kettle lake and onto a boardwalk towards the town of Cataract, where the Credit River drops over the edge of the Niagara Escarpment in a very impressive waterfall called the Cataract Falls.

Getting There

From Caledon Village on Highway 10, take Highway 24 (Charleston sideroad) west for 3km (2mi) to McLaren Road (2nd Line West). Turn left and drive for about 2.5km (1.6mi) to the park entrance.

Further Information

Forks of the Credit Provincial Park
c/o Earl Rowe Provincial Park
PO Box 966
Alliston, ON L0M 1A0
☎*(705)435-2498*
www.ontarioparks.com

Southern Ontario

Fanshawe Conservation Area

Location:	1424 Clarke Rd., London
Number of trails:	4
Total distance:	15km (9mi)
Level of difficulty:	●
Groomed:	100%
Trackset:	100% classic
Interesting features:	Woodlands, Fanshawe Lake
Fee:	$6/day, $60/season
Other activities:	Tobogganing
Services:	**(R)** *($10)*
Amenities and other services:	Parking, heated pavilion with maps, snack bar, toilets, telephones, waxing centre

Getting There

From London, take Airport Road north to Huron Street. Turn right (west). Drive to Clarke Sideroad, and turn right (north). Continue 1km (.6mi) to the park entrance.

Further Information

Upper Thames River Conservation Authority
1424 Clarke Rd.
London, ON N5V 5B9
☎ *(519) 451-2800*
⇆ *(519) 451-1188*
www.thamesriver.org

Goderich to Auburn Rail Trail (GART)

Location:	Menesetung Bridge in Goderich across Sharpe's Creek to Maitland River at Blind Line
Number of trails:	1
Total distance:	12km (7.5mi)
Level of difficulty:	●
Groomed:	No
Trackset:	No
Interesting features:	Sharpes Creek
Fee:	No
Other activities:	Snowmobiling
Amenities and other services:	Parking

Getting There

Park on North Harbour Road in Goderich, and walk to the converted CPR bridge that crosses the Maitland River.

Further Information

Maitland Trail Association
PO Box 443
Goderich, ON N7A 4C7

Gordon Glaves Memorial Pathway

Location:	Brantford
Number of trails:	1 linear
Total distance:	25km (16mi)
Level of difficulty:	●
Groomed:	No
Trackset:	No
Interesting features:	Brant River, Gilkison Flats, Lions Park
Fee:	No
Amenities and other services:	Parking

The Gordon Glaves Memorial Pathway includes five distinct sections that connect to one another directly or via footbridges across the Brant River. One linear section runs along Mohawk Street and Birkett Lane and then follows the north shore of the Brant River. A second linear section runs along the south shore of the river, from the Alexander Graham Bell Homestead past the Gilkison Flats and on to D'Aubigny Creek. Three loops connect to the south shore linear section in Lions Park: one skirts the top of an escarpment, another loops through a Carolinian forest, and a third leads around a pond that was created when an old Brant River meander separated from the main branch.

Getting There

Access the pathway along Ballantyne Drive, Erie Avenue, Gilkison Street, Grand River Avenue, Greenwich Street, Hardy Road, Heights Road, Market Street South, Parkside Drive, Water Street and through Bellview Park, Brant Conservation Area, Cockshutt Park, D'Aubigny Creek Park, D'Aubigny Creek Path, Fordview Park, Lions Park and Waterworks Park.

Further Information

Tourism Brantford
1 Sherwood Dr.
Brantford, ON N3T 1N3
☎ *(519) 756-1500*
☎ *800-265-6299*
www.city.brantford.on.ca

Southern Ontario

Hay Swamp Management Area

Location:	West of Exeter and Hensall
Number of trails:	2
Total distance:	41km (25mi)
Level of difficulty:	●
Groomed:	73% (by snowmobiles)
Trackset:	No
Interesting features:	Wetland
Fee:	$2/day, $5/family/day, $20/year, $35/family/year or Ontario Federation of Snowmobile Clubs permit
Other activities:	Hunting, snowmobiling
Amenities and other services:	Parking

Ontario's largest wetland is an area called Hay Swamp, which is made up of more than 2,000ha (4,940 acres) of forested wetlands, marsh, plantations and farmland just west of Lake Huron and north of Grand Bend. The area is very important for migrating birds, including tundra swans and ducks; other species of wetland birds also nest here.

The Ausable Bayfield Conservation Authority has two public trails that are closed to motorized vehicles. There are 10km (6.2mi) of trails in and around Black Creek at the Hay Swamp main entrance area on County Road 83 and Concession 4/5. There is also a new 1km (.6mi) loop in the Klopp Woodland Management Area near Hensall.

The Pineridge Snowmobile Club also operates another 30km (18.6mi) of trails through Hay Swamp, although their system goes through private and public land. To use these trails, you need an Ontario Federation of Snowmobile Clubs pass or a guest pass from the Pineridge Snowmobile Club.

Getting There

Drive west on Highway 83 from Exeter or on Highway 84 from Hensall for about 6km (4mi) to Hay Township Concession Road 4/5. There are two parking lots on Township

Concession Road 4/5: one is at the junction of Highway 83, and the other is just south from Highway 84.

Further Information

Ausable Bayfield Conservation Authority
RR 3
Exeter, ON N0M 1S5
☎*(519) 235-2610*
(519) 235-1963
www.execulink.com/~abca

Pineridge Snowmobile Club Inc.
☎*(519) 229-6283 (Rick Vandenbussche)*
http://pineridge.hypermart.net/index.html

Hullett Wildlife Area

Location:	North of Clinton
Number of trails:	3
Total distance:	12km (7mi)
Level of difficulty:	● ■
Groomed:	No
Trackset:	No
Interesting features:	Dykes
Fee:	No
Other activities:	Hunting, horseback riding
Amenities and other services:	Parking

Getting There

From Clinton, take Highway 4 north to Hullett Township Concession Road 1/2. Turn right (east), and drive for about 3km (2mi).

Further Information

Friends of Hullett Inc.
Clinton, ON
☎*(519) 482-7011*

Inverhuron Provincial Park

Location:	North of Kincardine
Number of trails:	1
Total distance:	10km (6.2mi)
Level of difficulty:	●
Groomed:	No
Trackset:	No
Interesting features:	Inverhuron Bay, hemlock forest, red pine plantation, sand dunes
Fee:	No
Other activities:	Snowmobiling

Inverhuron Provincial Park has been out of use for several years, but is now starting to be revived. The trails are not groomed, but many local cross-country skiers and snowshoers create their own trails along grown-in camping roads through the area.

Getting There

From Blyth, take County Road 4 to East Wawanosh Concession 6 and 7 (Nature Centre Road). Turn left (east) and drive 7km (4mi) to the entrance.

Further Information

Inverhuron
c/o MacGregor Point Provincial Park
RR 1
Port Elgin, ON N0H 2C5
☎ *(519) 389-9056*
☎ *800-667-1940*
www.OntarioParks.com

Kinghurst Management Unit

Location:	Dornoch
Number of trails:	1
Total distance:	5km (3mi)
Level of difficulty:	●
Groomed:	No
Trackset:	No
Interesting features:	Farmstead ruins and racoon, porcupine, deer, rabbit, fox, grouse and coyote tracks
Fee:	Donation
Amenities and other services:	Parking, maps

This 140ha (346-acre) site along part of the Singhampton moraine used to be part of the Lustig homestead that was settled in the 1840s. Now covered with conifer plantations and a maple woodlot, the area attracts cross-country skiers and snowshoers who are willing to create their own trails or follow others through the woods and across plains in search of old farm building remains. In fact, the area is very popular among Chesley area residents, who have created a good ungroomed cross-country ski trail that loops for about 5km (3mi).

Although you may not spot the raccoons, porcupines, white-tailed deer, snowshoe rabbits, red fox, ruffled grouse and coyotes that live here, you're sure to see their tracks. Also look for the great horned owls and woodpeckers that inhabit in the region year-round.

Getting There

Take Grey County Road 25 west from Dornoch or east from Chesley to the park entrance on the north side of the road.

Southern Ontario

Further Information

Saugeen Valley Conservation Authority
RR 1
Hanover, ON N4N 3B8
☎ *(519) 364-1255*
≈ *(519) 364-6990*
www.svca.on.ca

Laurel Creek Conservation Area

Location:	Waterloo
Number of trails:	3
Total distance:	8km (5mi)
Level of difficulty:	● ■ ◆
Groomed:	100%
Trackset:	100% classic
Interesting features:	pine, maple and beech forests
Fee:	$4/adult, $2.25/children 6-14yrs
Services:	**(R)** *($8)*
Amenities and other services:	Parking, toilets, telephones, heated lodge, snack bar

Getting There

From Waterloo, take Northfield Drive to Westmount Road, north. The park entrance is on the left.

Further Information

Laurel Creek Conservation Area
290 Laurel Wood Dr.
Waterloo, ON N2J 3Z4
☎ *(519) 884-6620*

Grand River Conservation Authority
400 Clyde Rd.
PO Box 729
Cambridge, ON N1R 5W6
☎ *(519) 621-2761*
www.grandriver.on.ca

Longwoods Road Conservation Area (♥)

Location:	Between Melbourne and Delaware
Number of trails:	2
Total distance:	6km (3.7mi)
Level of difficulty:	● ■
Groomed:	100%
Trackset:	100% classic
Interesting features:	River gorge, Ska-Nah-Doht Iroquoian village, hunting cabins
Fee:	Donation
Other activities:	Moonlight guided hikes, museum
Amenities and other services:	Parking, toilets, telephones and maps in visitor centre

Longwoods Road Conservation Area is a natural respite well worth exploring, especially since its location in a valley ensures good snow cover even when surrounding areas are bare.

Cross-country ski trails include a 2km (1mi) easy loop and a 4km (2.5mi) intermediate loop. The easy loop leads skiers through a Carolinian forest featuring walnut trees and enormous paperbark maples. A few of the more impressive specimens contain graffiti from misguided nature lovers who visited the area in the 1970s. The intermediate loop leads skiers through and alongside a frozen cattail marsh.

Snowshoers will prefer to take the boardwalk across the marsh or to explore the Carolinian woodlands on their own. Be sure to look for the boardwalk that leads over and around a mill river ravine that resembles a mini Grand Canyon, complete with winding creek at the bottom. Look for red fox dens in the ravine.

Snowshoeing is also the best way to explore the Ska-Nah-Doht Iroquoian Village. The name "Ska-Nah-Doht" means

Southern Ontario

"a village stands again" in Chippewa, and comes from the fact that today's reconstructed village is on the actual site where a two-longhouse village stood more than a thousand years ago. Today, the village features three longhouses, one to represent each of the Iroquoian bands that currently occupy the region.

Begin at three 100-year-old log cabins, which were donated by the chiefs of the local Oneida, Muncies and Chippewa First Nations when the village was built in 1972. From there, walk past a *V*-shaped branch fence once used by Iroquoian hunters to trap deer, a burial scaffold, a temporary shelter for the hunters, and a garden featuring the famous three sisters: beans, corn and squash. Once you reach the palisade, follow a maze to get inside the longhouse village. Imagine 150 people living in the three longhouses and using the storage hut, sweat lodge and the meat drying and stretching racks.

Getting There

Take County Road 2 (Longwoods Road) north from Melbourne or south from Delaware

Further Information

Longwoods Road Conservation Area
RR 1
Mount Brydges, ON N0L 1W0
☎*(519) 264-2420*
=*(519) 264-1562*
www.lowerthames-conservation.on.ca

Lynn Valley Trail

Location:	Between Simcoe and Dover in Norfolk
Number of trails:	1 linear
Total distance:	8km (5mi)
Level of difficulty:	●
Groomed:	No
Trackset:	No

Interesting features:	Lynn River, tundra swans, Carolinian forest
Fee:	Donation
Amenities and other services:	Parking

Getting There

Access the trail from Memorial Park or the Lynn Valley Trail parking lot on Blueline South (off of Victoria Street) in the town of Simcoe.

Further Information

Lynne Valley Trail Association
137 Decou Rd.
Simcoe, ON N3Y 4K2
☎ *(519) 428-3292*
www.kwic.com/~kwic/lynntrail

MacGregor Point Provincial Park

Location:	Port Elgin
Number of trails:	1
Total distance:	3km (2mi)
Level of difficulty:	■
Groomed:	No
Trackset:	No
Interesting features:	Lake Huron, cattail marsh, silver maple swamps
Fee:	$6/vehicle
Other activities:	Winter camping
Services:	**(A)** *(Yurts–year-round tents)*
Amenities and other services:	Parking, heated toilets and showers, telephone

Cross-country skiing is very popular along this 7km (4mi) stretch of land on the shores of Lake Huron. The entire park is either wetland or wet forest and features silver maple swamps, cattail marshes, beaver ponds and sand dunes.

Southern Ontario

Skiers who use the Saugeen Rail Trail (see p 186) are hoping to eventually extend it all the way to McGregor Point, which will enable them to travel between the park, Port Elgin and Southampton without having to remove any equipment.

Getting There

Take Highway 21 south from Port Elgin or north from Kincardine to County Road 40 or County Road 11. Turn east (towards Lake Huron) and follow the road to the entrance.

Further Information

MacGregor Point Provincial Park
RR 1
Port Elgin, ON N0H 2C5
☎ *(519) 389-9056*
☎ *800-667-1940*
www.OntarioParks.com

Maitland Trail and Menesetung Bridge

Location:	Bridge crosses the Maitland River in Goderich, Maitland Trail follows the river through Benmiller to Auburn
Number of trails:	3
Total distance:	48km (30mi)
Level of difficulty:	● ■
Groomed:	No
Trackset:	No
Interesting features:	Lake Huron, which is frozen in waves
Fee:	No
Amenities and other services:	Parking

The 1.5km (.9mi) Menesetung Bridge symbolizes a community's ability to work together to build a new reality. It was created in 1992, as a result of a concerted effort on the part of Goderich citizens, who obtained permission from the

Canadian Pacific Railway owners to convert the rail bridge to a walking bridge and then raised enough money to do the job.

Thanks to their efforts, the converted bridge continues to wind its way across the Maitland River, only now it's made up of wood decking for people, rather than rails for trains.

The track gets enough traffic to stay packed, so skiers should have no problem getting a fast glide. As you ski across the bridge, you can see Lake Huron and Goderich Bay on one side, and the Maitland River on the other. In the winter, the sandy shores of the "laughing waters" river that give the bridge its Chippewa name are frozen solid into cement-like chunks that are a strange natural juxtaposition to the Sifto salt mine and port elevator on the other side of the bridge.

At the bridge's end, you have a choice between the Sifto and the Tiger Dunlop loops. The Sifto loop is the part of the Maitland Trail that follows the Maitland River towards Lake Huron. It is not suitable for skiers because it begins with a staircase and then continues along a number of ridges towards a marina. Skiers will probably prefer to continue to the right to follow a section of the Tiger Dunlop Trail that leads to the entrance of the Goderich to Auburn Rail Trail. Take a short detour south at the appropriate marking to see the tomb of Dr. William "Tiger" Dunlop (1792-1848), a physician, author and soldier who opened up the Huron Tract and founded Goderich.

Getting There

Park on North Harbour Road in Goderich and walk to the converted CPR bridge.

Further Information

Maitland Trail Association
PO Box 443
Goderich, ON N7A 4C7

Southern Ontario

Maple Keys Conservation Area

Location:	Ethel
Number of trails:	2
Total distance:	2km (1mi)
Level of difficulty:	●
Groomed:	No
Trackset:	No
Interesting features:	Maple forest
Fee:	No
Other activities:	Hunting (except Feb 15-Apr 15)

Getting There

From Ethel, drive north on County Road 19 to the entrance.

Further Information

Maitland Valley Conservation Authority
PO Box 127
93 Marietta St.
Wroxeter, ON N0G 2X0
☎*(519) 335-3557*
⇥*(519) 335-3516*
www.mvca.on.ca

Mono Nordic Ski Club (♥)

Location:	Monora Park, Mono
Number of trails:	4
Total distance:	15km (9mi)
Level of difficulty:	● ■ ◆
Groomed:	100%
Trackset:	100% classic, 50% skating
Lighting:	2km (1mi), every day 5pm to 10pm, Jan-Apr

Interesting features: Orangeville moraine, headwater springs of the Credit River, beaver dam

Fee: $70/members, $10/day for guests

Services: **(R)** *($5)*, **(L)** *(for jackrabbits)*

Amenities and other services: A two-storey pavilion opens on weekends to register guests and serve hot cider and chocolate.

Note: **Entrance only to members and their guests**

The Mono Nordic Club is a private community club that started in the late 1980s when a group of local teachers and cross-country skiing enthusiasts asked the Mono Township for land that could be developed into a trail system.

Today, the club maintains a 15km (9m) circuit that includes an easy loop, an intermediate touring loop and a loop of twisting, hilly terrain for expert skiers. The most popular of these is the yellow trail for intermediate skiers. Sights featured along the way include a beaver dam and an old gravel pit.

Membership includes about 600 people, half of whom are individuals, while the rest are families. The club offers a program to encourage jackrabbit skiers on weekends and another that gets elementary school children skiing.

Getting There

Monora Park is on the west side of Highway 10 north of Orangeville. The entrance is 300m (984ft) north of the stop light at First Street in Orangeville.

Further Information

Mono Nordic Club
PO Box 115
Orangeville, ON L9W 2Z5
☎ *(519) 942-1468*
☎ *(519) 942-0425 (Alan White)*
☎ *(519) 941-0797 (Ross Martin)*

Monora Park
☎ *(519) 942-2465*

Southern Ontario

Credit Valley Conservation Authority
1255 Old Derry Rd. W.
Meadowvale, ON L5N 6R4
☎*800-668-5557*
⇌*(905) 670-2210*
www.mississauganews.com/conservation/index

Morrison Dam Conservation Area

Location:	East of Exeter
Number of trails:	1
Total distance:	5km (3mi)
Level of difficulty:	■
Groomed:	No
Trackset:	No
Interesting features:	Pine plantation, wetlands
Fee:	$2/day, $5/family/day, $20/year, $35/family/year
Amenities and other services:	Parking

Getting There

From Exeter, take Highway 83 east for 22km (14mi) to
Concession Road 2/3. Turn right (south).

Further Information

Ausable Bayfield Conservation Authority
RR 3
Exeter, ON N0M 1S5
☎*(519) 235-2610*
⇌*(519) 235-1963*
www.execulink.com/~abca

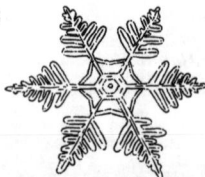

Naftel's Creek Conservation Area

Location: South of Goderich
Total distance: 3km (2mi)
Level of difficulty: ●
Groomed: Yes
Trackset: No
Interesting features: Mixed conifer plantations, marsh board-walks
Fee: No
Amenities and other services: Parking

Getting There

From Ethel, drive north on County Road 19 to the entrance.

Further Information

Maitland Valley Conservation Authority
PO Box 127
93 Marietta St.
Wroxeter, ON N0G 2X0
☎*(519) 335-3557*
✉*(519) 335-3516*
www.mvca.on.ca

Pinehurst Lake

Location: Between Cambridge and Paris
Number of trails: 5
Total distance: 13km (8mi)
Level of difficulty: ● ■ ◆
Groomed: 100%
Trackset: 100% classic, 25% skating (one trail groomed for both)

Southern Ontario

Interesting features: Pinehurst Lake (kettle lake), mature
Carolinian forest
Fee: $4/day
Services: **(R)** *($8)*
**Amenities and
other services:** Parking, toilets, telephones, heated
lodge, snack bar, waxing centre

Getting There

Take Highway 24A north from Paris or south from Cambridge.

Further Information

Area Superintendent
☎(519) 442-4721

Grand River Conservation Authority
400 Clyde Rd.
PO Box 729
Cambridge, ON N1R 5W6
☎(519) 621-3697 or 621-2761
www.grandriver.on.ca

Pinery Provincial Park (♥)

Location: Hwy. 21, south of Grand Bend
Number of trails: 5
Total distance: 38km (23.6mi)
Level of difficulty: ● ■ ◆
Groomed: 100%
Trackset: 100%, 27km (17mi) classic, 11km (7mi)
skating
Interesting features: Oak savanna, sand dunes, Old Ausable
Channel
Fee: $10/vehicle plus $2/person, $1/youth or
$25/season
Other activities: Ice-skating, walking, tobogganing,
camping, interpretive programs

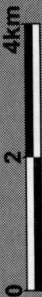

Pinery
Provincial Park

0   2   4km

Courtesy of Ontario Parks

Lake Huron

Grand Bend

21

N

5

©ULYSSES

Huron Trail

Heritage Trail

Old-Ausable Channel

Ausable Trail

5

Skate Trail

Cedar Trail

P

21

Dune Ridge Trail

Walker Woods

Walden Place

Port Franks

3

Services:	**(R)** *($15/adult or $10/children/day)*, **(A)** *(12 yurts–furnished year-round tents)*
Amenities and other services:	Parking, toilets, telephones, snack bar, maps and gift shop available weekends at the visitor information centre, 6 winter shelters along the trail have fire pits, toilets and picnic tables, heated lodge

The Pinery has southern Ontario's best classic cross-country skiing. Excellent groomed trails lead across huge sand dunes, between deep oak-pine forests, along a river and through a savanna forest. Be sure to look for the cedar waxwings that gather throughout the park in December and January. This brown medium-sized bird, which has a crest, black wings and a black mask over its eyes, enjoys eating the berries of red cedar and highbush cranberry that are common throughout the park. In midwinter, expect the trails to be scattered with snow fleas that gather on top of the snow to mate.

In addition to skiing, snowshoe or walk along the decked trails to view the world's largest intact example of oak savanna. Also be sure to take a winter walk along Lake Huron, which often freezes in waves (ice ridges as far as the eye can see). Late in the season, take the trails closest to the bog to watch white tundra swans and other waterfowl that are returning north on their spring migrations.

Four trails are groomed and trackset for classic skiers: the 3.2km (2mi) easy Chickadee Trail, the 4.7km (3mi) Ausable and the 9.6km (6mi) Huron trails for intermediate skiers, and the 9.4km (6mi) Dune Ridge Trail for advanced skiers. There's also one 11km (7mi) trail that's trackset for skaters and two packed trails for snowshoeing or winter hiking.

Getting There

Take Highway 21 north from Northville or south from Grand Bend. The park is on the west side of the highway.

Further Information

Pinery Provincial Park
RR 2
Grand Bend, ON N0M 1T0
☎ *(519) 243-2220*
☎ *800-667-1940 or 888-668-7275*
⇔ *(519) 243-3851*
www.ontarioparks.com

The Friends of Pinery Park
☎ *(519) 243-1521*
www.pinerypark.on.ca

Point Pelee National Park

Location:	County Road 33, south of Leamington
Number of trails:	7
Total distance:	11.3km (7mi)
Level of difficulty:	●
Groomed:	No
Trackset:	No
Interesting features:	Cattail marsh
Fee:	$2.25/person, $1.60/senior, $1.10/student or $5.35/family
Other activities:	Skating
Amenities and other services:	Parking, maps, snack bar, nature books, toilets, telephones, visitor centre

Getting There

From Leamington, take County Road 33 south to the park

Further Information

Point Pelee National Park
407 Robson St.
Leamington, ON N8H 3V4
☎ *(519) 322-2365*
☎ *(519) 322-2371 (snow conditions line)*
www.parcscanada.gc.ca/Parks/Ontario/Point_Pelee

Rankin Ski Trail

Location:	Hwy. 6, north of Wiarton
Number of trails:	6
Total distance:	18km (11mi)
Level of difficulty:	■ ◆
Groomed:	83%
Trackset:	83% classic
Interesting features:	Red Bay
Fee:	$4/day, $8/3-day weekend, $30/season; families: $12/day, $24/3-day weekend, $50/season
	Tickets available at Red Bay Lodge
Services:	(A)
Amenities and other services:	Parking

Getting There

Take Spry Lake Road north out of Wiarton. Turn right on Bryant Street. Turn right on Red Bay Road, at Red Bay Tent and Trailer Camp or at Red Bay Lodge.

Further Information

Bruce County Tourism
PO Box 844
Southampton, ON N0H 2L0
☎*(519) 797-2191*
☎*800-268-3838*
=*(519) 797-1602*
www.naturalretreat.com

Bruce Ski Club
PO Box 205
Wiarton, ON N0H 2T0
☎*(519) 534-2502 (Martha Martell)*

Red Bay Lodge
☎*(519) 534-1027*

Rondeau Provincial Park

Location:	At the end of Hwy. 51, south of Hwy. 3
Number of trails:	6
Total distance:	27km (16.8mi)
Level of difficulty:	●
Groomed:	No
Trackset:	No
Interesting features:	Rondeau Bay, Lake Erie, sand dunes, marsh, oak savanna
Fee:	$8.50/vehicle, $40/vehicle/season
Other activities:	Icefishing, winter camping
Amenities and other services:	Parking, toilets, telephones, lodge, snack bar, maps, gift shop

Getting There

Take exit 101 from Highway 401 to get onto County Road 15, which becomes Highway 51 after Highway 3. Continue driving straight into the park.

Further Information

Rondeau Provincial Park
RR 1
Morpeth, ON N0P 1X0
☎*(519) 674-1750, 800-667-1940 or 888-668-7275*
www.ontarioparks.com

Friends of Rondeau
RR 1
Morpeth, ON N0P 1X0
☎*(519) 674-1777*
(519) 674-1755

Southern Ontario

Sauble Beach Cross Country Ski Trail (♥)

Location:	Hwy. 21, north of Sauble Falls Provincial Park
Number of trails:	6
Total distance:	18km (11mi)
Level of difficulty:	● ■
Groomed:	100%
Trackset:	100% classic
Interesting features:	Scenic view, forest, damn, Rankin River
Fee:	$6/day; $9/day/family; $25/year; $35/year/family (Note: tickets sold at the chalet on weekends or at Sauble Home Hardware on weekdays)
Amenities and other services:	Heated lodge open on weekends

Classic skiers will love these trails, which are wide enough to be comfortable yet narrow enough to be scenic. The trails turn frequently and they also have lots of hills, including one that leads to a beautiful scenic view over the Rankin River. Old-fashioned coloured ribbon and map placards scattered at various points on the trails ensure that skiers don't get lost.

All the land is locally owned, both privately and publicly, who allow club members to use their property. There are maps posted throughout the trails to keep skiers from getting lost. A parking lot is in the planning stages, because the trails are becoming too crowded to continue allowing people to park on the highway, as they now do.

If you visit, expect to meet lots of friendly club members who will be happy to fill you in on local lore. Many of the stories feature an 84-year old skier from Owen Sound who is an inspiration for many of the local skiers. In fact, Bill Georges is so popular that he alone collects $14,000 of the roughly $60,000 the club usually raises in their annual Easter Seal skiathon.

Getting There

Take County Road 13 north from Sauble Beach past Sauble Falls Provincial Park. The trails are on the east side.

Further Information

Sauble Beach Cross Country Ski Club
931 Sauble Falls Pkwy.
Sauble Beach, ON N0H 2G0
☎*(519) 422-1405*
☎*(519) 422-2690*

Saugeen Bluffs Conservation Area

Location:	North of Paisley
Number of trails:	3
Total distance:	15km (9mi)
Level of difficulty:	■
Groomed:	No (skiers use the snowmobile trails)
Trackset:	No
Interesting features:	Saugeen Bluffs
Fee:	Donation
Other activities:	Snowmobiling
Amenities and other services:	Parking

Getting There

From Paisley, take Bruce County Road 3 north for 3km (2mi).

Further Information

Saugeen Valley Conservation Authority
RR 1
Hanover, ON N4N 3B8
☎*(519) 364-1255*
⇥*(519) 364-6990*
www.svca.on.ca

Southern Ontario

Saugeen Rail Trail

Location:	Port Elgin
Number of trails:	1 linear
Total distance:	11km (6.8mi)
Level of difficulty:	●
Groomed:	No
Trackset:	No
Interesting features:	Conifers, snow rabbits, deer
Fee:	No daily fee but a $10 individual or $20/family membership supports maintenance
Amenities and other services:	Parking, toilets, telephones, lodge, snack bar, maps, waxing centre, gift shop

Getting There

The trail begins on River Street in Port Elgin and continues to McNabb Street in Southampton. Skiers and snowshoers can begin at either end.

Further Information

Saugeen Rail Trail Association
Joyce Scammell
PO Box 2313
Port Elgin, ON N0H 2C0
☎ *(519) 832-6443 or 832-9193*

Sawmill Cross Country Ski Trail (♥)

Location:	Hepworth
Number of trails:	4
Total distance:	20km (12mi)
Level of difficulty:	● ■ ◆

Groomed:	100%
Trackset:	100% classic and 50% skating
Interesting features:	Hills
Fee:	$4/day, $8/3-day weekend, $30/season; families: $12/day, $24/3-day weekend, $50/season
	Tickets available at Suntrail Outfitters
Services:	**(R)** *(from Suntrail Outfitters)*
Amenities and other services:	Parking, heated lodge with telephones, toilets and waxing area

Sawmill Ski Trail is home to Ontario's current high school champion ski team, the West Hill Skiers, but the trails also attract lots of recreational skiers. That's why members have been very careful to design their trails so that all skiers, regardless of their level of expertise, can continuously ski for a set period of time without running into something they can't handle.

The beginner "orange" loop runs for 4.8km (3mi) and doesn't contain any hills. The short intermediate "yellow" loop runs for only 2km (1.2mi), but contains a sharp turn called the "little dipper." The long intermediate "blue" trail is a 6.5km (4mi) double loop run that includes the yellow and orange trails plus an additional hill (Halfway Hill), a slightly challenging curve called the "sidewinder" and a hill called the "yo-yo." The "red" trail gives an advanced skier a run of 9.3km (5.7mi) that includes the blue trail and a hill called "grunt," a twisting section called the "hardwood loop" and a downhill stretch called "free fall." It also includes "cardiac climb," "heart attack loop" and Sheldon's Trail.

The ski lodge, Jerry's Place, is named after Jerry Van Doors, who was only 18 years old when he died in 1998.

Getting There

Take Highway 6 south from Wiarton or north from Shallow Lake. The ski trails are on the north side of the highway.

Further Information

Bruce County Tourism
PO Box 844
Southampton, ON N0H 2L0
☎*(519) 797-2191*
☎*800-268-3838*
⇄*(519) 797-1602*
www.naturalretreat.com

Bruce Ski Club
PO Box 205
Wiarton, ON N0H 2T0
☎*(519) 534-0799 (Martin Kerr)*

Suntrail Outfitters
100 Spencer St.
Hepworth, ON
☎*(519) 935-2478*

Shade's Mills Conservation Area

Location:	412 Avenue Rd., east of Frankin Blvd. in Cambridge
Number of trails:	5
Total distance:	12km (7.4mi)
Level of difficulty:	● ■ ◆
Groomed:	100%
Trackset:	100% classic
Interesting features:	Conifer woodlands and plantations, well-protected trails
Fee:	$4/adult, $2.25/children 6-14yrs
Other activities:	Ice fishing, heated ice-hut rentals
Services:	(R) ($8)
Amenities and other services:	Parking, heated toilets, warmup lodge with waxing centre and snack bar

Getting There

From Toronto, take Highway 401 west. Just prior to Cambridge, get off on the Townline exit and turn left to head south on Townline Road. At the junction, turn right onto Avenue Road. The park entrance is on the left.

If you're heading east on Highway 401, get off on Franklin Boulevard. Head south. At the sixth set of lights, turn left onto Avenue Road. The park entrance is on the right.

Further Information

Grand River Conservation Authority
400 Clyde Rd.
PO Box 729
Cambridge, ON N1R 5W6
☎ *(519) 621-3697 or 621-2761*
www.grandriver.on.ca

South Trail, Kincardine

Location:	Aintree Rd., north of Kincardine, west of Aintree golf course
Number of trails:	4
Total distance:	10km (6.2mi)
Level of difficulty:	● ■
Groomed:	100%
Trackset:	No
Interesting features:	Bush (maple, beech, hemlock, cedar)
Fee:	No
Amenities and other services:	Parking

Getting There

From Kincardine, take Highway 21 north for 5km (3mi) to Aintree Road. The entrance is just past Aintree Golf Course.

Further Information

Kincardine Cross Country Ski Club
Karel Mika
187 Huron Ridge
Kincardine, ON N2Z 1K2
☎ *(519) 396-7383*
www.angelfire.com/co/kccsc

Stoney Island Conservation Area

Location:	Kincardine
Number of trails:	3
Total distance:	9.5km (6mi)
Level of difficulty:	● ■
Groomed:	100%
Trackset:	100% classic and skating
Interesting features:	Deciduous and cedar woodland
Fee:	Donation
Services:	**(L)** *(for jackrabbits)*
Amenities and other services:	Parking, heated ski lodge

Getting There

County Road 23 (B Line), 4km (2.5mi) north of Kincardine

Further Information

Saugeen Conservation Authority
RR 1
Hanover, ON N4N 3B8
☎ *(519) 364-1255*
≈ *(519) 364-6990*
www.svca.on.ca

Kincardine Cross Country Ski Club
187 Huron Ridge
Kincardine, ON N2Z 1K2
☎ *(519) 396-7383 (Karel Mika)*
www.angelfire.com/co/kccsc

Wawanosh Conservation Area

Location:	North of Blyth
Number of trails:	1

Total distance: 3km (2mi)
Level of difficulty: ●
Groomed: No
Trackset: No
Interesting features: Hemlock forest, red pine plantation
Fee: No

Getting There

From Blyth, take County Road 4 to East Wawanosh Concession 6 and 7 (Nature Centre Road). Turn left (east) and drive 7km (4mi) to the entrance.

Further Information

Maitland Valley Conservation Authority
PO Box 127
93 Marietta St.
Wroxeter, ON N0G 2X0
☎ *(519) 335-3557*
⇄ *(519) 335-3516*
www.mvca.on.ca

Southern Ontario

Wildwood Conservation Area

Location: East of St. Marys
Number of trails: 5
Total distance: 18km (11mi)
Level of difficulty: ● ■ ◆
Groomed: 100%
Trackset: 100% classic
Interesting features: Conifer plantation, rolling hills
Fee: No
**Amenities and
other services:**   Parking

Getting There

From St. Marys, take Highway 7 past Highway 119 to the park entrance.

Further Information

Wildwood Conservation Area
3995 Line 9
St. Marys, ON N4X 1C5
☎*(519) 284-2829*
☎*(519) 284-2292*
⇌*(519) 284-4711*
http://thamesriver.org

Central Ontario

C entral Ontario takes cross-country skiing so seriously that you should plan on wearing your skis just about everywhere! Snowshoeing is also catching on quite quickly in the area.

P erhaps it's not surprising that most of Ontario's major cross-country ski centres and many of its best snowshoe trails are located in this region, because the conditions are perfect for winter sports. It's cold enough most winters for a season that begins in November and ends in April. Also, the Niagara Escarpment, to the west of the region, works like a mountain range, ensuring that lots of snow gets dropped on much of central Ontario throughout the winter. Still, the region's success is built on more than good weather conditions. Central Ontario also contains a great many ski centres that not only keep their trails well maintained and carefully groomed, but also pay attention to meeting and exceeding visitors' demands for services. Innovative ski centres in central Ontario are helping rejuvenate the sport throughout the province.

T he three best examples of innovative cross-country ski centres are **Hardwood Hills** (see p 222), **Highlands Nordic** (see p 226) and **Mansfield Outdoor Centre** (see p 237). All three have invested in snowmaking equipment to improve track conditions and ensure as long a season as possible. They all groom most of their trails for both classic and skating techniques, although they also provide backcountry trails for snowshoers, skiers and, in Hardwood Hill's case, skijorers. These top-notch centres specialize in creating innovative programs for racers, recreational skiers and families, which continue to thrill experienced skiers and bring beginners into the fold. Women's weekends, club days, ski fitness programmes and hard-body challenges and other such special events cater to key target customers. Each centre holds popular loppets to enable newer and touring skiers to race. Then there are the extra imaginative features that provide visitors with unique outdoor experiences. Highlands Nordic, for example, has created a Hundred Acre Woods Trail with mail boxes that enable pint-sized visitors to send letters to Winnie the Pooh and all his friends.

The **Haliburton Highlands Nordic Trails** (see p 225), a cross-country skier's version of paradise, is also a trend-setter, especially when it comes to local partnership. Everyone in Haliburton, including hotel-owners, private citizens and town officials, has worked together to create an impressive 80km (50mi) network of trails that connects all the major Haliburton destinations together. One portion of this, a small 2km (1mi) section of the Haliburton Trail in Glebe Park, is lit from dusk until midnight every night from December until the end of the season for night skiing. No matter what your ability, there's a trail in Haliburton that will satisfy your every need.

People in Haliburton are so used to cooperating for success, they've even included two areas that aren't in their town on the official trail map, although there's no doubt that the **Leslie M. Frost Outdoor Centre** (see p 235) and the **Camp Wanakita YMCA Trail System** (see p 213), are important cross-country ski centres in the area.

Other ski centres are doing what they can to create an exciting atmosphere for cross-country skiers. **Lafontaine Cross-Country Ski Centre** (see p 235), which has a very impressive trail system, also offers moonlight ski tours. Lafon-taine also recently started catering to snowshoers with some new trails designed specifically for them.

A number of local and distant ski clubs maintain excellent trails in the area too, including the **Georgian Nordic Ski Club** (see p 218), **Kolapore Uplands** (see p 234), **Massie Hills**

Central Ontario

1. Algonquin Park
2. Arrowhead Provincial Park
3. Awenda Provincial Park
4. Beaver River Wetland Conservation Area
5. Blueberry Trails Nordic Centre
6. Blue Spruce Inn
7. Blue Water Acres
8. Bondi Village Resort
9. Bracebridge Resource Management Centre
10. Camp Wanakita YMCA Trail System
11. Cedar Grove Lodge Resort
12. Cranberry Resort
13. Deerhurst Resort
14. Devil's Elbow Ski Resort
15. Fern Resort
16. Georgian Nordic Ski Club
17. Georgian Bay Islands National Park
18. Georgian Trail
19. Grandview Inn
20. Gravenhurst KOA Trails
21. Hardwood Hills
22. Halimar Lodge
23. Haliburton Highlands Nordic Trails
24. Highlands Nordic
25. Horseshoe Resort
26. Inglis Falls Conservation Area
27. Jackson Creek Kiwanis Trail
28. Ken Reid Conservation Area
29. Kerr Park
30. Kolapore Uplands
31. Lafontaine Cross-Country Ski Centre
32. Leslie M. Frost Outdoor Centre
33. Mansfield Outdoor Centre
34. Massie Hills
35. Minesing Swamp Conservation Area
36. Mountain View Ski Hill
37. Muskoka Heritage Place
38. Muskoka Sands Resort
39. Nordic Inn
40. Norland Cross Country Ski & Recreation Park
41. PineStone Resort
42. Pow Wow Point Lodge
43. Scanlon Creek Conservation Area
44. Selwyn Conservation Area
45. Shamrock Lodge
46. Sherwood Inn
47. Springwater Provincial Park
48. Talisman Mountain Resort
49. Tawingo Trails
50. The Baldwins
51. The Briars Resort
52. Tiffin Centre for Conservation
53. Torrance Barrens Conservation and Dark Sky Reserve
54. Wigamog Inn Resort
55. Wye Marsh Wildlife Centre

Central Ontario

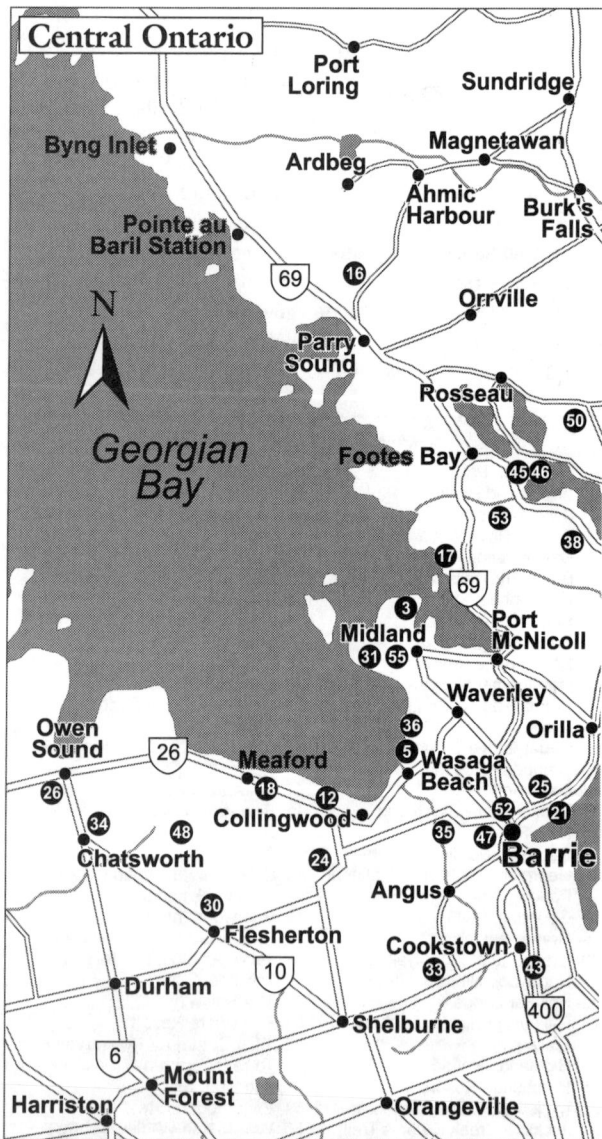

Algonquin Provincial Park

Sand Lake

Madawaska

60

Barry's Bay

Whitney

127

62

❶

❷ ❶⑨ ❻
Huntsville
❸⑦
❸⑦ ❶❶
⑬ ⑧
❹⑨
㊷

Maynooth

Dorset
㊴ ㉜

㊺❶
Haliburton

Bancroft

㉒
㉓ ❿

⑨
Bracebridge
㉙

Tory Hill

⑳
Gravenhurst

㊵ Minden

11

Kinmount

Coboconk

Bobcaygeon

Burleigh Falls

⑮

Kirkfield

Lake Simcoe

㉘
Lindsay

Norwood

㊹

Carrington

㉗

㊱ Sutton
Blackwater

❹

Bethany ⑭ Peterborough

Port Perry

Colborne

Port Hope

Cobourg

401

Aurora

Newcastle

Markham

Ajax

Oshawa

Lake Ontario

©ULYSSES

(see p 238) and the **Norland Cross Country Ski & Recreation Park** (see p 243). Kolapore Uplands offers what are considered to be the best backcountry trails in this region.

Conservation areas in central Ontario also promote cross-country skiing and snowshoeing on their properties, although like elsewhere in Ontario, they do so as a way of promoting activities that don't adversely affect water quality, plant cover or animal diversification efforts. The **Beaver River Wetland Conservation Area** (see p 207), **Ken Reid Conservation Area** (see p 232), **Minesing Swamp Conservation Area** (see p 239), **Scanlon Creek Conservation Area** (see p 245), **Selwyn Conservation Area** (see p 246), the **Tiffin Centre for Conservation** (see p 253) and the **Torrance Barrens Conservation and Dark Sky Reserve** (see p 253) are all popular locations for skiing and snowshoeing, although the trails are not groomed. Some of these conservation areas offer spectacular winter vistas. Visitors to **Inglis Falls**

Conservation Area (see p 230), for instance, start their tours at a stunning half-frozen waterfall. Skiing or snowshoeing through **Warsaw Caves Conservation Area** offers views of glacial formations at close range. Visitors to the **Wye Marsh Wildlife Centre** (see p 255) who stop by the pond where a group of white tundra swans over-winter get a rather disconcerting view that looks like a bunch of black beaks floating in air. Eventually, as your eyes begin to distinguish pure white feathers on bright white snow, a group of majestic birds appears.

All three levels of government promote cross-country skiing at their properties in central Ontario. The federal government, for instance, has a 30km (19mi) trail network at **Georgian Bay Islands National Park** (see p 219).

Provincial parks in the region that attract cross-country skiers include **Algonquin** (see p 201), **Arrowhead** (see p 205), **Awenda** (see p 205) and Wasaga Beach, which all offer excellent trail systems. **Springwater Provincial Park** (see p 248) also has trails in and among its animal refuge enclosures. Of all of these, Wasaga Beach Provincial Park is the one that stands out. They've partnered with members of the Ganaraska Trail Association to establish a superb cross-country ski centre called **Blueberry Trails Nordic Centre** (see p 208).

Even municipalities are in on the act these days, with cross-country skiing at the **Bracebridge Resource Management Centre** (see p 212), **Kerr Park** (see p 233) in Bracebridge, the **Jackson Creek Kiwanis Trail** (see p 232) in Peterborough and the **Georgian Trail** (see p 219) from Meaford to Collingwood.

The incredible importance of cross-country skiing to central Ontario residents has encouraged many alpine centres in the region to add one or two cross-country skiing trails that lead away from their alpine facilities, while a few have even opened separate cross-country ski centres with complete trail systems. The better of these include **Devil's Elbow Ski Resort** (see p 216), **Horseshoe Resort** (see p 228), **Mountain View Ski Hill** (see p 240) and **Talisman Mountain Resort** (see p 249). Horseshoe Resort's Cross-Country Centre, in particular, stands out from the crowd. The people in charge offer weekly ski fit programs, torch-led ski safaris through Copeland Forest, and moonlight skis throughout the season. The centre also employs several trained Nordic instructors to satisfy their clientele.

Many hotel resorts in central Ontario groom and trackset trails to lead right to their doors, including **Blue Spruce Inn** (see p 209), **Blue Water Acres** (see p 210), **Bondi Village Resort** (see p 211), **Cedar Grove Lodge Resort** (see p 213), **Cranberry Resort** (see p 214), **Deerhurst Resort** (see p 215), **Fern Resort** (see p 217), **Grandview Inn** (see p 220), **Halimar Lodge** (see p 224), **Muskoka Sands Resort** (see p 241), **Nordic Inn** (see

Central Ontario

p 242), **Paquana Cottages**, **PineStone Resort** (see p 243), **Pow Wow Point Lodge** (see p 244), **Shamrock Lodge** (see p 246), **Sherwood Inn** (see p 247), **The Baldwins** (see p 251), **The Briars Resort** (see p 252) and **Wigamog Inn Resort** (see p 254). Many of these trails are open to the public, for a fee. In the case of Halimar Lodge, Pinehurst and Wigamog, the trails they've built are included in the main Haliburton Highlands Nordic Trails system. Guests pay for a daily trail pass to access the entire system.

One Muskoka campground, **Gravenhurst KOA Trails** (see p 221), maintains some very good groomed and trackset trails on their property. The owners have discovered that the winter ski season is a nice complement to their busy summer camping season.

Camping and education centres in central Ontario, such as **Tawingo Trails** (see p 250) and Wildfire Outdoor Education Centre, focus on cross-country skiing and snowshoeing for their winter outdoors education programs to such an extent that they've developed some good trails to support this effort.

Even attractions that are closed for the season, such as the **Muskoka Heritage Place** (see p 240) in Huntsville, have reputations as cross-country skiing destinations.

Tourist Information

Georgian Triangle Tourist Association
601 First St.
Collingwood, ON L9Y 4L2
☎ *(705) 445-7722*
⇥ *(705) 445-6158*
www.georgiantriangle.org

Kawartha Lakes Chamber of Commerce
175 George St. N.
Peterborough, ON K9J 3G6
☎ *(705) 652-6963*
☎ *887-53-LAKES (52537)*

Muskoka Tourism
RR 2
Kilworthy, ON P0E 1G0
☎*(705) 689-0660*
☎*800-267-9700*
www.muskoka-tourism.on.ca

Rice Lake Tourist Association
PO Box 42R
Roseneath, ON K0K 2X0
☎*800-461-6424*
www.ricelakecanada.com

Algonquin Park

Location:	N. of Haliburton, east of Huntsville, west of Pembroke
Number of trails:	18 loops in 3 areas
Total distance:	137km (85mi)
Level of difficulty:	● ■ ◆
Groomed:	100%
Trackset:	75%: 80km (50mi) classic, 23km (14mi) skating
Interesting features:	Cliffs, rock faces, waterfalls, rapids, homestead ruins
Fee:	$10/person/day, $8 senior or persons with disabilities
Other activities:	Dogsledding, camping
Services:	**(A)** *(7 yurts, furnished year-round tents; resort rooms on Leaf Lake section in Whitney)*
Amenities and other services:	Parking, toilets, telephones, visitor centre (weekends), snack bar, maps, waxing centre, gift shop, shelters, emergency barrels that contain first-aid kit, spare ski tip, duct tape, matches, fire starter, kindling, candles, blankets, sleeping bag and emergency rations
Note:	No sleighs or baby gliders permitted.

Central Ontario

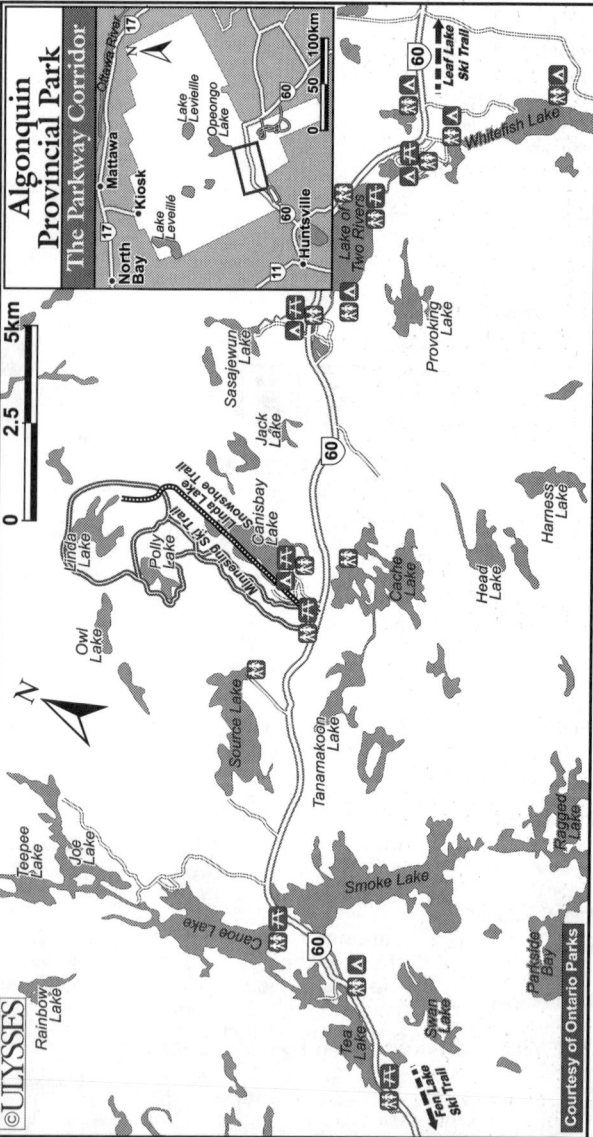

Algonquin Provincial Park
The Parkway Corridor

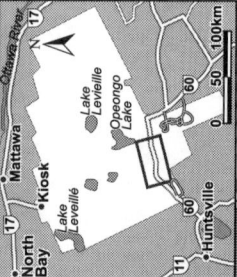

Courtesy of Ontario Parks

© ULYSSES

Algonquin Park has three different skiing areas off of Highway 60: Fen Lake, Leaf Lake, and the Minnesing Wilderness Ski Trail.

Fen Lake begins at the West Gate parking lot. Skiers travel through a mixed forest of maple, birch, beech and hemlock along four different loops—1.25km (.8mi), 5km (3mi), 11km (6.8mi) and 13km (8mi). All four loops are trackset for classic skiing, while skaters can enjoy a 6.2km (3.8mi) section. A shelter and an emergency barrel are located at different points on the most distant loop.

The **Leaf Lake** Trail System provides 10 loops that begin in Whitney for classic or backcountry skiers or from the Logging Museum parking lot for skaters and classic or backcountry skiers. The Bear Trail Inn and the Algonquin Park Skiers Association groom and maintain the southern portion, which includes the 5km (3mi) **Moose**, the 3km (2mi) **Farm**, the 6km (3.7mi) **Galeairy Lake**, the David Thompson and the Fraser Lake loops. Most of the 12km (7.5mi) **David Thompson** and the 6km (3.7mi) **Fraser Lake** loops are groomed but not trackset, and so are suitable for advanced skiers only. There's only one toilet and one shelter at the southern end, at the junction between the David Thompson, Fraser Lake and Thistle Lake loops. Park staff is responsible for the northern five loops. They trackset the outer edge of the 5km (3mi) **Jack Rabbit** and the 6km (3.7mi) **Leaf Lake** loops for skating and classic skiers, although the dividing line is only trackset for classic skiers, as are the 4km (2.5mi) **Clark Lake** and the 6km (3.5mi) **Thistle Lake** loops. The four loops share three toilets and one shelter. The highly recommended 13km (8mi) **Pine Tree Loop** is groomed, but not trackset, and is suitable for advanced skiers only. Three toilets, a shelter and an emergency barrel are located on it.
C
The **Minnesing Wilderness Ski Trail** provides four loops of ungroomed backcountry trails for advanced skiers. Begin at the Minnesing Ski Trail parking lot, on Highway 60, 21km (13mi) from the West Gate or 35km (21.7mi) from the East Gate. One of the two shelters and one of the six toilets are

located at this point. The shortest loop is the 5km (3mi) **Sugar Bush Loop**. The 7km (4mi) **Timber Slide Loop** follows. True backcountry enthusiasts can then complete the 8km (5mi) **Polly's Pitch** or the 13km (8mi) **Callighen's Corners**. Camping is not permitted close to the trail or in either of the shelters.

Although visitors can snowshoe almost anywhere in Algonquin Park, there is one established 8km (5mi) **Linda Lake snowshoe trail** for **overnight campers**. The Linda Lake Trail begins at the Minnesing Ski Trail parking lot.

Getting There

Enter the park on Highway 60 at the East Gate, 1.6km (1mi) north of Whitney or the West Gate, 69km (43mi) north of Huntsville.

Further Information

Algonquin Provincial Park
PO Box 219
Whitney, ON K0J 2M0
☎(705) 633-5572
☎800-667-1940
☎888-668-7275 (yurt reservations)
www.ontarioparks.com

The Friends of Algonquin Park
PO Box 248
Whitney, ON K0J 2M0
☎(613) 637-2828
=(613) 637-2138
www.algonquinpark.on.ca

The Bear Trail Inn Resort
couples only
☎(613) 637-2662
www.beartrailresort.com

The Algonquin Park Skiers Association
☎(613) 637-2114 (Patsy Shalla)

Arrowhead Provincial Park

Location:	Hwy. 11, north of Huntsville
Number of trails:	6
Total distance:	27km (16.7mi)
Level of difficulty:	● ■ ◆
Groomed:	100%
Trackset:	100%, 27km (16.7mi) classic and 7km (4mi) skating
Interesting features:	Stubb's Falls, Big East River Valley, maple forests, deer, rabbits, chickadees, grosbeaks
Fee:	$8.50/vehicle
Other activities:	Skating, tobogganing, tubing, ice fishing
Services:	**(R)**, **(L)**
Amenities and other services:	Parking, toilets, telephones, heated lodge, Canadian Ski Patrol

Getting There

From Huntsville, take Highway 11 north and drive for 8km (5mi).

Further Information

Arrowhead Provincial Park
RR 3
Huntsville, ON P0A 1K0
☎(705) 789-5105
☎800-667-1940
www.ontarioparks.com.

Central Ontario

Awenda Provincial Park

Location:	15min from Penetanguishene
Number of trails:	4

Total distance:	30km (18.6mi)
Level of difficulty:	● ■
Groomed:	100%
Trackset:	75%
Interesting features:	Nipissing Bluff, Algonquin Bluff, Giant's Tomb Island, homestead ruins
Fee:	$8.50/vehicle, $6.50/ vehicle (senior), $4.25/ vehicle (persons with disabilities)
Amenities and other services:	Parking, toilets, telephone, red pine cabin trail centre (occasionally open)

Awenda Provincial Park sits on the edge of the Penetanguishene Peninsula, which juts into Georgian Bay to create Nottawasaga Bay and Severn Sound. Almost all the trails leave from the trail centre, which is located in a red pine log cabin near the entrance parking lot.

An intermediate-level, moderately challenging trail, the 4km (2.5mi) **Brûlé Loop**, follows the Nipissing and Bluff trails across the summer road. It then turns off before the stairwell to cross the main road and then continues through a mature deciduous forest along an old logging road from the 1880s. The easy 5km (3mi) **Wendat Trail** circumvents the largest lake in the park, once known as Second Lake, but rededicated "Kettle Lake" on June 24, 2000. It also passes the ruins of the Brabant family homestead, then through marshes and forest. Another moderate trail, the **Bluff Trail** loops past several forested sand dunes for 13km (8mi), providing some impressive lookouts of Georgian Bay. The **Beach Trail** is a difficult trail that travels 5km (3mi) down the face of the Nipissing Bluff. Continue to Methodist Point on the Georgian Bay shoreline for a good view of Giant's Tomb Island.

Getting There

Take Highway 93 to Penetanguishene. Follow the park signs left onto Robert Street (the street name is not indicated). Then turn right on Lafontaine Road (Concession 16) and turn right again at the first stop sign. Awenda Park road is the first road on the left. The park is about 5min further along, on the left.

Further Information

Awenda Provincial Park
PO Box 5004
Penetanguishene, ON L9M 2G2
☏(705) 549-2231
☏800-667-1940
www.ontarioparks.com

Beaver River Wetland Conservation Area

Location:	Blackwater to Cannington
Number of trails:	1 linear
Total distance:	17km (10.5mi)
Level of difficulty:	●
Groomed:	No
Trackset:	No
Interesting features:	Signs of abandoned railway
Fee:	No
Amenities and other services:	Parking

Getting There

Access the trail on Highway 7 at either Blackwater or
Sunderland or on Regional Road 12 at Cannington.

Further Information

Lake Simcoe Region Conservation Authority
120 Bayview Pkwy.
PO Box 282
Newmarket, ON L3Y 4X1
☏(905) 895-1281
⇌(905) 853-5881
www.lsrca.on.ca

Central Ontario

Blueberry Trails Nordic Centre (♥)

Location:	Wasaga Beach
Number of trails:	8
Total distance:	29km (18mi)
Level of difficulty:	● ■ ◆
Groomed:	100%
Trackset:	100% classic, 7% skating
Interesting features:	Ganaraska Trail, dune forest, blueberry plains, raised beaches, fore dunes, high dunes, deer, wild turkey
Fee:	$8.50/vehicle plus $2/person, $1/youth or $25/season
Services:	**(R)** *($15)*, **(L)** *($10/30min)*
Amenities and other services:	Parking, heated lodge with toilets, telephone, snack bar, waxing centre and pro shop, two shelters with barbecues, fireplaces, firewood and toilets

Every Wednesday throughout the winter, members of the Ganaraska Trail Association meet at the Blueberry Trails Nordic Centre for a couple of hours' skiing. They also help to maintain the trails, especially in the spring and fall, when there's lots of work to be done.

Two easy, four intermediate and two difficult trails meander through the dunes. Only two, the 3km (2mi) easy **Skating Trail** and the 4km (2.6mi) intermediate **Skating Trail**, cater to skaters. They are marked in green. Families, novices and the curious will want to ski on the 4km (2.5mi) **Blueberry Plains Trail,** which gave the Nordic centre its name. Intermediate skiers can extend their ski by tagging on the 2.4km (1.5mi) **Pine Trail** that leads through a thick pine forest, the .4km (.2mi) **Schrei Ski** (named for Joe Schrei, who started the trails in 1975) or the 1.1km (.7mi) **Gill's Gulch**. Be careful though. The Schrei Ski

leads to one of the easier sections on the difficult **High
Dunes Trail**, which is 5.8km (3.6mi) long in total. Gill's
Gulch leads to an easy section on the 4.5km (2.8mi) **Monument Hill Trail**, which goes to the top of the most prominent
parabolic sand dune for a scenic view of the countryside.
You'll also see lots of rolling hills extending beyond the
trail.

Plan on stopping by the clubhouse for a chat after you've
finished skiing these wonderfully versatile trails. The
friendly atmosphere ensures that even strangers are welcomed like old friends any day of the week.

Getting There

Go into Wasaga Beach and travel west on River Road
West. Turn right (south) onto Blueberry Trail Road and
drive to the park entrance on the left (east) side of the
road.

Further Information

Blueberry Trails Nordic Centre
Wasaga Beach Provincial Park
PO Box 183
Wasaga Beach, ON L0L 2P0
☎ *(705) 429-0943 (trail centre)*
☎ *(705) 429-2516 (park office)*
☎ *800-667-1940*
⇝ *(705) 429-7983*
www.OntarioParks.com

Blue Spruce Inn

🛏 **Access to trails reserved for overnight guests**

Location:	Algonquin Park
Number of trails:	3
Total distance:	10km (6mi)
Level of difficulty:	● ■
Groomed:	No

Trackset:	No
Interesting features:	Oxtongue Lake
Fee:	No
Other activities:	Sleigh rides, snowmobiling
Services:	**(A)**
Amenities and other services:	Parking, toilets, telephones, inn, spa, restaurant

Further Information

Blue Spruce Inn
RR 1
Dwight, ON P0A 1H0
☎*(705) 635-2330*
⇌*(705) 635-9443*

Blue Water Acres

🛏 **Access to trails reserved for overnight guests**

Location:	Huntsville
Number of trails:	4
Total distance:	12km (7mi)
Level of difficulty:	● ■
Groomed:	100%
Trackset:	100% classic
Interesting features:	Lake of Bays
Fee:	No
Other activities:	Snowmobiling, ice fishing, skating, alpine skiing, tubing, snowboarding, dogsledding, indoor pool
Services:	**(R)** *($20)*, **(A)**
Amenities and other services:	Parking, toilets, telephones, inn, spa, restaurant

Getting There

From Barrie, take Highway 11 north to Highway 60. Take Highway 60 east for 18km (11mi) to South Portage

Muskoka Road 9. Turn right (south). Drive about 3km
(2mi) to the entrance.

Further Information

Blue Water Acres
RR 4
PO Box 34
Huntsville, ON P1H 2J6
☎*(705) 635-2880*
☎*800-461-4279*
www.bwacres.com

Bondi Village Resort

Location:	Huntsville
Number of trails:	5
Total distance:	16km (10mi)
Level of difficulty:	● ■
Groomed:	100%
Trackset:	No
Interesting features:	Lake of Bays, swamp, beaver ponds, sugar bush and lookout over Bondi Bay
Fee:	$8/day
Other activities:	Snowmobiling, ice-skating, tobogganing
Services:	(A)
Amenities and other services:	Parking, toilets, telephones, inn, spa, restaurant

Central Ontario

Getting There

From Dwight, take Highway 35 south to Muskoka Road 21.
Turn right (west). Follow the road as it curves to the west
to the resort entrance.

Further Information

Bondi Village Resort
RR 1
Dwight, Lake of Bays, ON P0A 1H0
☎ *(705) 635-2261*
☎ *800-300-2132*
www.bondi-cottage-resort.com

Bracebridge Resource Management Centre

Location:	Muskoka Forest
Number of trails:	5
Total distance:	9.5km (6mi)
Level of difficulty:	● ■ ◆
Groomed:	100%
Trackset:	100% classic
Interesting features:	Muskoka River, marshes, gravel pits
Fee:	Donation
Amenities and other services:	Parking

Five different trails traverse the 607ha (1,499 acres) of marsh, river, forests, sand and rock that make up the Bracebridge Resource Management Centre. Five trails, a 3.3km (2mi) main trail, three 1km (.6mi) and one 3km (2mi) side trails lead skiers around the property. Trail two, which leads along the shore of the Muskoka River, is highly recommended.

Getting There

Take Highway 11 north from Bracebridge past High Falls Road. The entrance is on the right.

Further Information

Bracebridge Culture and Recreation
111 Wellington St.
PO Box 2079
Bracebridge, ON P1L 1V9
☎ *(705) 645-3037*
⇄ *(705) 645-3030*

Camp Wanakita YMCA Trail System

Location: South of Haliburton
Number of trails: 5
Total distance: 20km (12.4mi)
Level of difficulty: ● ■ ◆
Groomed: 100%
Trackset: 100% classic and skating
Interesting features: Koshlong Lake
Fee: $12/person, $10/student, free for children less than 12yrs
Other activities: children's camp, family camp, hockey camp
Services: **(A)**
Amenities and other services: Parking; heated lodge with waxing centre; visitor centre with snack bar, maps, toilets, telephones and gift shop

Getting There

Take Regional Road 1 west and south of Haliburton to Donald. Turn right (east) and follow the signs to Camp Wanakita YMCA.

Further Information

YMCA Wanakita
RR 2
Haliburton, ON K0M 1S0
☎(705) 457-2132
☎800-387-5081
www.ymca-wanakita.on.ca

Central Ontario

Cedar Grove Lodge Resort

🛏 Access to trails reserved for overnight guests

Location:	Huntsville
Number of trails:	10
Total distance:	12km (7mi)
Level of difficulty:	● ■ ◆
Groomed:	No
Trackset:	No
Interesting features:	Peninsula Lake
Fee:	No
Other activities:	Ice-skating, ice fishing, tobogganing
Services::	**(A)**
Amenities and other services:	Parking, toilets, telephones, inn, spa, restaurant

Further Information

Cedar Grove Lodge Resort
P. O. Box 5104
Huntsville, ON P1H 2K5
☎*(705) 789-4036*
☎*800-461-4269*
www.cedargrove.on.ca

Cranberry Resort

🛏 **Access to trails reserved for overnight guests**

Location:	Between Craiglaith and Collingwood
Number of trails:	10
Total distance:	20km (12mi)
Level of difficulty:	● ■
Groomed:	100%
Trackset:	No
Interesting features:	Georgian Bay, Blue Mountain
Fee:	No
Other activities:	Sleigh rides, snowmobiling
Services:	**(R)** *($14)*, **(A)**
Amenities and other services:	Parking, toilets, telephones, inn, spa, restaurant, recreation centre with snack bar, wood-burning stove, billiards, ping pong, arcade games, darts, air hockey

Getting There

From Barrie, take Highway 26 west for about 1.6km (1mi)
past the town of Collingwood to the entrance of the resort.

Further Information

Cranberry Resort
19 Keith Ave.
RR 4
Collingwood, ON L9Y 4T9
☎(705) 445-6600
☎800-465-9077
www.cranberry-resort.on.ca

Deerhurst Resort

Location:	Huntsville
Number of trails:	5
Total distance:	13km (8mi)
Level of difficulty:	● ■
Groomed:	100%
Trackset:	No
Interesting features:	Highland hills, hardwood forest, Peninsula Lake, lookout
Fee:	$10
Other activities:	Ice-skating, pool, fitness room, sleigh rides, snowmobiling and snow tubing
Services:	(A)
Amenities and other services:	Parking, toilets, telephones, pavilion with snack bar and maps

Central Ontario

Getting There

From Huntsville, take Highway 60 west to Deerhurst Canal
Road. Turn right (south) and drive to the resort entrance
on the left.

Further Information

Deerhurst Resort
1235 Deerhurst Dr.
Huntsville, ON P1H 2E8
☎*(705) 789-6411*
☎*800-461-4393*
www.deerhurst.on.ca

Devil's Elbow Ski Resort

Location:	West of Peterborough
Number of trails:	2
Total distance:	8km (5mi)
Level of difficulty:	● ■ ◆
Groomed:	100%
Trackset:	100% classic
Interesting features:	Oak Ridges Moraine
Fee:	$5
Other activities:	Alpine skiing
Services:	**(R)**
Amenities and other services:	Parking, heated lodge with toilets, telephone, snack bar, waxing centre and pro shop

Getting There

From Bethany at Highway 7A, take County Road 38 north for 5km (3mi).

Further Information

Devil's Elbow Ski Resort
Bethany, ON L0A 1A0
☎*(705) 277-2012*
www.devilselbow.com

Fern Resort

🛏 **Access to trails reserved for overnight guests**

Location:	Orillia
Number of trails:	10
Total distance:	20km (12.4mi)
Level of difficulty:	● ■
Groomed:	100%
Trackset:	100% classic
Interesting features:	Mixed forest, lakes and lookouts
Fee:	No
Other activities:	Bird walks, spa, "torch light safari," skating, dogsledding
Services:	**(A)**
Amenities and other services:	Parking, toilets, telephones, restaurant, spa, hot tub

Getting There

From Barrie, take Highway 11 north to Orillia. Then turn south onto Highway 12, continuing until Rama Road, where you turn left (east). Fern Resort Road is just before the casino. Turn left.

Further Information

Fern Resort
4432 Fern Resort Rd., RR 5
Orillia, ON L3V 6H5
☎*(705) 325-2256*
☎*800-567-3376*
⇋*(705) 327-5647*
www.fernresort.com

Central Ontario

Georgian Nordic Ski Club

Location:	Parry Sound
Number of trails:	8
Total distance:	30km (18.6mi)
Level of difficulty:	● ■ ◆
Groomed:	100%
Trackset:	100% classic and skating
Interesting features:	Granite ridges, conifer forest and lakes
Fee:	$8/person/day; $20/family/day; $65 annual; $130 annual family
Other activities:	member newsletter, potluck suppers, moonlight skiing events, races, canoeing
Services:	(L)
Amenities and other services:	Parking, heated lodge with toilets and waxing area

The Georgian Nordic Ski and Canoe Club maintains trails on more than 81ha (200 acres) of land on top of the Canadian Shield in the scenic Parry Sound area.

Getting There

From Parry Sound, head east on Highway 124 for 7km (4.3mi) to Nine Mile Lake Road. Turn left. The lodge is on the left-hand side of the road.

Further Information

Georgian Nordic Ski and Canoe Club
PO Box 42
Parry Sound, ON P2A 2X2
☎*(705) 746-5067*
www.georgiannordic.com

Georgian Bay Islands National Park

Location:	Beausoleil Island
Number of trails:	6
Total distance:	30km (19mi)
Level of difficulty:	● ■ ◆
Groomed:	4%
Trackset:	No
Interesting features:	Hardwood forests, wind-swept conifers and rocks, animal tracks
Fee:	No
Other activities:	Winter camping, snowmobiling
Amenities and other services:	Parking at Honey Harbour, visitor centre at Cedar Spring on Beausoleil Island with snack bar, maps, toilets, telephones, docks, campsites

Getting There

Take a snowmobile or ski from Honey Harbour across the ice to the island. Many skiers ski around the perimeter.

Further Information

Georgian Bay Islands National Park
PO Box 28
Honey Harbour, ON P0E 1E0
☎*(705) 756-2415*
☎*(705) 756-5909 (reservations)*
www.parcscanada.gc.ca/parks/ontario/georgian_bay

Central Ontario

Georgian Trail

Location:	Meaford to Collingwood
Number of trails:	1 linear
Total distance:	32km (19.8mi)

Level of difficulty: ●
Groomed: 100%
Trackset: No
Interesting features: Abandoned rail line
Fee: No
Other activities: Snowmobiling

Getting There

Access at Meaford, Thornbury, Craiglaith or Collingwood.

Further Information

Georgian Triangle Tourist Association
19 Mountain Rd., Unit 3B
Collingwood, ON L9Y 4M2
☎ *(705) 445-7722*
www.georgiantriangle.org

Grandview Inn

🛏 **Access to trails reserved for overnight guests**

Location: Huntsville, north side of Highway 35/60
Number of trails: 7
Total distance: 15km (9mi)
Level of difficulty: ● ■ ◆
Groomed: 100%
Trackset: 100%
Interesting features: Fairy Lake
Fee: No
Other activities: Sleigh rides, snowmobiling
Services: (A)
**Amenities and
other services:**   Parking, toilets, telephones, inn, spa,
                          restaurant

Further Information

Grandview Inn (Club Link)
939 Hwy. 60
Huntsville, ON P1H 1Z4
☎ *(705) 789-4417*
☎ *800-461-4454*
⇌ *(705) 789-1674*
www.clublink.ca

Gravenhurst KOA Trails

Location:	Hwy. 11 at Gravenhurst
Number of trails:	8
Total distance:	17km (10.5mi)
Level of difficulty:	● ■ ◆
Groomed:	100%
Trackset:	100% classic and skating
Fee:	$6/person
Other activities:	Winter camping
Services:	**(R)**, **(A)** *(camping cabins)*
Amenities and other services:	Parking, heated toilets and showers, telephones, heated barn with waxing centre and woodstove, convenience store, Canadian Ski Patrol

KOA Gravenhurst Trails provides a relatively uncrowded place for good family skiing in a convenient location just off Highway 11. The groomed and trackset trails curve through woodland and fields and range from easy to moderate, with Canadian Ski Patrol volunteers to ensure everyone's safety.

Eight trails begin at a parking lot across the street from the store and barn. Beginners, or those warming up, will appreciate the 1.4km (.9mi) **Muskoka Road**, the 1.6km (1mi) **Marsh Trail**, the 1.3km (.8mi) **Peterson Road**, the 1.6km (1mi) **Inside Track** and the 2km (1.2mi) **Tamarack Trail**. For a more vigorous ski, try the intermediate trails, which are the 2.2km (1.4mi) **Burnt Pine Trail** and the 3.2km (2mi) **Mohawk**

Central Ontario

Trail. The **Boundary Trail** offers 3.2km (2mi) of challenging hills and curves for advanced skiers.

Getting There

Take Highway 11 north from Gravenhurst or south from Bracebridge to Reay Road East. Look for the Gravenhurst KOA sign on the right side of the street. Buy your passes at the convenience store.

Further Information

Paul Cook and Marcel Waters
Gravenhurst KOA
RR 3
Gravenhurst, ON P1P 1R3
☎ *(705) 687-2333*

Hardwood Hills (♥)

Location:	Oro Station
Number of trails:	11
Total distance:	42km (26mi)
Level of difficulty:	● ■ ◆
Groomed:	100%
Trackset:	82% classic and skating
Interesting features:	Racing atmosphere
Fee:	$15/day; $12.50/day students 13-19yrs and seniors over 60yrs; $8/day children 8-12yrs; free for children less than 8yrs, $75/six days
Other activities:	Skijoring, dogs and pulkas
Services:	**(R)** *($20)*, **(L)** *($30/45min)*, **(A)**
Amenities and other services:	Parking, heated lodge with cafeteria, maps, pro shop, toilets, telephones and waxing centre; snowmaking, Canadian Ski Patrol, babysitting

Ontario's elite cross-country skiers choose Hardwood Hills as their prime destination. The facility caters to racers, touring skiers, backcountry skiers and family skiers with four separate trail systems that are rated between one and 10 for both technical and physical difficulty.

The Olympic system offers five curving fast trails for classic and freestyle competitors: the 7.5km (5mi) **Hardwood Trail**, the 2km (1.2mi) **Tower Loop**, the 3km (1.9mi) **Roller Coaster Loop**, the .5km (.3mi) **DVP Loop** and the 1.5km (.9mi) **Bowl Loop**. Expect a workout—sections along the trail have nicknames such as the Berlin wall, eliminator, black hole and vertigo.

Touring enthusiasts who enjoy classic or freestyle skiing will enjoy the recreational trail system's four trails, which are well laid out and include enough curves and hills to offer a challenge. The main **Pine Trail** runs for 6km (3.7mi) and has a tunnel shortcut along the way. Extend your route by adding one or several additional trails from among the 2km (1.2mi) **Beaver Pond Loop**, the 3.5km (2mi) **Kim's Loop** and the 1km (.6mi) **Lookout Loop**. Many of the curves and hills on these recreational trails also have nicknames. Expect to slip along the little dipper, cruise the rapids and slide down the banister of the stairway to heaven.

Slower skiers, younger skiers, those pulling young children in pulkas and snowshoers should choose the 7.5km (5mi) **Meadowlands Trail**, which passes by ponds, meadows, a cedar grove and Blue Heron Creek.

Skijorers, snowshoers and other backcountry enthusiasts should choose the 6km (3.7mi) **Wilderness Trail**.

Every night, five sets of guests stay at The Inn at Hardwood, where they can jump out of bed, enjoy a hearty breakfast and ski right onto the trails at a discounted rate.

Getting There

Take Highway 400 north past Barrie to the Forbes Road/Simcoe 11 exit. Take Simcoe 11 Road through Dalston and Edgar to Hardwood Hills on the right.

Central Ontario

Further Information

Hardwood Hills Cross Country Ski Centre
RR 1
Oro Station, ON L0L 2E0
☎*(705) 487-3775*
=*(705) 487-2153*

The Inn at Hardwood
☎*888-INN-ATHH (466-2844)*

Halimar Lodge

Location:	South side of Kashagawigamog Lake in Haliburton
Number of trails:	2
Total distance:	2km (1mi)
Level of difficulty:	■
Groomed:	100%
Trackset:	No
Interesting features:	Mixed forest, lookout onto Kashagawigamog Lake, mature jack pines
Fee:	$12/day, $10/student 13-18yrs, free for children
Other activities:	Outdoor hot tub, sauna and exercise room
Services:	**(R)**, **(A)**
Amenities and other services:	Parking; inn, maps, restaurants, toilets and telephones

Getting There

From Haliburton, take Regional Road 1 west to Regional Road 18. Continue on Regional Road 18 until you see Halimar Lodge on the right.

Further Information

Halimar Lodge
RR 2
Haliburton, ON K0M 1S0
☎ *(705) 457-1300*
☎ *800-233-7322 (reservations)*
⇒ *(705) 457-2559*
www.halimar.com

Haliburton Highlands Nordic Trails (♥)

Location:	Haliburton, south of Algonquin Park and east of Bracebridge
Number of trails:	22
Total distance:	80km (50mi)
Level of difficulty:	● ■ ◆
Groomed:	100%
Trackset:	100% classic and skating
Interesting features:	Lakes, forests, hills, mixed forests, wolves, 2km (1.2) night-lit trails
Fee:	$12/day, $10/student 13-18yrs, free for children
Other activities:	Snowmobiling
Services:	**(R), (L), (A)**
Amenities and other services:	Parking, toilets, telephones, lodges, snack bars, maps, restaurants, waxing centres, gift shops, hotels

If you're a cross-country skier, Haliburton is heaven—although the noise from snowmobiles can be a minor annoyance. Whether you're a classic skier or a skater, you can ski for days on these impeccably groomed and trackset trails without seeing everything. The trail system extends throughout the region, although most of the trails are located in the centre of town on the north side of Head, Grass and Kashagawigamog lakes. It includes both private lands and public parkland, including all of Glebe Park.

Central Ontario

The **Jim Beef Trail** leads 11km (7mi) from Glebe Park and the Lakeview Motel onto property owned by the Wigamog (see p 254) and PineStone (see p 243) resorts. The difficult 6km (3.7mi) **Olympic Loop West** and the 7km (4mi) **Olympic Loop East**, the intermediate 1.5km (.9mi) **Moonshine Loop East** and the 1.1km (.7mi) **Moonshine Loop West** lead skiers north of the Jim Beef Trail. **Glebe Park** has 10km (6mi) of trails, including 2km (1mi) that are lit for evening skiing.

Trails at Halimar Lodge (see p 224) on the south side of Kashagawigamog Lake, south of Haliburton at Camp Wanakita YMCA (see p 213) and west of Haliburton at the Leslie M. Frost Outdoor Centre (see p 235) also form part of the Haliburton Highlands Nordic Trails.

Getting There

Take Regional Road 21 northeast from Minden, or west from Tory Hill or take Highway 118 south from West Guilford.

Further Information

Haliburton Nordic Trail Association
PO Box 670
Haliburton, ON K0M 1S0
☎ *(705) 457-1640*
Skihaliburton.8m.com

Haliburton Highlands Cross Country Ski Club
☎ *(705) 457-1640 (Blake Paton)*
www3.sypatico.ca/bpaton/Nordic/hscfr1

Haliburton Chamber of Commerce
☎ *800-461-7677*

Highlands Nordic (♥)

Location:	Duntroon Side Rd., southwest of Collingwood
Number of trails:	5
Total distance:	17km (11mi)

Level of difficulty:	● ■ ◆
Groomed:	100%
Trackset:	100% classic and skating
Interesting features:	Hundred Acre Woods, Biathlon range
Fee:	$12/day, $8/day seniors and juniors 8-19yrs
Other activities:	Toboggan Park, women's ski fit programme
Services:	**(R)**, **(L)**, **(A)** *(farmhouse)*
Amenities and other services:	Parking, heated lodge with snack bar, toilets, telephones, maps, waxing centre and pro shop, Canadian Ski Patrol, snowmaking

Larry Sinclair, along with his family and friends, has created a superb cross-country ski destination that appeals to everyone. His success is due to a four-part philosophy of simplicity, maintenance, imagination and change.

The trails reflect simplicity. Highlands Nordic has only five cross-country ski trails: the 2.5km (1.6mi) easy **green** one; the 4km (2.5mi) **blue** and 5km (3mi) **yellow** trails for intermediate skiers, and the 7km (4mi) **orange** and 11km (7mi) **red** trails for advanced skiers. Each trail was carefully designed, however, to provide a workout while challenging the technical skills of skiers of every level of expertise.

Constant maintenance ensures that skiers who try Highlands Nordic will want to return. Snowmaking equipment keeps the trail surfaces as smooth as possible and all five trails are impeccably groomed and trackset. All the buildings on site are newly painted and clean, with washrooms that are well-maintained and fully equipped. The snack bar is clean, with cold water, hot chilli and freshly baked goods to offer. The rental equipment is clean and in good repair. After a while, regulars begin to rely on such top conditions and don't trust other locations to match them.

Sinclair uses his imagination every time he adds a new trail, activity or service. The most innovative trail he's created so far, for example, is an ungroomed path through the

Hundred-Acre Wood. Signs, doorbells and other props identify the homes of Eeyore, Piglet, Owl, Tigger, Kanga and Roo, Rabbit and Winnie the Pooh (Saunder's House). Christopher Robin lives in a small cabin, complete with a porch to climb on. Mailboxes enable visitors to leave letters for their friends or read what's already there. They'll try thinking in Pooh's "thoughtful spot" or playing Pooh sticks on Pooh Sticks Bridge. Many mini-skiers are keen on returning to Nordic Highlands again and again.

Change comes in with all the types of activities offered. Loppets, ski fit programs, a biathlon range—the opportunities for different events are endless and people appreciate the new opportunities and atmospheres that each event creates. Of course, once the event is created, people don't want it to change—that's where simplicity and upkeep come in…again.

Getting There

From Duntroon, take County Road 91 west and turn left (south) on Concession 10. Highlands Nordic is on the right.

Further Information

Highlands Nordic
PO Box 110
Duntroon, ON L0M 1H0
☎ *(705) 444-5017*
☎ *800-263-5017*
www.highlandsnordic.on.ca

Horseshoe Resort (♥)

Location:	North of Barrie
Number of trails:	12
Total distance:	75.5km (47mi)
Level of difficulty:	● ■ ◆
Groomed:	100%
Trackset:	65% classic, 69% skating
Interesting features:	Lots of hills, Copeland Forest

Fee:	$14/day, $10/day 13-18yrs, $7/day senior over 65yrs, children 7-12yrs
Other activities:	Alpine, snowboarding, moonlight and fitness skis
Services:	**(R)** *($19)*, **(L)** *($37/hr)*, **(A)**
Amenities and other services:	Babysitting, parking, heated lodge, pro shop, telephones, toilets, snack bar, maps, waxing centre, Canadian Ski Patrol

Horseshoe Resort spends as much effort on their cross-country facilities as they do on their alpine facilities—and that's a lot.

There are three distinct areas for cross-country trails, although they all connect.

The **South Trails** lie south of Regional Road 22 and circumvent the small Horseshoe Inn (the resort includes this inn plus other facilities), Carriage Hills Resort and the alpine slopes. Horseshoe Resort grooms the four trails for skating, primarily for the benefit of telemark skiers. The **red** expert trail is 14km (8.7mi); the **green** intermediate trail is 5.4km (3.4mi), the **blue** intermediate trail is 3.3km (2mi) and the **Farm Loop** is 3.5km (2mi) for intermediate skiers.

The four **West Trails** are groomed and trackset for skating and classic. They include a **red** 9.5km (5.9mi) expert trail, a **green** 7km (4mi) intermediate trail, a **blue** 6km (3.7mi) intermediate trail and a **yellow** 3.8km (2.4mi) beginner trail.

The four **North Trails** are groomed and trackset for classic skiing only. They include a 12km (7mi) **red** trail for experts, a 5.8km (3.6mi) **green** trail and a 3.7km (2.3mi) **blue** trail for intermediate skiers and a 1.5km (.9mi) **yellow** trail for beginners.

The trails are groomed with precision and everything offered here—rentals, washrooms, waxing area—is clean, well maintained and stocked. For a real treat, join instructors for a fitness ski which is held every Thursday evening or for a moonlight ski every Saturday night when the moon is full.

Central Ontario

Getting There

Take Highway 400 north from Barrie to Horseshoe Valley Road. Take the eastbound exit and drive for 6km (4mi).

Further Information

Horseshoe Resort
PO Box 10, Horseshoe Valley, RR 1
Barrie, ON L4M 4Y8
☎*(705) 835-2790*
☎*800-461-5627*
www.horseshoeresort.com

Inglis Falls Conservation Area (♥)

Location:	Owen Sound
Number of trails:	3
Total distance:	10km (6.2mi)
Level of difficulty:	● ■
Groomed:	No
Trackset:	No
Interesting features:	Inglis Falls, stone foundation of a three-storey mill, Niagara Escarpment, Sydenham River, Bruce Trail
Fee:	Donation
Other activities:	Yes
Amenities and other services:	Parking, toilets, nature shop occasionally open

The Sydenham River falls over the Niagara Escarpment just west of Owen Sound in an 18m-high (59ft) cascade known as Inglis Falls, after entrepreneur Peter Inglis who built two gristmills, a sawmill and a woollen mill on the site in the mid 1800s. The gristmill was famous during World War I because it supplied the flour for Canadian troops overseas.

In the winter, the view of the falls from the wooden platform looks like something out of a fairy tale; most of the water stays frozen in sheets of heavy icicles while a torrent of liquid falls in the centre. The limestone remains of the circa-1862 four-storey mill provide a man-made backdrop to the natural wonder.

To begin cross-country skiing, cross the bridge to the Nature Shop. Unless you have snowshoes, ignore the trail that follows the Sydenham River upstream. This is the Bruce Trail (see p 351) and it turns left into the park about 100m (328ft) along.

The most scenic trail, **Inglis Trail**, follows the Sydenham River downstream for 6km (3.7mi) and offers several good hills. To get to this trail, you need to ski behind the nature store, turn to the left and ski for a short while before the trail leads to the left and back down to the river farther along. (It turns towards this trail twice.)

The Inglis Trail leads to several bridges across the Sydenham River. Take the third crossing along (the first are stairs, the second and third are bridges) to get to the 2km (1.2mi) **west trail** on the opposite side of the river (although this trail may close).

Continue straight behind the nature shop to stay on the 2km (1.2mi) loop that leads to **Harrison Park** and another selection of cross-country ski trails.

Getting There

From Owen Sound, take Highway 6 south to Rockford. Turn right (west) on County Road 18, and then right again (north) on Inglis Falls Road. The conservation area parking lot is to the right.

Further Information

Grey Sauble Conservation Authority
RR 4, Inglis Falls Rd.
Owen Sound, ON N4K 5N6
☎(519) 376-3076
www.greycounty.on.ca/tourism/greysauble

Central Ontario

Jackson Creek Kiwanis Trail

Location: Along Jackson Creek between Peterborough's Jackson Park and Ackison Rd.
Number of trails: 1 linear
Total distance: 4km (2.5mi)
Level of difficulty: ●
Groomed: No
Trackset: No
Interesting features: Jackson Creek, forest, farms, wetland
Fee: No

Getting There

Access the trail from Jackson Park in Peterborough.

Further Information

Otonabee Conservation
250 Milroy Dr.
Peterborough, ON K9H 7M9
☎*(705) 745-5791*
📠*(705) 745-7488*
www.otonabee.com

Ken Reid Conservation Area

Location: North of Lindsay
Number of trails: 2
Total distance: 7km (4mi)
Level of difficulty: ●
Groomed: 100%
Trackset: No
Interesting features: McLaren Creek, forest, snowshoe hare, deer, marsh boardwalk, Sturgeon Lake
Fee: Donation

**Amenities and
other services:**   Parking, toilets

Getting There

From Lindsay, drive north on Highway 35 for 3km (1.9mi).
When you reach Kenrei Park Road, turn left and drive to
the parking lot.

Further Information

Kawartha Region Conservation Authority
Kenrei Park Rd., RR 1
Lindsay, ON K9V 4R1
☎*(705) 328-2271*
☎*800-668-5722 (705 and 416 area codes only)*

Kerr Park

Location: Bracebridge
Number of trails: 4
Total distance: 10km (6mi)
Level of difficulty: ● ■
Groomed: 100%
Trackset: No
Interesting features: Woodland, lagoons
Fee: No
**Amenities and
other services:**   Parking, toilets, telephones, chalet

Getting There

From Highway 11, take Highway 118 west (Ecclestone
Drive) to Beaumont Drive.

Further Information

Kerr Park
☎*(705) 645-3037*

Central Ontario

Kolapore Uplands

Location:	Eastern edge of Beaver Valley, near Collingwood
Number of trails:	12
Total distance:	50km (31mi)
Level of difficulty:	● ■ ◆
Groomed:	No
Trackset:	No
Interesting features:	45m-high (147ft) limestone cliffs, waterfall, Bruce Trail
Fee:	Donation
Other activities:	Alpine skiing
Services:	(A) *(University of Toronto cabin)*
Amenities and other services:	Parking

Getting There

From Feversham, drive north on County Road 2 (8th Line) for about 8km (5mi) until you reach the parking lot.

Further Information

Kolapore Ski Trails
PO Box 6647, Station A
Toronto, ON M5W 1X4

Ravenna General Store
maps available
Grey County Rd. 2
Kolapore
☎*(519) 599-2796*

University of Toronto Outing Club
www.campuslife.utoronto.ca/groups/utoc

Grey Sauble Conservation Authority
RR 4, Inglis Falls Rd.
Owen Sound, ON N4K 5N6
☎*(519) 376-3076*
www.greycounty.on.ca/tourism/greysauble

Lafontaine Cross-Country Ski Centre

Location:	Penetanguishene
Number of trails:	9
Total distance:	45km (28mi)
Level of difficulty:	● ■ ◆
Groomed:	100%
Trackset:	100%, 45km (28mi), classic, 7km (4mi) skating
Interesting features:	Lookout over Thunder Bay in the Christian Channel of Georgian Bay
Fee:	$10/day, $7 child or senior, $30 family
Services:	**(R)** *($12)*
Amenities and other services:	Parking, toilets, telephones, lodge with snack bar (weekends) and waxing centre

How to Get There

Take Highway 93 to Penetanguishene. Follow the signs to Awenda Provincial Park that lead you to turn left on Robert Street (which is not indicated). Then turn left on Lafontaine Road (Concession 16).

Further Information

Lafontaine Cross Country Ski Trails
240 Lafontaine Rd. E.
Penetanguishene, ON L9M 1R3
☎ *(705) 533-2961*
⇌ *(705) 533-2961*
www.lafontaine-ent.on.ca

Central Ontario

Leslie M. Frost Outdoor Centre (♥)

Location:	Between Minden and Dorset
Number of trails:	7

Total distance:	22km (13.7mi)
Level of difficulty:	● ■ ◆
Groomed:	100%
Trackset:	100% classic
Interesting features:	Canadian Shield, white pine and hemlock forests, cliff top lookouts, frozen waterfall, McKewen Lake, Dan Lake, Three Island Lake, marsh
Fee:	$8/day, free for children under 17yrs and Haliburton Trail pass holders
Services:	**(A)** *(Frost Centre for groups)*
Amenities and other services:	Parking, toilets, telephones, maps, two shelters with wood stoves

Anyone who enjoys classic skiing should put the Frost Centre's cross country ski trails on their list of things to do. To get to the trails, you have to climb a huge limestone cliff. At the top, you get a great view of St. Nora Lake on the other side of Highway 35, a view that's worth stopping for. The trails through the woods are also pretty, but there are also even more beautiful scenic lookouts over lakes and a blue cascade to admire along the trails.

The trail system includes seven linked loops. The 2.2km (1.3mi) **Fox** and the 1.1km (.7mi) **Bunny**, at the beginning, are the only easy trails on the course. If you follow the sawmill signs from the Bunny Trail, you will have one tough bridge to cross, but after that you just follow a road to a rather unimpressive sawmill. You're better to stick with the views from the marked trails.

The 2.7km (1.7mi) **Beaver** and the 4km (2.5mi) **Bear** are intermediate trails. The 6.5km (4mi) **Deer** and the 4km (2.5mi) **Moose** are difficult trails. Also, although it's only 1.6km-long (1mi), two steep hills on the **Marten Trail** make it the hardest trail on the course.

Getting There

Take Highway 35 north from Minden or south from Dorset. The Nordic trails are on the east side, across the street from the Leslie M. Frost Natural Resources Centre.

Further Information

Ski Friends of the Frost Centre
c/o Frost Centre
RR 2
Minden, ON K0M 2K0
☎ *(705) 766-9677*
☎ *(705) 754-2351 (Margaret)*
☎ *(705) 766-0545 (Shirley)*

Mansfield Outdoor Centre

Location:	Airport Rd., north of Hwy. 89
Number of trails:	8
Total distance:	35km (22mi)
Level of difficulty:	● ■ ◆
Groomed:	100%
Trackset:	100%, 35km (22mi) double-tracked classic, 10km (6mi) skating
Interesting features:	Mixed forest on rolling terrain, Boyne River
Fee:	$8.50/day, $7 children
Services:	**(R)**, **(L)**
Amenities and other services:	Parking, heated lodge, snack bar, maps, toilets, telephones, waxing centre, snowmaking equipment, Canadian Ski Patrol

The Mansfield Outdoor Centre was the first of the new style cross-country centres to focus on good trail and facility maintenance so skiers can concentrate on technique and stamina.

Most of the Mansfield trails run to the north of the field centre, where hills are numerous. For that reason, the beginners' trails run to the south and east of the field centre. They include the orange 2km (1mi) **River Run** and the green 4.5km (2.8mi) **Cedar Trail**.

Central Ontario

There are two intermediate trails, a 3.7km (2.3mi) red **Lookout Trail** and a 9.5km (5.9mi) blue **Logger Trail**, although if you take a **shortcut** the **Logger** is only 7.8km (4.8mi).

Advanced skiers can choose either the 11.4km (7mi) **Deer Trail** or the 8km (5mi) **Deer shortcut**. The Deer and the Logger trails link for a total trail length of 15.8km (10mi).

Skaters have one 9.9km (6mi) **Black** trail to follow.

Getting There

From Highway 89, take Airport Road north 10km (6mi).

Further Information

Mansfield Outdoor Centre
PO Box 95
Mansfield, ON L0N 1M0
☎*(705) 435-4479*
www.mansfield-outdoors.com

Massie Hills

Location:	Southeast of Owen Sound on Hwy. 10
Number of trails:	6
Total distance:	7km (4.3mi)
Level of difficulty:	● ■ ◆
Groomed:	100%, but only weekly
Trackset:	No
Interesting features:	Deer, hare, jack rabbits
Fee:	Donation

Getting There

From Owen Sound, take Highway 26 east and turn right (south) on Regional Road 11. Turn left (east) on Regional Road 18 and turn right (south) on the 6th Concession. Massie Hills is on your right.

Further Information

Owen Sound Cross Country Ski Club
PO Box 1033
Owen Sound
☎ *(519) 372-8046 (Chris Hughes)*

Minesing Swamp Conservation Area

Location:	George Johnston Rd. (Simcoe Rd. 28), south of the village of Minesing
Number of trails:	1 linear
Total distance:	1km (.6mi)
Level of difficulty:	●
Groomed:	100%
Trackset:	No
Interesting features:	Overview of the old Algonquin shore-line, marsh
Fee:	Donation
Amenities and other services:	Parking, toilets

Getting There

From Barrie, travel west on Highway 26 to the village of Minesing. Turn right (south) on Simcoe Road 28 (George Johnston Road) to get to the Willow Creek access point.

Further Information

Nottawasaga Valley Conservation Authority
266 Mill St. (Simcoe Rd. 90), RR 1
Angus, ON L0M 1B0
☎ *(705) 424-1479*
⇄ *(705) 424-2115*
www.nvca.on.ca

Central Ontario

Mountain View Ski Hill

Location:	Midland
Number of trails:	4
Total distance:	20km (12mi)
Level of difficulty:	● ■ ◆
Groomed:	100%
Trackset:	100% classic and skating
Interesting features:	Georgian Bay, Blue Mountain
Fee:	$12
Other activities:	Alpine skiing and snowboarding on weekends
Services:	**(R)**
Amenities and other services:	Parking, heated lodge with toilets, telephone, snack bar, waxing centre and pro shop

Getting There

Take Highway 93 to Midland. After entering the town, take Foster's Road west.

Further Information

Mountain View Ski Hill
RR 2
Midland, ON L4K 4K4
☎*(705) 526-8149*

Muskoka Heritage Place

Location:	Huntsville
Number of trails:	1
Total distance:	2km (1mi)
Level of difficulty:	●
Groomed:	No

Trackset:	No
Interesting features:	Log cabins, Cann Lake
Fee:	Donation
Amenities and other services:	Parking

Getting There

From downtown Huntsville, walk to Brunel Road.

Further Information

Muskoka Heritage Place
88 Brunel Rd.
Huntsville, ON P1H 1R1
☎ *(705) 789-7576*
✆ *(705) 789-6169*
www.muskokaheritageplace.org

Muskoka Sands Resort

🛏 **Access to trails reserved for overnight guests**

Location:	Gravenhurst
Number of trails:	2
Total distance:	6km (4mi)
Level of difficulty:	● ■
Groomed:	No
Trackset:	No
Interesting features:	Lake Muskoka
Fee:	No
Other activities:	Snowmobiling, indoor pool, ice-skating, dogsledding
Services:	(R)
Amenities and other services:	Parking

Getting There

From Gravenhurst, take Bethune Drive north to Muskoka Beach Road. Follow the road towards the lake to the entrance of the resort.

Central Ontario

Further Information

Muskoka Sands Resort
Muskoka Beach Rd.
Gravenhurst, ON P1P 1R1
☎ *(705) 687-2253*
☎ *800-461-0236*
⇆ *(705) 687-7474*
www.muskokasands.com

Nordic Inn

🛏 **Access to trails reserved for overnight guests**

Location:	Hwy. 35, Dorset
Number of trails:	3
Total distance:	10km (6mi)
Level of difficulty:	●
Groomed:	100%
Trackset:	No
Interesting features:	Lake of Bays, Dorset Observation Tower
Fee:	No
Other activities:	Snowmobiling, ice-skating, alpine skiing and curling
Services:	(A)
Amenities and other services:	Parking, toilets, telephones, lodging, restaurant

Getting There

Take Highway 35 north from Halls Lake or south from Dwight to Dorset.

Further Information

Nordic Inn
Hwy. 35
PO Box 155
Dorset, ON P0A 1E0
☎ *(705) 766-2343*
☎ *888-392-7777*
www.thenordicinn.com

Norland Cross Country Ski & Recreation Park

Location:	Norland
Number of trails:	9
Total distance:	40km (25mi)
Level of difficulty:	● ■ ◆
Groomed:	100%
Trackset:	100%, classic
Interesting features:	Marshland, lakes, woods
Fee:	$15
Amenities and other services:	Parking, toilets, telephones, heated lodge with waxing centre

Getting There

Take Highway 503 west from Norland for 6km (4mi).

Further Information

Norland Cross Country Ski and Recreation Park
PO Box 177
Norland, ON K0M 2L0
☎ *(705) 454-9518*
☎ *800-486-9808*

Pinestone Resort

Location:	Hwy. 21, west of Haliburton
Number of trails:	3
Total distance:	15km (9mi)
Level of difficulty:	● ■
Groomed:	100%
Trackset:	100% classic
Interesting features:	Kashagawigamog Lake

Central Ontario

Fee:	$12/day, $10/student 13-18yrs, free for children
Other activities:	Tobogganing, dogsledding
Services:	**(R)**, **(A)**
Amenities and other services:	Parking, heated ski centre, maps, toilets, telephones, restaurants, indoor pool

Getting There

Take Highway 121 west from Haliburton.

Further Information

Pinestone Golf and Conference Resort
PO Box 809
Haliburton, ON K0M 1S0
☎ *(705) 457-1800*
☎ *800-461-0357*
✉ *(705) 457-3136*
www.pinestone.on.ca

Pow Wow Point Lodge

🛏 **Access to trails reserved for overnight guests**

Location:	Huntsville
Number of trails:	2
Total distance:	12km (7mi)
Level of difficulty:	●
Groomed:	100%
Trackset:	100%, classic
Interesting features:	Peninsula Lake
Fee:	No
Other activities:	Ice-skating, snowmobiling, tobogganing
Services:	**(R)**, **(A)**
Amenities and other services:	Parking, toilets, telephones, inn, spa, restaurant

Getting There

Take Highway 60 to Regional Road 23. Follow the signs to the resort.

Further Information

Pow Wow Point Lodge
RR 4, 207 Grassmere Resort Rd.
Huntsville, ON P1H 2J6
☎ *(705) 789-4951*
☎ *800-461-4263*
⇄ *(705) 789-7123*
www.powwowpointlodge.com

Scanlon Creek Conservation Area

Location:	North of Bradford
Number of trails:	1
Total distance:	5km (3mi)
Level of difficulty:	●
Groomed:	No
Trackset:	No
Interesting features:	Forests, marsh and glacial erratics
Fee:	No
Amenities and other services:	Parking

Getting There

From Bradford, take County Road 4 to Concession Road 9 and follow the signs to the entrance.

Further Information

Lake Simcoe Region Conservation Authority
120 Bayview Pkwy.
PO Box 282
Newmarket, ON L3Y 4X1
☎ *(705) 895-1281*
⇄ *(705) 853-5881*
www.lsrca.on.ca

Central Ontario

Selwyn Conservation Area

Location:	Selwyn
Number of trails:	1
Total distance:	3km (2mi)
Level of difficulty:	●
Groomed:	No
Trackset:	No
Interesting features:	Chemong Lake
Fee:	No
Amenities and other services:	Parking

Getting There

Take Highway 507 south from Buckhorn or north from Lakefield.

Further Information

Otonabee Conservation
250 Milroy Dr.
Peterborough, ON K9H 7M9
☎*(705) 745-5791*
⇌*(705) 745-7488*
www.otonabee.com

Shamrock Lodge

🛏 Access to trails reserved for overnight guests

Location:	Port Carling
Number of trails:	8
Total distance:	20km (12mi)
Level of difficulty:	● ■
Groomed:	100%
Trackset:	No

Interesting features: Lake Rosseau
Fee: No
Other activities: Snowmobiling, ice fishing
Services: **(A)**
**Amenities and
other services:** Parking, toilets, telephones, inn, spa, restaurant

Getting There

From Port Carling, drive 4.5km (3mi) along Ferndale, Johnston and Shamrock roads.

Further Information

Shamrock Lodge
PO Box 160
Port Carling, ON P0B 1J0
☎ *(705) 765-3177*
☎ *800-668-8885*
⇌ *(705) 765-6267*
www.shamrocklodge.com

Sherwood Inn

🛏 **Access to trails reserved for overnight guests**

Location: Port Carling
Number of trails: 7
Total distance: 16km (10mi)
Level of difficulty: ● ■
Groomed: No
Trackset: No
Interesting features: Lake Rosseau
Fee: No
Other activities: Ice-skating, tobogganing
Services: **(A)**
**Amenities and
other services:** Parking, toilets, telephones, restaurant

Central Ontario

Getting There

From Port Carling, take Highway 118 west to Highway 169. Turn north and drive for 2km (1mi).

Further Information

Sherwood Inn
PO Box 400
Port Carling, ON P0B 1J0
☎*(705) 765-3131*
☎*800-461-4233*

Springwater Provincial Park

Location:	Midhurst
Number of trails:	5
Total distance:	15km (9mi)
Level of difficulty:	●
Groomed:	100%
Trackset:	No
Interesting features:	Birds of prey, bears, beavers, coyotes, owls, porcupine, raccoons, turkeys and wolves
Fee:	$8.50/vehicle
Amenities and other services:	Parking, toilets

If you have kids, Springwater Provincial Park is an absolute must for cross-country skiing. The Ministry of Natural Resources houses injured, orphaned and human-imprinted birds and wildlife that can't be released into nature in specially designed enclosures that provide the animals with appropriate space. The deer enclosure, for instance, spans .8ha (2 acres).

Children can spend hours watching snowy owls, hawks, porcupines, beavers, raccoons, turkeys,

wolves, coyotes, bears and other wild animals up close. They also enjoy seeing the employees clean the enclosures and provide the animals with fresh food, including alfalfa from the neighbouring fields in the summer. Every animal receives daily care.

Trails include the 1km (.6mi) **Animal Display Path**, the 5.5km (3.4mi) **Red Trail**, the 4km (2.5mi) **Green Trail**, the 2.5km (1.6mi) **Blue Trail** and the 1.5km (.9mi) **William R. Wilson Snowshoe Trail**.

Getting There

Take Highway 26 north from Barrie.

Further Information

Springwater Provincial Park
Hwy. 26
Midhurst, ON L0L 1X0
☎ *(705) 728-7393*
☎ *800-667-1940*
⇋ *(705) 728-5444*
www.ontarioparks.com

Talisman Mountain Resort

Location:	Hwy. 7 north of Kimberley
Number of trails:	3
Total distance:	10km (6mi)
Level of difficulty:	● ■ ◆
Groomed:	100%
Trackset:	100% classic and skating
Interesting features:	Beaver Valley
Fee:	$8/day
Other activities:	Alpine skiing, snow tubing, snowboarding
Services:	**(R)**, **(L)**, **(A)**
Amenities and other services:	Parking, toilets, telephones, heated lodge with snack bar, maps, waxing centre, pro shop, babysitting service, Canadian Ski Patrol

Central Ontario

Getting There

From Kimberley, drive on Grey Road 13 west for 2km (1.2mi) until you get to Grey Road 7, where the resort is located.

Further Information

Talisman Mountain Resort
150 Talisman Mountain Dr.
Kimberley, ON N0C 1G0
☎ *(519) 599-2520*
☎ *800-265-3759*
www.talisman.ca

Tawingo Trails

Location:	Huntsville
Number of trails:	8
Total distance:	15km (9mi)
Level of difficulty:	●
Groomed:	100%
Trackset:	100% classic
Interesting features:	Lake Vernon, three streams
Fee:	Donation
Services:	**(A)**
Amenities and other services:	Parking, maps

Getting There

From Huntsville, take Muskoka Road No. 2 (Ravenscliffe Road) for 8km (5mi) past Ravenscliffe to the Camp Tawingo gate.

Further Information

Camp Tawingo
RR No. 1
Huntsville, ON P1H 2J2
☎ *(705) 789-5612*
⇌ *(705) 789-6624*
www.tawingo.net

The Baldwins

🛏 **Access to trails reserved for overnight guests**

Location:	Windermere
Number of trails:	5
Total distance:	20km (9mi)
Level of difficulty:	● ■ ◆
Groomed:	100%
Trackset:	100% classic, 25% skating
Interesting features:	Lake Rosseau
Fee:	No
Other activities:	Ice-skating, tobogganing, kick-sledding and ice fishing
Services:	(R), (A)
Amenities and other services:	Parking, toilets, telephones, inn, indoor pool, sauna, whirlpool, restaurant

Getting There

From Bracebridge, take Regional Road 4 to Windermere.

Further Information

Bob and Deanne Rainville
PO Box 61
Windermere, ON P0B 1P0
☎ *(705) 769-3371*
☎ *800-461-1728*
www.travelmuskoka.com/baldwins

The Briars Resort

📖 Access to trails reserved for overnight guests

Location:	Jackson's Point
Number of trails:	1
Total distance:	10km (6mi)
Level of difficulty:	■
Groomed:	100%
Trackset:	100% classic
Interesting features:	Lake Simcoe, 150yr-old historic inn, woodlands
Fee:	No
Other activities:	Tobogganing, snow golf, walking, ice-skating on the lake, horse-drawn sleigh rides
Services:	**(R)** *($17)*, **(A)**
Amenities and other services:	Parking, heated toilets, telephones, gourmet restaurant

Getting There

Take Highway 48 north to Sutton. Turn left onto High Street. Drive until the street ends at Dalton Road. Turn right and follow Dalton Road to Jackson's Point. The second stop sign is Lake Drive. Turn right and drive about 1km (.6mi) to the entrance gates on Hedge Road.

Further Information

The Briars Resort
55 Hedge Rd., RR 1
Jackson's Point, ON L0E 1L0
☎ *(905) 722-3271 or (416) 493-2173*
☎ *800-465-2376*
⇄ *(905) 722-9698*
www.briars.ca

Tiffin Centre for Conservation

Location:	Barrie
Number of trails:	3
Total distance:	7km (4mi)
Level of difficulty:	●
Groomed:	100%
Trackset:	No
Interesting features:	Conifer forest
Fee:	Donation
Amenities and other services:	Parking, toilets, telephones, lodge, snack bar, maps

Getting There

From Barrie, take the 8th Concession of Essa Township south. Pass Highway 90 and continue driving for another 4km (2.5mi) to the park entrance.

Further Information

Tiffin Centre for Conservation
☎ *(705) 424-1485*

Nottawasaga Valley Conservation Authority
266 Mill St. (Simcoe Rd. 90), RR 1
Angus, ON L0M 1B0
☎ *(705) 424-1479*
⇒ *(705) 424-2115*
www.nvca.on.ca

Central Ontario

Torrance Barrens Conservation and Dark Sky Reserve

Location:	Southwood Rd. between Bala and Gravenhurst

Number of trails: 3
Total distance: 8km (5mi)
Level of difficulty: ■ ◆
Groomed: No
Trackset: No
Interesting features: Marsh, bare bedrock, stars, northern lights
Fee: No
Other activities: snowmobiling
**Amenities and
other services:**   Parking

Getting There

Take Muskoka Road 169 north from Gravenhurst or south from Bala. Turn south on Muskoka Road 13 (Southwood Road). Torrance Barrens is 7km (4mi) along.

Further Information

The Muskoka Heritage Foundation
9 Taylor Rd.
PO Box 482
Bracebridge, ON P1L 1T8
☎ *(705) 645-7393*
⇌ *(705) 645-7888*

Wigamog Inn Resort

Location: Haliburton
Number of trails: 2
Total distance: 10km (6mi)
Level of difficulty: ● ■ ◆
Groomed: 100%
Trackset: 100% classic and skating
Interesting features: Mixed forest
Fee: $12/day, $10/student 13-18yrs, free for children
Other activities: Snowmobiling
Services: **(R)**, **(A)** *(couples only)*

**Amenities and
other services:**   Parking, toilets, telephones, lodge with
pro shop, restaurant, snack bar,
babysitting

Getting There

Take Regional Road 121 southwest of Haliburton.

Further Information

Wigamog Inn Resort
RR 2
Haliburton, ON K0M 1S0
☎ *(705) 457-2000*
☎ *800-661-2010*
www.wigamoginn.on.ca

Wye Marsh Wildlife Centre

Location: Across from the Martyrs Shrine in Mid-
land
Number of trails: 5
Total distance: 10km (6mi)
Level of difficulty: ● ■
Groomed: 100%
Trackset: 100% classic
Interesting features: Trumpeter Swans, chickadees, Wye
Valley
Fee: $5.50/day, $5/day seniors and children
3-17yrs
Other activities: Sugar shack, floating boardwalk
Services: **(R)** *($12)*
**Amenities and
other services:**   Parking; heated lodge with waxing cen-
tre; visitor centre with snack bar, maps,
toilets, telephones and gift shop

The Wye Marsh 1,000ha (150-acre) nature discovery centre
features 10km (6mi) of cross-country ski trails and another
5km (3mi) of snowshoe paths that leads to a pond shelter-

ing 25 rare Trumpeter swans during the winter. You can also snowshoe across the floating boardwalk, visit a sugar shack or enjoy lots of great winter birding.

Getting There

Take Highway 12 east from Midland.

Further Information

Wye Marsh Wildlife Centre
PO Box 100
Midland, ON L4R 4K6
☎*(705) 526-7809*
⇌*(705) 526-3294*
www.bpm.on.ca/wyemarsh

Eastern Ontario

Skiers and snowshoers experience three distinct types of scenery in eastern Ontario.

That's because the area is divided into three by the **Frontenac Axis**, a point of solid gneiss/granite jutting out southward from the Canadian Shield. The **Ottawa–St. Lawrence Lowlands** lie to either side of the Frontenac Axis, but the section downriver used to be covered with salt water, while the upriver portion used to be covered with fresh water.

If you visit a park located on the Frontenac Axis, you'll often find yourself skiing along plains of granite covered as much with lichens and moss as with snow. Expect to pass many lakes, shallow bogs and marshes. Typical vegetation includes conifers, with roots capable of circumventing rock to reach tiny bits of soil, and shallow-rooted trees, such as silver maples. **Frontenac Provincial Park** (see p 267) is the largest park in this area, with beautiful scenery surrounding more than 22 lakes. There are six different groomed skiing trails for a total of 13km (8mi) of classic skiing and another seven ungroomed trails for backcountry skiing and snowshoeing. **Silent Lake Provincial Park** (see p 285), also located on the Frontenac Axis, has become quite famous for its cross-country skiing. The park grooms 48.5km (30mi) of trails for novice, intermediate and expert skiers. Classic skiers have the most choice, including a 19km (12mi) trail that circumvents three lakes. Skate skiers aren't left out either, with one 8km (5mi) trail groomed just for them. **Murphys Point Provincial Park** (see p 278) also specializes in cross-country skiing, and offers 21km (13mi) of groomed trails in the classic style. Other good skiing areas on the Frontenac Axis are **Depot Lakes Conservation and Campground** (see p 263), **Gould Lake Conservation Area** (see p 269), **Mill Pond Conservation Area** (see p 276), and **Twin Wheels Farm** (see p 289).

The once-salty section of the Ottawa–St. Lawrence Lowlands lies in a triangular area of eastern Ontario between the Ottawa and Rideau rivers and the Frontenac Axis edge that runs along a rough line between Arnprior and Brockville. Here, the shield rock dips below what was once a great glacial body of saltwater called the Champlain Sea. The bedrock is limestone plain rather than gneiss and granite, and it's covered with a deep layer of clay. Farms are quite prevalent throughout the region, which is comprised of mixed forests containing white pine, eastern hemlock, sugar maples, red maples, red oak and white cedar. The parks in this area include the **Mill of Kintail Conservation Area** (see p 275) along the Indian River and the **Terry Fox Athletic Facility** (see p 287) on Mooney's Bay in Ottawa.

The third region in eastern Ontario is the Ottawa–St. Lawrence Lowlands, which lies south of the Frontenac Axis and east of the Oak Ridges Moraine. It includes the regions immediately surrounding Belleville, Kingston, Picton, Trenton and Tweed. This part of the province used to be covered by freshwater glacial lakes that were the precursors to today's Great Lakes. The area sits on limestone bedrock covered by a deep layer of sand that was dropped by water flowing from the glacial lakes as they made their

Eastern Ontario

1. Baxter Conservation Area
2. Bonnechere Provincial Park
3. Depot Lakes Conservation and Campground
4. Foley Mountain
5. Forest Lea Cross Country Ski Trails
6. Frink Centre
7. Frontenac Provincial Park
8. Gooderich-Loomis Conservation Area
9. Gould Lake Conservation Area
10. Gray's Creek Conservation Area
11. K&P Trail
12. Lemoine Point Conservation Area

13. Little Cataraqui Creek Conservation Area
14. Macaulay Mountain Conservation Area
15. Mac Johnson Wildlife Area
16. Mill of Kintail Conservation Area
17. Mill Pond Conservation Area
18. Mount Pakenham
19. Murphys Point Provincial Park
20. Nakkertok Cross Country Ski Club
21. Nagor Resort
22. Parrott's Bay Conservation Area
23. Perth Wildlife Reserve
24. Rideau Trail
25. Sandbanks Provincial Park
26. Silent Lake Provincial Park
27. Silver Fox Nordic
28. Terry Fox Athletic Facility
29. Triangle Cross Country Ski Club of Brockville
30. Twin Wheels Farm
31. Vanderwater Conservation Area
32. Voyageur Provincial Park

© ULYSSES

QUÉBEC

N

0 25 50km

Pembroke, Buckingham, Hull, Ottawa, Hawkesbury, Cornwall, Kemptville, Arnprior, Renfrew, Edganville, Denbigh, Merrickville, Smith Falls, Carleton Place, Perth, Maitland, Brockville, Perth Road, Gananoque, Eastview, Kingston, Bancroft, Kaladar, Tweed, Madoc, Marmora, Stirling, Campbellford, Burleigh Falls, Lakefield, Peterborough

Petroglyphs Provincial Park

St. Lawrence River

Ottawa River

way towards the Champlain Sea. While the area once supported oak savanna and sugar maple, much of it was cleared for farming, and it now contains pine plantations that were introduced to stabilize the sand. Cross-country skiing locations in the area include: the **Frink Centre** (see p 266), **Gooderich-Loomis Conservation Area** (see p 268), **Gray's Creek Conservation Area** (see p 270), **Lemoine Point Conservation Area** (see p 272), **Little Cataraqui Creek Conservation Area** (see p 272), **Macaulay Mountain Conservation Area** (see p 273), **Parrott's Bay Conservation Area** (see p 281), **Perth Wildlife Reserve** (see p 281), **Sandbanks Provincial Park** (see p 284), the **Triangle Cross Country Ski Club of Brockville** (see p 288), and **Vanderwater Conservation Area** (see p 290).

Skiing locations that are located in transition areas between the three regions combine traits that are typical of the Frontenac Axis locations with those typical of the Ottawa–St. Lawrence Lowlands. **Baxter Conservation Area** (see p 261), with its silver maple forests on one hand, and its nut groves on the other, is one such example. **Foley Mountain's** (see p 264) transitional location on a fault line between the Canadian Shield and the Great St. Lawrence Lowlands provides visitors with a 65m-high (200ft) view over Westport. The linear **K&P Trail** (see p 271) begins in the sandy Ottawa-St. Lawrence Lowlands, but most of the trail leads across the Frontenac Axis. You can actually ski or snowshoe over two sand dunes that were formerly beaches on the Champlain Sea at the **Mac Johnson Wildlife Area** (see p 274), which is also a major site for granite outcrops. **Mount Pakenham** (see p 277), the well-known ski destination that combines alpine hills with cross-country trails, also benefits from its position on a fault line between the Canadian Shield and the limestone lowlands, as does **Voyageur Provincial Park** (see p 291).

Visitors can see elements of all three regions, both separately and in different combinations within the transition zones, by travelling the entire 300km (186mi) length of the linear **Rideau Trail** (see p 282).

There is one other major rock formation that's noticeable on trails in eastern Ontario. Known as the Ottawa-Bonnechere Graben, this formation formed the Ottawa and Bonnechere river valleys, which were created when the rock between the Algonquin Dome to the south and the Gatineau Hills to the north collapsed into a fault line. To see all the sides of this process, you might want to ski on the trails at **Bonnechere Provincial Park** (see p 262), at **Forest Lea Cross Country Ski Trails** (see p 265) in Pembroke, at **Nangor Resort** (see p 280) on the Ottawa River or at the Deep River trails maintained by the **Silver Fox Nordic** (see p 287) ski club. To see what the area may have looked like before the collapse, try visiting the trails owned by the Ottawa-based **Nakkertok Cross Country Ski Club** (see p 279) in the Gatineau Hills.

Tourist Information

Ontario East Tourism Association
108 St. Lawrence St.
Merrickville, ON K0G 1N0
☎ *800-567-EAST (3278)*
www.ontarioeast.com

Baxter Conservation Area

Location:	Between Manotick and Kemptville
Number of trails:	3
Total distance:	5km (3mi)
Level of difficulty:	●
Groomed:	100%
Trackset:	No

Eastern
Ontario

Interesting features: Rideau River; nut groves with Kentucky coffee, ginko and Chinese chestnut trees; conifer plantations; marsh board-walk; natural flood plain of silver maple and cedar

Fee: $5/day, $35/year Rideau Valley Pass

Other activities: Solar Energy Display

Amenities and other services: Parking, toilets, telephones, snack bar, McManus Conservation Centre

Getting There

Take Highway 416 south from Manotick or north from Kemptville. Turn east on Dilworth Road and drive 3km (2mi) to the park. The entrance is on the right.

Further Information

Baxter Conservation Area
☎*(613) 489-3592*

Rideau Valley Conservation Authority
PO Box 599
1128 Mill St.
Manotick, ON K4M 1A5
☎*(613) 692-3571*
☎*800-267-3504*
www.rideauvalley.on.ca

Bonnechere Provincial Park

Location: Southwest of Pembroke
Number of trails: 2
Total distance: 5km (3mi)
Level of difficulty: ● ■
Groomed: 100%
Trackset: 100% classic
Interesting features: Forest and wetland, mouth of Little Bonnechere River, Round Lake
Fee: $8.50/vehicle, $2 walk-in

Other activities:	Ice-skating, ice fishing and winter camping
Services:	**(A)** *(rustic cabins or Okum House lodge)*
Amenities and other services:	Parking, toilets, warm-up hut, heated showers, laundry

Getting There

Take County Road 58 (formerly Highway 62) 37km (23mi) southwest of Pembroke to Round Lake Road. Turn left into the park.

Further Information

Bonnechere Provincial Park
4024 Round Lake Rd.
Bonnechere, ON
☎ *(613) 757-2103 (reservations)*
☎ *800-667-1940*
www.ontarioparks.com

Friends of Bonnechere Park
PO Box 220
Pembroke, ON K8A 6X4
www.bonnecherepark.on.ca

Depot Lakes Conservation and Campground

Location:	North of Kingston
Number of trails:	5
Total distance:	9km (6mi)
Level of difficulty:	● ■
Groomed:	No
Trackset:	No
Interesting features:	Canadian Shield
Fee:	Donation
Amenities and other services:	Parking, toilets

Eastern Ontario

Getting There

From Verona, take Highway 38 north to Snider Road. Turn left (west).

Further Information

Quinte Conservation
2061 Old Highway 2, RR 2
Belleville, ON K8N 4Z2
☎*(613) 968-3434*
⇌*(613) 968-8240*
www.pec.on.ca/conservation/nrca.html

Foley Mountain

Location:	Off County Rd. 58 (Round Lake Rd.) southwest of Pembroke
Number of trails:	5
Total distance:	20km (12mi)
Level of difficulty:	● ■ ◆
Groomed:	55%
Trackset:	55% classic
Interesting features:	Spy Rock, view over Big Rideau Lake and the city of Westport
Fee:	$5/vehicle, $2 walk-in
Amenities and other services:	Parking, toilets

Two groomed cross-country ski trails and three nature trails that might be more appropriate for snowshoes criss-cross Foley Mountain. Before heading to the **two groomed cross-country ski trails**, you'll probably want to visit the **Scenic Rock Trail** near the first parking lot. A wooden ramp and stairs enable you to see the view over Westport, 65m (200ft) below. The trail continues to the left in a double loop around the mountain and can get quite slippery at times. While on Spy Rock, you'll also be on the **Rideau Trail** (see p 282), which heads to the right towards Grady Road or to the left toward the interpretive centre and the beach. The short portion leading from this trail to the interpretive centre is known as the **Nature Trail**.

While skiing, look for some of the 70 to 100 white-tailed deer that winter in the park and watch for white-tailed rabbits and snowshoe hares.

Getting There

Take Highway 42 until it ends at Westport and continue across the bridge to County Road 10 or take County Road 10 from Perth. The entrance is to the east on the hill.

Further Information

Friends of Foley Mountain
Area supervisor Barry McQuay
PO Box 244
Westport, ON K0G 1X0
☎*(613) 273-3255*
www.kingston.org/foleymountain

Rideau Valley Conservation Authority
PO Box 599
Manotick, ON K4M 1A5
☎*(613) 692-3571*
☎*800-267-3504*
www.rideauvalley.on.ca

Forest Lea Cross Country Ski Trails

Location:	West of Pembroke
Number of trails:	7
Total distance:	19km (12mi)
Level of difficulty:	● ■ ◆
Groomed:	100%
Trackset:	100% skating, 73% classic
Interesting features:	Canadian Shield outcrops, mixed forest, porcupines, deer, chickadees and blue jays
Fee:	$2/day, $5/family, $25/season
Services:	(L) *($20/child, adult lessons on demand)*
Amenities and other services:	Parking, toilets, warm-up lodge

Eastern Ontario

Getting There

Take Highway 17 west from Pembroke or east from Petawawa to Forest Lea Road. Turn south and drive to the park
entrance at the end of the street.

Further Information

Pembroke and Area Cross Country Ski Club
☎(613) 735-8466 (Brian Mottershead)
www.valleynet.on.ca/Sports/PAXC

Frink Centre

(Formerly known as Plainfield Conservation Centre)

Location:	North of Belleville
Number of trails:	3
Total distance:	8km (5mi)
Level of difficulty:	● ■ ◆
Groomed:	No
Trackset:	No
Interesting features:	Drumlin, class-one wetland
Fee:	Donation
Amenities and other services:	Parking, toilets

Getting There

Take Highway 37 north from Belleville or south from Plainfield. Turn east on Thrasher Road and travel about 2km
(1mi) to the entrance.

Further Information

Quinte Conservation
2061 Old Highway 2, RR 2
Belleville, ON K8N 4Z2
☎(613) 968-3434
↔(613) 968-8240
www.pec.on.ca/conservation/nrca.html

Courtesy of Ontario Parks

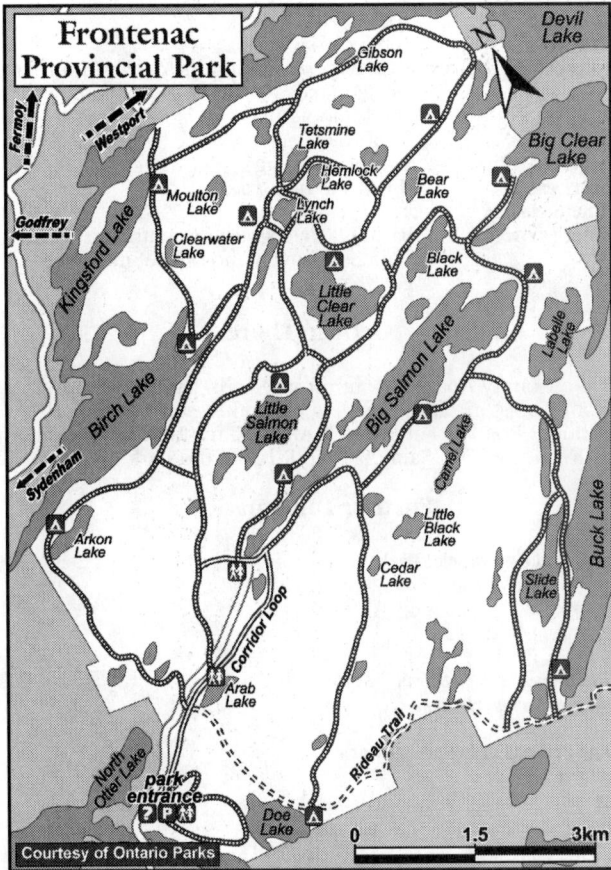

Frontenac Provincial Park

Location:	Sydenham, north of Kingston
Number of trails:	6
Total distance:	13km (8mi)
Level of difficulty:	● ■ ◆

Eastern Ontario

Groomed:	100%
Trackset:	100% classic
Interesting features:	Beaver ponds, trappers' cabin, Moulton Gorge, lakes, waterfalls, Canadian Shield, lookouts
Fee:	$8.50/day
Other activities:	Winter camping
Services:	**(L)** *(wilderness skills)*
Amenities and other services:	Parking, toilets, visitor centre with telephones, convenience store, maps and gift shop

Getting There

Take County Road 38 south from Sharbot Lake or north from Kingston. Turn, heading east on Desert Lake Road (County Road 19) at Verona. After 22km (14mi), turn right to head north on Salmon Lake Road to the park entrance.

Further Information

Frontenac Provincial Park
1090 Salmon Lake Rd.
PO Box 11
Sydenham, ON K0H 2T0
☎*(613) 376-3489*
☎*888-668-7275 or 800-667-1940*
www.ontarioparks.com

The Friends of Frontenac Park
PO Box 2237
Kingston, ON K7L 5J9

Gooderich-Loomis Conservation Area

Location:	North of Brighton
Number of trails:	4
Total distance:	18km (11mi)
Level of difficulty:	● ■ ◆
Groomed:	No
Trackset:	No

Interesting features: Deer, rabbits
Fee: Donation
Amenities and
other services: Parking, toilets

Getting There

Take Highway 30 north from the Brighton exit of Highway 401 or south from Cambellford. Take the Gooderich Side Road west.

Further Information

Lower Trent Conservation Authority
441 Front St.
Trenton, ON K8V 6C1
☎ *(613) 394-4829*
⇌ *(613) 394-5226*
www.ltc.on.ca

Gould Lake Conservation Area

Location: Gould Lake Rd. north of Sydenham
Number of trails: 10
Total distance: 20km (12mi)
Level of difficulty: ● ■ ◆
Groomed: No
Trackset: No
Interesting features: Millhaven Creek headwaters, Canadian Shield, Rideau Trail
Fee: Donation
Amenities and
other services: Parking, toilets, barn recreation centre (rarely open)

Getting There

Take County Road 5 east from Harrowsmith or west from Sydenham to Wheatley Street. Turn, heading north and continue to Alton Road. Turn left. Turn right on Rosedale Road, left on Freeman Road and right on Gould Lake Road.

Eastern Ontario

There's a huge hill on this road. You shouldn't have any problem getting in, but you'll stand a much better chance of getting out if you have a four-wheel drive. Turn right at the bottom of the hill and go down another short hill (this is the last one) and drive to the entrance. Most of the trails start at the barn beside the lake.

Further Information

Cataraqui Region Conservation Authority (CRCA)
1641 Perth Rd.
PO Box 160
Glenburnie, ON K0H 1S0
☎*(613) 546-4228*
www.cataraquiregion.on.ca

Rideau Trail Association
PO Box 15
Kingston, ON K7L 4V6
☎*(613) 730-2229*
www.ncf.carleton.ca/rta

Gray's Creek Conservation Area

Location:	6589 Boundary Rd., Cornwall
Number of trails:	1
Total distance:	2.3km (1.4mi)
Level of difficulty:	●
Groomed:	No
Trackset:	No
Interesting features:	Mouth of Gray Creek at the St. Lawrence River
Fee:	No
Other activities:	Marina
Amenities and other services:	Parking, toilets

Getting There

From Cornwall, take County Road East to the edge of the city limits. When you see the sign for Boundary Road, turn left (north).

Further Information

Raisin Region Conservation Authority
6589 Boundary Rd.
PO Box 429
Cornwall, ON K6H 5T2
☎ *(613) 938-3611*
www.rrca.on.ca

K&P Trail

Location:	Along the old Kingston-Pembroke rail line between Kingston and Renfrew
Number of trails:	1 linear
Total distance:	40km (25mi)
Level of difficulty:	●
Groomed:	100%
Trackset:	No
Interesting features:	Lakes, marsh
Fee:	No
Other activities:	Snowmobiling
Amenities and other services:	None

The public part of this trail is the part through Snow Road Station, Lavant Station, Flower Station and Barryvale.

Getting There

From Snow Road Station, take Highway 7 north for about 3km. The signed entrance is on the right.

Further Information

Mississippi Valley Conservation Authority
PO Box 268
Lanark, ON K0G 1K0
☎ *(613) 259-2421*
www.mvc.on.ca

Eastern Ontario

Lemoine Point Conservation Area

Location:	Coverdale Rd., Kingston
Number of trails:	4
Total distance:	11km (7km)
Level of difficulty:	●
Groomed:	No
Trackset:	No
Interesting features:	Collins Bay, Lake Ontario
Fee:	Donation
Amenities and other services:	Parking, toilets

Getting There

In Kingston, take Highway 33 west to the Collins Bay exit and turn left (south), or take Front Road past the airport, and turn right (north).

Further Information

Cataraqui Region Conservation Authority (CRCA)
1641 Perth Rd.
PO Box 160
Glenburnie, ON K0H 1S0
☎ *(613) 546-4228*
www.cataraquiregion.on.ca

Little Cataraqui Creek Conservation Area

Location:	North of Hwy. 401 and Division St., Kingston
Number of trails:	5
Total distance:	13km (8mi)
Level of difficulty:	● ■
Groomed:	100%
Trackset:	100% classic

Interesting features: Dam
Fee: $6/vehicle
Other activities: Ice-skating on the reservoir, bonfire pit and sugar shack
Services: **(R)**, **(L)**
**Amenities and
other services:** Parking, toilets, telephones, outdoor centre, warming huts

Getting There

In Kingston, take Division Street north. It becomes Perth Road (County Road 10) north of Highway 401. The entrance is on the left.

Further Information

Cataraqui Region Conservation Authority (CRCA)
1641 Perth Rd.
PO Box 160
Glenburnie, ON K0H 1S0
☎ *(613) 546-4228, ext. 501 (trail conditions)*
www.cataraquiregion.on.ca

Macaulay Mountain Conservation Area

Location: Picton
Number of trails: 3
Total distance: 12km (7.4mi)
Level of difficulty: ● ■
Groomed: No
Trackset: No
Interesting features: Milford Pond, dam, Scott's Mill, Birdhouse City, shrubs and mixed forest
Fee: Donation
Other activities: Tobogganing
**Amenities and
other services:** Parking, toilets, telephones, lodge, Snack bar, maps, waxing centre, gift shop

Eastern
Ontario

Getting There

From Picton, take County Road 8 (Union Street) east and follow the signs to the entrance of the park

Further Information

Quinte Conservation
2061 Old Highway 2, RR 2
Belleville, ON   K8N 4Z2
☎ *(613) 968-3434*
⇌ *(613) 968-8240*
www.pec.on.ca/conservation/nrca.html

Mac Johnson Wildlife Area

Location:	North of Brockville
Number of trails:	5
Total distance:	11km (7mi)
Level of difficulty:	● ■
Groomed:	No
Trackset:	No
Interesting features:	Buells Creek headwaters, reservoir doesn't freeze so Trumpeter swans breed on it, old foundations of Hamilton Joyce's circa-1860s farmstead (house, well, shed or barn wall), abandoned railway bed, mill
Fee:	Donation
Other activities:	Ice-skating
Amenities and other services:	Parking, toilets, nature centre

The Mac Johnson Wildlife Area commemorates a Brockville resident with 532ha (1,314 acres) of wetland, field and forest in and around Beulls Creek. The area was the site of peat-moss extraction in the 1800s, but it is

now rejuvenated and has become a major nesting area for mallards, teals and wood ducks.

None of the trails are groomed, so you can ski or snow-shoe wherever you like, although it will be easier if you follow the marked trails. You have a choice between swamp deciduous forest in the northeast, mixed woods (where lots of deer and snowshoe hares live) in the north-west or sugar maple woods in the west.

Getting There

From Highway 401 at Brockville, take Highway 29 north and drive for 4km (2.5mi) to Tincap. Turn right to head east on Debruge Road and continue to the entrance of the Mac Johnson Conservation Area.

Further Information

Cataraqui Region Conservation Authority (CRCA)
1641 Perth Rd.
PO Box 160
Glenburnie, ON K0H 1S0
☎*(613) 546-4228*
www.cataraquiregion.on.ca

Friends of Mac Johnson Wildlife Area
4671 Debruge Rd.
Elizabethtown, ON K6T 1AS
☎*(613) 342-3062*

Mill of Kintail Conservation Area

Location:	Indian Rd., east. of Hwy. 29 between Almonte and Pakenham
Number of trails:	7
Total distance:	12km (7mi)
Level of difficulty:	●
Groomed:	No
Trackset:	No
Interesting features:	Indian River, hills of cedar birch, hemlock, white cedar swamps

Eastern Ontario

Fee:	$3/day
Other activities:	Robert Tait McKenzie Museum
Amenities and other services:	Parking, toilets, telephones, conference centre, pioneer cabin

Getting There

Take Highway 29 north from Almonte or south from
Pakenham. Turn to head west on Clayton Road and follow
the signs.

Further Information

Mill of Kintail Conservation Area
RR 1
Almonte, ON K0A 1A0
☎ *(613) 256-3610*
(613) 256-5087
www.trytel.com/~kintail

Mississippi Valley Conservation Authority
PO Box 268
Lanark, ON K0G 1K0
☎ *(613) 259-2421*
(613) 259-3468
www.mvc.on.ca

Mill Pond Conservation Area

Location:	Hwy. 15, between Portland and Lombardy
Number of trails:	7
Total distance:	15km (9mi)
Level of difficulty:	● ■
Groomed:	No
Trackset:	No
Interesting features:	Otter Lake
Fee:	Donation
Other activities:	Sugar bush
Amenities and other services:	Parking

Getting There

Take Highway 15 north from Portland or south from Lombardy. Exit at Briton-Houghton Bay Road and follow the signs to the entrance.

Further Information

Rideau Valley Conservation Authority
PO Box 599
1128 Mill St.
Manotick, ON K4M 1A5
☎ *(613) 692-3571*
☎ *800-267-3504*
www.rideauvalley.on.ca

Mount Pakenham

Location:	Pakenham
Number of trails:	3
Total distance:	20km (12.4mi)
Level of difficulty:	● ■ ◆
Groomed:	100%
Trackset:	100% classic and skating
Fee:	$7
Other activities:	Alpine skiing
Services:	**(R)** *($20)*
Amenities and other services:	Parking, toilets, telephones, heated lodge with snack bar and waxing centre, babysitting, Canadian Ski Patrol

Getting There

From Pakenham, take Highway 15 east for 3km (1.9mi).

Further Information

Mount Pakenham
PO Box 190
Pakenham, ON K0A 2X0
☎ *(613) 624-5290*
www.mountpakenham.com

Murphys Point Provincial Park (♥)

Location:	South of Perth
Number of trails:	5
Total distance:	21km (13mi)
Level of difficulty:	● ■ ◆
Groomed:	100%
Trackset:	100% classic
Interesting features:	McParlan House, Silver Queen Mine and Bunkhouse, Rocky Narrows Beach, waterfall
Fee:	$6/vehicle
Services:	**(A)** *(lodge for groups)*
Amenities and other services:	Parking, toilets, telephones, two warm-up lodges

Murphys Point's location, directly on top of the Frontenac Axis, meant that European settlers attracted to the area had to focus on mining and logging, rather than farming. Snow-shoeing along the trails is a good way to explore the many remnants of the settlers' lives including: McParlan House, a fully restored log cabin and shed originally built by Reuben Sherwood in 1812 along the **McParlan House Trail,** the Silver Queen mine and the Lally cabin along the **Silver Queen Mine Trail**.

The Tay Valley Ski Club maintains the cross-country ski trails for the park.

Getting There

Take County Road 1 from Perth or the Rideau Ferry to Lanark County 21, also known as Elm Grove Road. Turn onto Lanark County 21 and drive for 12km (7.4mi). The Provincial Park is on the left.

Further Information

Murphys Point Provincial Park
RR5
Perth, ON K7H 3C7
☎ *(613) 267-5060*
☎ *800-667-1940*
www.ontarioparks.com

Nakkertok Cross Country Ski Club

Location:	North of Ottawa
Level of difficulty:	●
Total distance:	75km (47mi)
Level of difficulty:	● ■ ◆
Groomed:	100%
Trackset:	100% classic, 50% skating
Nightlit:	1.5km (.9mi)
Interesting features:	Gatineau Hills, coniferous and mixed forests, backcountry trails, Johannsenhus clubhouse, Bradford Bunker, Ostromhus cabin
Fee:	Members only—$80/person $150/family, $120/couple
Services:	**(L)** *(bunnyrabbit $25, jackrabbit $35, challengers $35, racing rabbits $50, junior racing $70, adult $35)*, **(A)**
Amenities and other services:	Parking, toilets, cabins

Getting There

To get to Nakkertok South from Ottawa, take Highway 5 north to 50 East. Exit at La Verendrye and turn left (north) at the lights. After crossing Highway 50, take the first right (east) onto Gatineau Avenue. After about 4km (2.5mi) the main road forks left. Continue driving straight on the dirt road to the club entrance.

Further Information

Nakkertok Ski Club
PO Box 4476
Postal Station E.
Ottawa, ON K1S 5B4
www.nakkertock.ca

Nangor Resort

Location:	On the Ottawa River between Westmeath and La Passe
Total distance:	10km (6mi)
Level of difficulty:	● ■
Groomed:	100%
Trackset:	100% classic
Interesting features:	Woodland trails with pine, cedar, spruce and maples
Fee:	$5/day or free with accommodation
Other activities:	Ice-fishing (huts for rent), snowmobiling
Services:	**(R)**, **(A)** *(cottages)*
Amenities and other services:	Parking, toilets, telephones, bar and restaurant (weekends), fireplace

Getting There

At the stop sign in Westmeath, turn to head north on Gore Line. Turn left (west) on Wright Road and drive to the entrance.

Further Information

Nangor Resort
Westmeath, ON K0J 2L0
☎ *(613) 587-4455*
☎ *800-268-5302*
www.ottawavalleyonline.com/sites/snowcountry_02/snogoers/sponsors/nangor.html

Parrott's Bay Conservation Area

Location: West of Kingston
Number of trails: 4
Total distance: 5km (3mi)
Level of difficulty: ●
Groomed: 100%
Trackset: 100%
Interesting features: Lake Ontario inlet, marsh and woodland
Fee: Donation
Amenities and other services: Parking, toilets

Getting There

Take Highway 33 east from Bath or west from Amherstview.

Further Information

Cataraqui Region Conservation Authority (CRCA)
1641 Perth Rd.
PO Box 160
Glenburnie, ON K0H 1S0
☎ *(613) 546-4228*
www.cataraquiregion.on.ca

Perth Wildlife Reserve

Location: Off County Rd. 1 between Perth and the Rideau Ferry
Number of trails: 1
Total distance: 5km (3mi)
Level of difficulty: ●
Groomed: 100%
Trackset: No

Eastern Ontario

Interesting features: Tay Marsh, deer, wood ducks
Fee: $5/day, $35/year Rideau Valley Pass
**Amenities and
other services:**   Parking, toilets

The Perth Wildlife Reserve includes about half of the Tay Marsh along 2km (1.2mi) of the Tay River. It opened in 1974 as a refuge for migrating Canada geese and snow geese, as well as ducks. Since then, many improvements have been made, especially along Jebb's Creek, which runs through the area. Wildlife friendly plants, such as the red elderberry, have been planted; new ponds with goose nesting areas have been created; grazing areas have been planted; and nesting boxes have been set up to encourage wood ducks to nest along the creek. You'll also see deer, fox dens and a great variety of other birds as the trail weaves its way through the bush and along the marsh.

Getting There

Take County Road 1 south from Perth or north from the town of Rideau Ferry. Turn to head east on County Road 18.

Further Information

Friends of the Perth Wildlife Reserve
Jean Griffin
Rideau Valley Conservation Authority
PO Box 599
1128 Mill St.
Manotick, ON K4M 1A5
☎ *(613) 692-3571*
☎ *800-267-3504*
www.rideauvalley.on.ca

Rideau Trail

Location: Links Kingston and Ottawa
Number of trails: 1 linear
Total distance: 300km (186mi)

Markers:	Orange isosceles triangles with yellow tips in the Kingston direction, oriented so that the point indicates trail direction. Side trails and loops marked with blue triangles
Level of difficulty:	●
Groomed:	25%
Trackset:	25%
Interesting features:	Graves of Canada's first prime minister Sir John A. Macdonald and Father of Confederation, Sir Alexander Campbell; Chaffey's Lock on the Rideau Canal; the Beverige Dam and Locks
Fee:	$20 membership
Other activities:	Snowmobiling
Trailheads:	Parking lot at the Cataraqui Marshlands Conservation area, on the north side of King St., west of the Cataraqui Golf course in Kingston; or Richmond Landing, near the parking lot of The Mill Restaurant, on The Parkway in Ottawa or in any of the conservation areas along the trail

The Rideau Trail is a hiking trail that began as a vision of Kingston resident Doug Knapp and now has 1,100 members throughout eastern Ontario. During the winter, it is very popular for skiing and snowmobiling, although some snowshoers also try completing several parts of it. The groomed sections are all within provincial parks and conservation areas that have portions of the trail passing through their properties.

Getting There

Access the trail from Ottawa, Richmond, Merrickville, Smith's Falls, Port Elmsley, Perth, Westport, Sydenham or Kingston or from the parks it passes through, including: Marlborough Forest, Mica Mine Conservation Area, Murphys Point Provincial Park (see p 278), Foley Mountain Conservation Area (see p 264), Frontenac Provincial Park (see p 267), Gould Lake Conservation Area (see p 269) or Cataraqui Bay Conservation Area.

Eastern Ontario

Further Information

Rideau Trail Association
PO Box 15
Kingston, ON K7L 4V6
☎*(613) 730-2229*
www.ncf.carleton.ca/rta

Kingston Rideau Trail Club
PO Box 15
Kingston, ON K7L 4V6
☎*(613) 545-0823*

Central Rideau Trail Club
PO Box 213
Perth, ON K7H 3E4
☎*(613) 264-8338*

Ottawa Rideau Trail Club
PO Box 4616, Station E.
Ottawa, ON K1S 5H8
☎*(613) 730-2229*

Sandbanks Provincial Park

Location:	South of Picton
Number of trails:	6
Total distance:	11km (7mi)
Level of difficulty:	● ■ ◆
Groomed:	100%
Trackset:	100% classic
Interesting features:	World's largest freshwater baymouth barrier sand dune, with some dunes ranging from 15m (49ft) to 25m (82ft) in height
Fee:	$1 donation/day
Amenities and other services:	Parking, toilets, telephones, warm-up lodge and snack bar

Cross-country skiers travel through and over the sand dunes on the West Lake side of Sandbanks Provincial Park.

There are six groomed trackset trails: the **yellow** 5km (3mi) trail that goes around the outer perimeter; the **blue** 2km (1mi) trail, the **green** 1.5km (.9mi) trail, the **orange/yellow** 1km (.6mi) trail, the **red** .75km (.5mi) trail and the **orange** .5km (.3mi) trail.

Getting There

From Picton, follow County Road 10 to County Road 11. Turn right. Continue to County Road 18. Turn left. The park is on your left.

Further Information

Sandbanks Provincial Park
RR 1
Picton, ON K0K 2T0
☎ *(613) 393-3319*
☎ *800-667-1940*
www.ontarioparks.com

Friends of Sandbanks
PO Box 20007
219 Main St.
Picton, ON K0K 2T0
☎ *(613) 393-3319*

Silent Lake Provincial Park (♥)

Location:	Highway 28 north of Apsley and south of Bancroft
Number of trails:	5
Total distance:	48.5km (30mi)
Level of difficulty:	● ■ ◆
Groomed:	100%
Trackset:	84% classic, 16% skating
Interesting features:	Sunset over Silent Lake, Quiet Lake, Bear nests
Fee:	$8.50/vehicle plus $2/person, $1/youth or $25/season
Other activities:	winter camping

Services:	**(R)**, **(L)**, **(A)** *(a lodge and a yurt; year-round tent)*
Amenities and other services:	Parking, toilets, telephones, pro shop, three warm-up huts

Silent Lake has one of the most comfortable, calming atmospheres in all of Ontario, especially during the ski season. To best experience this feeling, avid skiers will want to complete the 19km (12mi) **Blue Trail** that circumvents Silent, Quiet and Soft lakes. There's often no traffic at all along the way, and three areas with warm-up huts and toilets make for pleasant places to stop and rest.

The **Yellow Loop** takes intermediate skiers along the early sections of the Blue Trail and then loops back to the parking lot for a total of 13km (8mi).

There's also a 6km (4mi) **Red Loop** for beginning skiers or those who want to warm up, and a 2.5km (1.6mi) **Green Loop** for novices.

Skaters will enjoy the 8km (5mi) trail set up specifically for them.

Getting There

Take Highway 28 north from Apsley or south from Bancroft.

Further Information

Silent Lake Provincial Park
PO Box 500
Bancroft, ON K0L 1C0
☎ *(613) 339-2807*
☎ *800-667-1940*
www.ontarioparks.com

Trips & Trails Nordic Ski and Cycle
PO Box 1650
258 Hastings St. N.
Bancroft, ON L0L 1C0
☎ *(613) 332-1969*
☎ *800-481-2925*
⇌ *(613) 339-2807*
www.mwdesign.net/tipstail

Silver Fox Nordic

Location:	Deep River
Number of trails:	2
Total distance:	17.5km (11mi)
Level of difficulty:	● ◆
Groomed:	100%
Trackset:	100% classic, 43% skating
Interesting features:	Welsh Bay on the Ottawa River
Fee:	Members and guests only—$35/person, $85/family
Other activities:	tobogganing, snowboarding
Amenities and other services:	Parking, toilets, telephones, heated chalet

Getting There

Take Highway 17 east from North Bay or west from Deep River. Turn to head south on Josie Lane, which is just east of the Pines Motel and Valley Ventures, and follow the road to the parking lot.

Further Information

Silver Fox Nordic
PO Box 1222
Deep River, ON K0J 1P0
☎ *(613) 584-3619*
www.magma.ca/~meadow

Terry Fox Athletic Facility

Location:	Mooney's Bay, Ottawa
Number of trails:	1
Level of difficulty:	●
Total distance:	5km (3mi)

Level of difficulty: ● ■
Groomed: 100%
Trackset: 100% classic and skating
Lit: 2km (1mi)
Fee: $2.50/day
Services: **(R)**, **(L)** *($20/hr for individuals or group programme fee)*

**Amenities and
other services:**   Parking, toilets, change rooms, pro shop, showers, lockers, canteen

Getting There

Take Highway 417 to Ottawa and exit at Riverside Drive. Continue south to the facility.

Further Information

Terry Fox Athletic Facility
2960 Riverside Dr.
Mooney's Bay Park
☎ *(613) 247-4883*
⇄ *(613) 247-4883*
http://city.Ottawa.on.ca/city_services/recreation

Triangle Cross Country Ski Club of Brockville

Location: McIntosh Mills, off Marsh Rd.
Number of trails: 18
Total distance: 40km (25mi)
Level of difficulty: ● ■ ◆
Groomed: 55%
Trackset: 35% classic, 20% skating
Interesting features: Frontenac Axis, marsh, woods
Fee: Donation, members $25/yr
Services: **(L)**, **(A)**
**Amenities and
other services:**   Parking, toilets, warm-up chalet

Getting There

Take Highway 401 east from Kingston or west from Brockville to Exit 675, Mallorytown. Drive north to Highway 2. Turn right to head east on Highway 2 to County Road 5. Turn left to head north to McIntosh Mills. Turn left at Marsh Road and drive to the chalet.

Further Information

Triangle Cross Country Ski Club of Brockville
PO Box 1277
Brockville, ON K6Y 5W2
http://communities.msn.com/TriangleCrossCountrySkiClubofBrockville &naventry

Twin Wheels Farm

🛏 **Access to trails reserved for overnight guests**

Location:	Northeast of Barry's Bay
Number of trails:	3
Total distance:	10km (6mi)
Level of difficulty:	● ■ ◆
Groomed:	100%
Trackset:	No
Interesting features:	Canadian Shield, Murphy Lake
Fee:	No
Other activities:	skating, horse-drawn sleigh rides
Services:	(A) *(cottages)*
Amenities and other services:	Parking, toilets, telephones

Getting There

Take Highway 60 south from Pembroke or west from Renfrew to Killaloe. Turn onto Highway 512 and continue for 16km (10mi) to Drohan Road.

Further Information

Twin Wheels Farm
RR 3
483 Drohan Rd.
Killaloe, ON K0J 2A0
☎ *(613) 757-2107*
⇄ *(613) 757-0802*
www.holidayjunction.com/canada/on/con0092.html

Vanderwater Conservation Area

Location:	South of Tweed
Number of trails:	4
Total distance:	15km (9mi)
Level of difficulty:	● ■ ◆
Groomed:	No
Trackset:	No
Interesting features:	Moira River, rapids
Fee:	Donation
Amenities and other services:	Parking, toilets

Getting There

From Tweed, take Highway 37 to Thomasburgh and head east, following the signs to the conservation area.

Further Information

Quinte Conservation
2061 Old Highway 2, RR 2
Belleville, ON K8N 4Z2
☎ *(613) 968-3434*
⇄ *(613) 968-8240*
www.pec.on.ca/conservation/nrca.html

Voyageur Provincial Park

Location: On the Ottawa River between Chutes-à-
                         Blondeau and Pointe Fortune
Number of trails: 3
Total distance: 10km (6mi)
Level of difficulty: ● ■ ◆
Groomed: 100%
Trackset: 100% classic
Interesting features: Beaver ponds, Ottawa River, St. Law-
                          rence Lowlands, Canadian Shield
Fee: $6/vehicle
**Amenities and
other services:**   Parking, toilets

Getting There

From Hawkesbury, take Highway 417 east to Exit 5. Head
north on County Road 4 to the park.

Further Information

Voyageur Provincial Park
PO Box 130
Chutes-à-Blondeau, ON K0B 1B0
☎(613) 674-2825
☎800-667-1940
www.ontarioparks.com

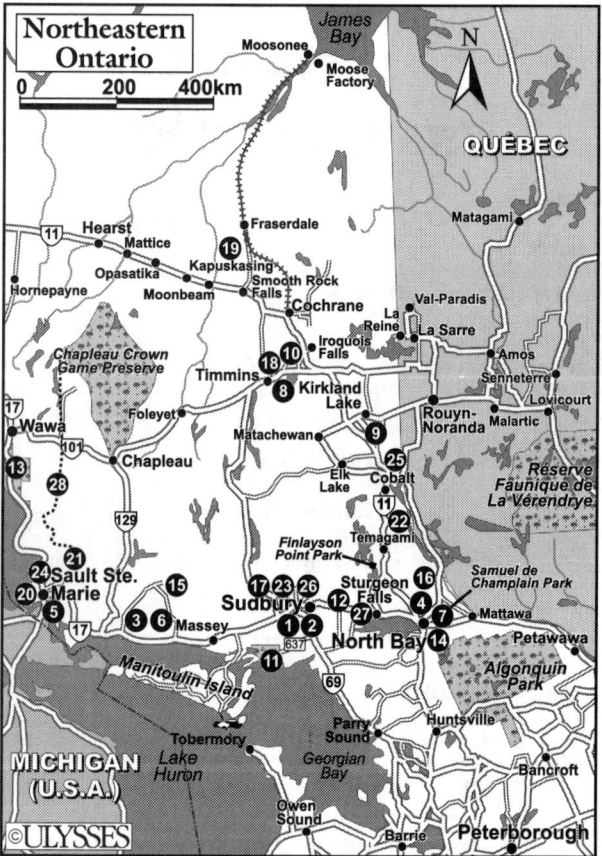

Northeastern Ontario

0 — 200 — 400km

James Bay

QUÉBEC

MICHIGAN (U.S.A.)

Lake Huron

Georgian Bay

Algonquin Park

Réserve Faunique de La Vérendrye

Chapleau Crown Game Preserve

Manitoulin Island

Moosonee
Moose Factory
Fraserdale
Hearst
Mattice
Opasatika
Moonbeam
Kapuskasing
Smooth Rock Falls
Cochrane
Iroquois Falls
La Reine
La Sarre
Val-Paradis
Matagami
Amos
Senneterre
Lovicourt
Rouyn-Noranda
Malartic
Hornepayne
Timmins
Kirkland Lake
Matachewan
Foleyet
Chapleau
Elk Lake
Cobalt
Temagami
Wawa
Sault Ste. Marie
Massey
Sudbury
Sturgeon Falls
North Bay
Mattawa
Petawawa
Samuel de Champlain Park
Finlayson Point Park
Parry Sound
Huntsville
Tobermory
Owen Sound
Barrie
Peterborough
Bancroft

©ULYSSES

1. Cambrian College
2. Capreol Cross-Country Ski Club
3. Cedar Rail Ranch Resort
4. Education Centre Ski Trails
5. Fort Creek Conservation Area
6. Iron Bridge Ski Trail System
7. Jack Pine Hill
8. Kamiskotia Ski Resort
9. Kap-Kig-Iwan
10. Kettle Lakes Provincial Park
11. Killarney Provincial Park
12. Kukagami Lodge
13. Lake Superior Provincial Park
14. Laurentian Park Footpath
15. Mississagi Provincial Park
16. North Bay Nordic Trails
17. Onaping Falls Nordic Ski Club
18. Porcupine Ski Runners
19. René Brunelle Provincial Park
20. Sault Trails and Recreation System
21. Searchmont Ski Resort
22. Smoothwater Ecolodge
23. South Shore Rim Nordic Ski System
24. Stokely Creek Lodge and Ski Touring Centre
25. Temiskaming Nordic Ski Club
26. Walden Cross-Country Fitness Club
27. West Nipissing Nordic Ski Club
28. Windy Lake Lodge

Northeastern Ontario

Northeastern Ontario was made for cross-country skiing and snowshoeing adventures.

This region has the snow, the scenery, and many enthusiastic people—in short, everything needed to ensure an exciting wilderness retreat. Locals in this region are used to winter isolation and they know how to make the most of the snow and cold. Visitors will find a friendly warm welcome, wherever they go.

A long winter, heavy snowfalls and very little humidity ensure that the trails are deeply covered with a 4m (13ft) base of snow that lasts from early December until early April. This region has never suffered from the trail closures that plague southern parts of the province. **Stokely Creek Lodge and Ski Touring Centre** (see p 321), which

sits just beyond the peaks of King Mountain, averages even more snow than the rest of the region—a total of 5m (16ft) per year. The centre began in 1977 as a partnership between Americans and Canadians who loved Nordic skiing in the region. With 130km (81mi) of trails groomed for classic and skating, the area has achieved a worldwide reputation for excellent cross-country skiing. When you arrive, you'll hand your luggage to staff and either climb into a sled or ski to the lodge, whichever you prefer.

In terms of scenery, most of Ontario's northeastern region sits on the hard precambrian granite and gneiss that make up the Canadian Shield, which accounts for its many ice-laden waterfalls, tall lookouts and jutting rock formations. Add that to the Sudbury Nickel Irruptive, a huge basin thought to be caused by a meteor impact a couple of billion years ago, and you get even more variety.

Group of Seven members A.Y. Jackson, Arthur Lismer, Franz Johnston, J.E.H. MacDonald and Lawren Harris immortalized the scenery of this area in their paintings. The Group of Seven painters are famous in Temagami and they are also known for the summers they spent in a cabin-equipped boxcar they rented from the Algoma Central Railway. Although it isn't always obvious which

views they painted, locals have tried to indicate a few with markers. On the way to the trails that the **Onaping Falls Nordic Ski Club** (see p 313) maintains in Windy Lake Provincial Park, for example, be sure to stop along Highway 144 at the A.Y. Jackson Lookout for a view of a scenic falls as the river tumbles from the Canadian Shield down into the Sudbury Basin.

People in northeastern Ontario are used to a very limited road and rail network that can be shut down for days at a time when a storm hits. The speed and convenience of cross-country skiing gives them an advantage when it comes to transportation in this region, one that compares only with snowmobiling for practicality, and they're used to taking full-advantage of it. Consequently, they have an "anything goes" attitude.

If you have any doubts that cross-country skiing reigns in this region, visit Hearst, a city that grooms 24km (15mi) of cross-country trails to enable anyone to travel quickly and easily around town. This is also the home of Nordcan 250, a 402km (250mi) cross-country ski race.

You can drive to Hearst, if you want, but you're better off to take the "tour of the line" run by **Algoma Central Railway**. This is the same company that operates a one-day "snow train" into the Agawa Canyon on Saturdays and Sundays from the end of December until mid-March. Both train excursions leave from the Algoma Railway Station on Bay Street in Sault Ste. Marie, and both offer breathtaking views of northeastern Ontario's beautiful scenery. Winter visitors also get to view something summer visitors don't see—the Agawa Canyon's north portal. The train skirts along rock walls that are less than 15m (50ft) apart. The Agawa River flows within spitting distance of the train windows around the foot of the east wall.

In fact, the Algoma train and cross-country skis are the only way to travel to **Windy Lake Lodge** (see p 325), a cross-country skier's paradise at mile 122.5. Visitors to Windy Lake Lodge have access to more than 50km (31mi) of cross-country ski trails, including a 2km (1.2mi) trail leading from the train station to the lodge. (Don't worry, the lodge sends people to lug your luggage with snowmobiles so that you can ski unencumbered.) There are other lodges along the line that also offer cross-country skiing, including Achigan Lake Outpost and Loon Pointe (mile 44.5); Spruce Haven Wilderness Lodge (mile 71.5); and Chadwick's Kwagama Lake Lodge (mile 118.5).

Snowmobilers will also carry your luggage so that up to six people can ski from lodge to lodge in Temagami along the more than 60km (37mi) of trails at **Smoothwater Ecolodge** (see p 319). Snowshoers are welcome too, and they have the option of exploring the areas between the trail.

If you prefer exploring trails right outside your door, choose the more luxurious accommodation at Smoothwater or stay at **Cedar Rail Ranch Resort** (see p 299), **Kukagami Lodge** (see p 307) or the **Searchmont Ski Resort** (see p 318). Those who stay at Kukagami Lodge are in for a bit of an adventure; accommodation is in rustic cabins with no electricity or toilets. A large outhouse cabin has been provided for the use of the 10 to 12 guests that Kukagami accommodates. To begin the adventure, guests ski in 7km (4mi) from the parking lot at the road to the lodges, although again, the hosts will transport your luggage for you.

You don't have to enjoy backcountry living to visit northeastern Ontario, however. There are also short, invigorating trails for the more urbanized cross-country ski enthusiast in many major cities. Sudbury has trails at **Cambrian College** (see p 298), the **Walden Cross-Country Fitness Club** (see p 323) and at the **South Shore Rim Nordic Ski System** (see p 320). Sault Ste. Marie runs the **Fort Creek Conservation Area** (see p 301) and the **Sault Trails and Recreation System** (see p 316), which lights a 2km (1mi) section of trail for night skiing. North Bay has the **Education Centre Ski Trails** (see p 300) and the **Laurentian Park Footpath** (see p 310).

Several clubs also maintain classic and skating trails that are suitable for everyone from children to racers. Some of the best systems include the **Capreol Cross-Country Ski Club** (see p 299), **The Iron Bridge Ski Trail System** (see p 302), **North Bay Nordic Trails** (see p 312), **The Porcupine Ski Runners** (see p 314), the **Temiskaming Nordic Ski Club** (see p 322) and the **West Nipissing Nordic Ski Club** (see p 324).

Alpine resorts, such as **Jack Pine Hill** (see p 302) and the **Kamiskotia Ski Resort** (see p 303) also have good cross-country ski trails.

Provincial parks offer great trails both for the casual skier and the wilderness expert. Casual skiers can enjoy the trails at **Fushimi Lake Provincial Point**, **Kap-Kig-Iwan** (see p 304), **Kettle Lakes Provincial Park** (see p 305) and **René Brunelle Provincial Park** (see p 315).

Experienced wilderness skiers will prefer **Killarney Provincial Park** (see p 305), **Lake Superior Provincial Park** (see p 308) and **Mississagi Provincial Park** (see p 311).

Tourist Information

Algoma Kinniwabi Travel Association
485 Queen St. E., suite 204
Sault Ste. Marie, ON P6A 1Z9
☎*(705) 254-4293*
☎*800-263-2546*
⇌*(705) 254-4892*
www.algomacountry.com

Rainbow Country Travel Association
2726 Whippoorwill Ave.
Sudbury, ON P3G 1E9
☎*(705) 522-0104*
☎*800-465-6655*
www.rainbowcountry.com

Almaguin Nipissing Travel Association
PO Box 351
Seymour St. & North Bay Bypass
North Bay, ON P1B 8H5
☎*(705) 474-6634*
☎*800-387-0516*
⇌*(705) 474-9271*
www.ontariosnearnorth.on.ca

Conchrane-Timiskaming Travel Association
76 McIntyre Rd.
PO Box 920
Schumacher, ON P0N 1G0
☎*(705) 360-1980 or 360-1989*
☎*800-461-3766*
⇌*(705) 268-5526*
www.jamesbayfrontier.com

Cambrian College

Location:	Cambrian Athletics Centre
Number of trails:	4
Total distance:	5km (3mi)
Level of difficulty:	● ■
Groomed:	100%
Trackset:	100% classic
Interesting features:	Sudbury
Fee:	$5/day
Other activities:	Weight training, cardio equipment, gym, saunas and showers
Amenities and other services:	Parking, toilets, telephones, change rooms

Getting There

Take the side entrance of the main building at Cambrian College and follow the signs to the Athletics Centre.

Further Information

Cambrian Athletic Centre
1,400 Barrydowne Rd.
Sudbury, ON P3A 3V8
☎*(705) 524-7378*
www.cambrianc.on.ca

Capreol Cross-Country Ski Club

Location:	Sudbury
Number of trails:	6
Total distance:	32km (20mi)
Level of difficulty:	● ■ ◆
Groomed:	100%
Trackset:	100% classic
Interesting features:	Vermillion River, forests, Black Bird Lagoon
Fee:	$5/day, $15/day/family, $35/year
Amenities and other services:	Parking, toilets, telephones, warm-up lodge, snack bar

Getting There

Take Route 84 north from Sudbury to Capreol. Turn left onto Yonge Street and then right onto Ski Capreol Road.

Further Information

Capreol Cross-Country Ski Club
☎ *(705) 858-1595 (Stan Finnson)*
☎ *(705) 858-4289 (ski line)*
www.capreolonline.com/sports/Xski/xski.htm

Cedar Rail Ranch Resort

🛏 **Access to trails reserved for overnight guests**

Location:	North of Thessalon
Number of trails:	3
Total distance:	10km (6mi)
Level of difficulty:	● ■
Groomed:	100%
Trackset:	100% classic

Interesting features: Pasture, mixed forest, Mississagi Valley
Fee: No
Other activities: Sleigh rides, cutter rides, ice fishing and snowmobiling
Services: **(A)** *(cottages or lodge)*
Amenities and other services: Parking, toilets

Getting There

From Thessalon, take Highway 129 north for 26km (16mi) to Wharncliffe. Exit onto Wharncliffe Road, cross the bridge, and turn onto the first driveway at the right.

Further Information

Lynn and Cathy Jarratt
RR 3
Thessalon, ON P0R 1L0
☎ *(705) 842-2021*
www.cedarrailranch.com

Education Centre Ski Trails

Location: North Bay
Number of trails: 3
Total distance: 10km (6mi)
Level of difficulty: ● ■
Groomed: 100%
Trackset: 100% classic
Interesting features: Duchesnay Falls, George's Gulch, Knome's Gnoll
Fee: No
Amenities and other services: Parking, toilets, telephones, snack bar

Getting There

Exit Highway 17 at North Bay, onto College Drive. Turn left at Canadore College and Nipissing University. Access the trails from parking lot 7.

Further Information

Canadore College
☎*(705) 474-7600 (Steve Laughlin)*

Discovery Routes Partnership
North Bay-Mattawa Conservation Authority
701 Oak St. E.
North Bay, ON P1B 9T1
☎*(705) 474-5420*
(705) 474-9793

Fort Creek Conservation Area

Location:	Second Line West in Sault Ste. Marie
Number of trails:	6
Total distance:	6km (3.7mi)
Level of difficulty:	● ■
Groomed:	No
Trackset:	No
Interesting features:	Fort Creek, mixed forest of birch, balsam, poplar and maple, marsh
Fee:	Donation
Amenities and other services:	Parking, toilets

Getting There

The entrance to the park is on Second Line West just east of People's Road.

Further Information

Sault Ste. Marie Region Conservation Authority
1100 Fifth Line E.
Sault Ste. Marie, ON P6A 5K7
☎*(705) 946-8530*
www.city.sault-ste-marie.on.ca/links/conservation/lands.shtml

Iron Bridge Ski Trail System

Location:	Between Blind River and Thessalon
Number of trails:	4
Total distance:	13km (8mi)
Level of difficulty:	● ■
Groomed:	100%
Trackset:	100% classic
Interesting features:	Mississaugi River, rock bluff, rabbits, deer
Fee:	$2/day, $20/year
Amenities and other services:	Parking, toilets, telephones, lodge, snack bar and waxing centre

Skiers have the choice of four trails at Iron Bridge. They include the 8.9km (5.5mi) **River Run** and the 5km (3mi) **Mountain Loop** for intermediate skiers, and the 4.9km (3mi) **Plantation Loop** and the 2.1km (1mi) **Rabbity Loop** for novice skiers. Many of the trails cross each other.

Getting There

From the town of Iron Bridge, take Highway 546 north for 2km (1.2mi) and turn left into the parking area.

Further Information

Iron Bridge Cross-Country Ski Club
www.adss.on.ca/ironbridge/skiclub.htm

Jack Pine Hill

Location:	North Bay
Number of trails:	4
Total distance:	10km (6mi)
Level of difficulty:	● ■ ◆

Groomed: 100%
Trackset: 100% classic and skating
Interesting features: Jack pines
Fee: $7
Other activities: Alpine skiing, snow tubing, snowboarding, snowmobiling

**Amenities and
other services:**   Parking, toilets, telephones, lodge, snack bar, maps and waxing centre

Getting There

Drive east on Ski Hill Road in North Bay.

Further Information

North Bay-Mattawa Conservation Authority
701 Oak St. E.
North Bay, ON P1B 9T1
☎ *(705) 474-5420*
🖷 *(705) 474-9793*
www.nbmca.on.ca

Kamiskotia Ski Resort

Location: Thunder Bay
Number of trails: 2
Total distance: 7km (4mi)
Level of difficulty: ■
Groomed: 100%
Trackset: 100% classic
Fee: $8 (applicable on Wed, Fri, weekends and holidays); trails are open the rest of the week, but no services are available
Other activities: Alpine skiing, snowboarding
**Amenities and
other services:**   Parking, toilets, telephones, heated lodge, snack bar, Canadian Ski Patrol (Wednesdays, Fridays, weekends and holidays)

Getting There

From Timmins, take Highway 576 east for 19km (12mi).

Further Information

Kamiskotia Ski Resort
☎*(705) 268-9057*

Kap-Kig-Iwan

Location:	Hwy. 560 north of New Liskeard
Number of trails:	1
Total distance:	4km (6.8mi)
Level of difficulty:	■
Groomed:	100%
Trackset:	100% classic
Interesting features:	Englehart River, waterfall, rapids, ravines and outcrops
Fee:	$6/vehicle
Amenities and other services:	Parking, toilets

Getting There

Take Highway 11 south from Englehart for about 2km (1mi).

Further Information

Kap-Kig-Iwan Provincial Park
PO Box 910
10 Government Rd. E.
Kirkland Lake, ON P2N 3K4
☎*(705) 544-2050 (May to Sep)*
☎*(705) 642-9702 (Oct to Apr)*
☎*(705) 544-2050*
☎*800-667-1940*
www.ontarioparks.com.

Kettle Lakes Provincial Park

Location:	East of Timmons
Number of trails:	3
Total distance:	12km (7mi)
Level of difficulty:	● ■
Groomed:	100%
Trackset:	100% classic
Interesting features:	Kettle lakes, boreal forest
Fee:	$6/vehicle
Amenities and other services:	Parking, toilets, telephones

Getting There

From Timmins, take Highway 101 east to Highway 67.
Drive north to the entrance of the park on the right.

Further Information

Kettle Lakes Provincial Park
Ontario Government Complex
PO Bag 3090
S. Porcupine, ON P0N 1H0
☎*(705) 363-3511 (summer)*
☎*(705) 235-1353 (winter)*
☎*800-667-1940*
www.ontarioparks.com

Killarney Provincial Park

Location:	North shore of Georgian Bay, south of Sudbury
Number of trails:	4
Total distance:	109km (68mi)
Level of difficulty:	◆
Groomed:	No

Trackset:	No
Interesting features:	Ivory-white quartzite hills called the La Cloche Mountains
Fee:	Donation
Other activities:	Winter camping
Amenities and other services:	Parking, toilets
Note:	Park closed in April for ice break-up

This 48,500ha (119,842-acre) wilderness park preserves a ring of huge white ridges that are the eroded remains of the La Cloche Mountains. In the two billion years since they were formed, four different glaciers and 11,000 years of wind have eroded them to the ridges you see now.

The park is officially closed for the winter, although interior campsites are always available. Backcountry enthusiasts can snowshoe or ski on any of the summer hiking trails. The 3km (1.9mi) Chikanishing Trail, which is named after a creek that flows into Georgian Bay, begins in the second parking lot off the access road south of Highway 637, near the summer boat launch. The 4km (2.5mi) **Cranberry Bog Trail** begins on the east side of George Lake campground, just south of the La Cloche Silhouette Trail trailhead. The 2km (1mi) **Granite Ridge Trail** begins south of the park office, past Highway 637, towards Georgian Bay and includes a good view over Philip Edward Island and Georgian Bay. Or, if you have three or four days to spare, try the 100km (62mi) **La Cloche Silhouette Trail,** which begins east or west of the George Lake campground. You'll pass five different lakes along the way, including the one that gave the park its name.

Getting There

Take Highway 69 south from Sudbury or north from Parry Sound to Highway 637. Turn, heading west towards the town of Killarney. It's another 68km (42mi) to the campground.

Further Information

Killarney Provincial Park
Killarney, ON P0M 2A0
☎ *(705) 287-2900*
☎ *800-667-1940*
✉ *(705) 287-2893*
www.ontarioparks.com

or

The Friends of Killarney Park
www.friendsofkillarneypark.ca

Kukagami Lodge

🛏 **Access to trails reserved for overnight guests**

Location:	East of Sudbury
Number of trails:	9
Total distance:	28km (17mi)
Level of difficulty:	■ ◆
Groomed:	100%
Trackset:	100% classic
Interesting features:	Maple sugar bush, balsam forest, white pines, lookout over Kukagami Lake
Fee:	No
Other activities:	Log sauna
Services:	**(A)** *(cabins without electricity accommodate 10 or 12 people)*
Amenities and other services:	Parking, outhouse, porta-potty, main lodge with dining and living rooms

Getting There

From Sudbury, Take Highway 17 east for 30km (19mi) to
Kukagami Road. Turn left (north) and drive about 18km.
Turn right at the sign and drive 2km (1.2mi) to a big parking lot. Allan or Vicki Mather will be there to meet you at a
prearranged time, and they'll transport your luggage while
you ski 7km (4mi) into the lodge.

Further Information

Kukagami Lodge
Kukagami Lake
Wahnapitae, ON P0M 3C0
☎ *(705) 853-4929*
☎ *(705) 853-4742 (answering machine)*

Lake Superior Provincial Park

Location:	Hwy. 17 between Sault Ste. Marie and Wawa
Number of trails:	11
Total distance:	128km (80mi)
Level of difficulty:	■ ◆
Groomed:	No
Trackset:	No
Interesting features:	Waterfalls, Old Woman's face rock formation, Agawa Falls, Agawa Valley cliffs, Algoma Central Railway
Fee:	Donation
Amenities and other services:	Parking

Lake Superior Provincial Park, a 155,600ha (384,482-acre)
region on the shores of Lake Superior, has several trails
that can be used by expert skiers or snowshoers, and only
a couple of shorter ones that can be attempted by those
with intermediate skills. All of them can be accessed along
Highway 17.

Lake Superior Provincial Park

Michipicoten River
Michipicoten Post Provincial Park
Michipicoten River
Treeby Lake
Anjigami Lake
17
Old Woman River
Nokomis
Old Woman Bay
South Old Woman River
Sand Lake
Peat Mountain
Almonte Lake
Maquon Lake
Mijinemungshing Lake
Old Woman Lake
17
Trapper's
Pinguisibi Trail
Leach Island
Coastal
Canyon
Black Beaver Lake
Awausee
Towab
Agawa Rock Indian Pictographs
Agawa Canyon
Frater
Lake Superior
Montreal Island
Agawa Bay
17
Crescent Lake
Crescent Lake
Montreal River

N

0   10   20km

The shorter trails include: the 1.5km (.9mi) **Trappers Trail**, which circuits the Renner brothers' trap line that was active until 1975; the 2km (1mi) **Crescent Lake Trail** that leads through an 80- to 100-year-old birch, maple, beech and white pine forest; the 3km (1.9mi) **Pinguisibi Trail** along the shore of the Sand River; the 2.5km (1.6mi) **South Old Woman River Trail** through an old glacial spillway; the 5km (3mi) **Nokomis Trail** past human-made depressions in the rocks called Pukaskwa Pits, and up across a granite cliff; and the 11km (6.8mi) **Peat Mountain Trail**, which leads to the highest point in the park.

Difficult trails include: the 8km (5mi) **Orphan Lake Trail**, which climbs to the top of a cliff above Orphan Lake and then leads to the Coastal Trail; the 10km (6.2mi) **Awausee Trail** along an old logging road and a ravine; and the 63km (39mi) linear **Coastal Trail**, which leads along the shore of Lake Superior between Agawa Bay and Chalfant Cove.

Getting There

Take Highway 17 north from Sault Ste. Marie or south from Wawa.

Further Information

Lake Superior Provincial Park and
Niijkiwenhwag **– Friends of Lake Superior**
PO Box 267
Wawa, ON P0S 1K0
☎ *(705) 856-2284 or 800-667-1940*
⇥ *(705) 856-1333*
www.ontarioparks.com

Laurentian Park Footpath

Location:	North Bay
Number of trails:	3
Total distance:	1.25km (.8mi)
Level of difficulty:	●
Groomed:	100%
Trackset:	100%

Interesting features: Urban forest, wetland
Fee: No
Services: **(L)**
**Amenities and
other services:** Parking, toilets, lodge and snack bar

Getting There

Park at the ploughed parking lot on Carruthers Street at the
junction with Bromely.

Further Information

Discovery Routes Partnership
North Bay-Mattawa Conservation Authority
701 Oak St. E.
North Bay, ON P1B 9T1
☎ *(705) 474-5420*
⇌ *(705) 474-9793*

Mississagi Provincial Park

Location: Hwy. 639 north of Elliot Lake
Number of trails: 4
Total distance: 20km (12mi)
Level of difficulty: ● ■ ◆
Groomed: 100%
Trackset: 100% classic
Interesting features: Exposed fossils on ripple rock, old
pines, solar heating for the gatehouse
Fee: Donation
**Amenities and
other services:** Parking, toilets

Getting There

From Elliott Lake, take Highway 546 north for 25km
(16mi).

Further Information

c/o Chutes Provincial Park
PO Box 37
Massey, ON P0P 1P0
☎*(705) 848-2806 (Jun-Sep)*
☎*(705) 865-2021 (Oct-May)*
☎*800-667-1940*
www.ontarioparks.com

Friends of Mississagi Provincial Park
PO Box 552
Elliott Lake, ON P5A 2J9

North Bay Nordic Trails

Location:	North Bay
Number of trails:	8
Total distance:	42km (26mi)
Level of difficulty:	● ■ ◆
Groomed:	100%
Trackset:	100% classic, 42% skating
Interesting features:	Trout Lake, scenic lookouts
Fee:	$7/weekday, $10/weekend day, $25/families, $95/year
Services:	**(R)**
Amenities and other services:	Parking, toilets, telephones, lodge, snack bar and waxing centre

North Bay Nordic Trails grooms three novice trails and four intermediate trails, all named for colours, and one expert trail that's called **Cook's Mountain Return**. This club obviously wants to challenge its members!

The novice trails include the 1.3km (.8mi) **yellow**, the 2km (1mi) **gold** and 3km (2mi) **purple** trails. The intermediates are the 4.3km (2.7mi) **brown**, the 5km (3mi) **red**, the 8.1km (5mi) **blue** and the 17.6km (10.9mi) **green** trails.

Getting There

From North Bay, take Highway 63 (Trout Lake Road) east
to Peninsula Road and turn right (south). Pass the Portage
Hotel and then take the next left (east) onto Northshore
Road. Continue driving to the entrance.

Further Information

North Bay Nordic Ski Club
630 Northshore Rd.
North Bay, ON P1B 8G4
☎ *(705) 495-0332*

Discovery Routes Partnership
North Bay-Mattawa Conservation Authority
701 Oak St. E.
North Bay, ON P1B 9T1
☎ *(705) 474-5420*
⇋ *(705) 474-9793*

Onaping Falls Nordic Ski Club

Location:	North of Sudbury
Number of trails:	5
Total distance:	20km (12mi)
Level of difficulty:	● ■ ◆
Groomed:	100%
Trackset:	100% classic and skating
Interesting features:	Sand plains, rocky outcrops, Sudbury Nickel Irruptive, Canadian Shield, annual loppet
Fee:	$5/day
Amenities and other services:	Parking, toilets, telephones, warm-up lodge with waxing area

Getting There

From Sudbury, take Highway 144 north for 55km (34mi)
and turn left at the Windy Lake Motel towards Windy Lake
Provincial Park, where the trails are located.

Further Information

Onaping Falls Nordic Ski Club
PO Box 180
Dowling, ON P0M 1R0
☎*(705) 855-2094 (Lise LeBlanc)*
⇌*(705) 855-0145*

Windy Lake Provincial Park
Northeast Zone
c/o 199 Larch St., Suite 404
Sudbury, ON P3E 5P9
☎*(705) 522-7823*
☎*(705) 966-0563 (Oct-May)*
☎*(705) 966-2315 (Jun-Sep)*
www.ParksOntario.com

Porcupine Ski Runners

Location:	Timmins
Number of trails:	9
Total distance:	30km (18.6mi)
Level of difficulty:	● ■
Groomed:	100%
Trackset:	100% classic and skating
Interesting features:	Dense forest
Fee:	$10/day
Amenities and other services:	Parking; heated chalet with change rooms, toilets and snack bar (weekends); wax hut and Canadian Ski Patrol

Getting There

From Schumacher, take Highway 101 east to Ski Runners
Road.

Further Information

Porcupine Ski Runners
Ski Runners Rd.
PO Box 250
Schumacher, ON P0N 1G0
☎ *(705) 360-1444*
www.porcupineskirunners.com

René Brunelle Provincial Park

Location:	East of Kapuskasing
Number of trails:	2
Total distance:	10km (6.2mi)
Level of difficulty:	● ■
Groomed:	100%
Trackset:	100% classic
Interesting features:	1922 plane crash, black spruce, fir, aspen, tamarack
Fee:	$6/vehicle
Amenities and other services:	Parking, toilets

Getting There

Take Highway 11 east from Kapuskasing or west from Cochrane.

Further Information

René Brunelle Provincial Park
RR 2, Hwy. 11 W.
Kapuskasing, ON P5N 2X8
☎ *(705) 367-2692 (May-Sep)*
☎ *(705) 372-2232 (Oct-Apr)*
☎ *800-667-1940*
≈ *(705) 856-1333*
www.ontarioparks.com

Sault Trails and Recreation System (♥)

Location:	5th line, 3km (1.9mi) east of Hwy. 17 in Sault Ste. Marie
Number of trails:	13
Total distance:	38km (24mi)
Level of difficulty:	● ■ ◆
Groomed:	100%
Trackset:	100% classic and skating
Nightlit:	2km (1mi)
Interesting features:	The Voyageur Trail (see p 371), waterfalls, red and white pines, 2 lookouts
Fee:	$14/day, $86/season
Other activities:	Sugaring off
Services:	(R)
Amenities and other services:	Parking, toilets, telephones, warm-up lodge, snack bar and waxing centre

The Sault Trails and Recreation System (STAR) covers Hiawatha Highlands, Kinsmen Park, Wishart Park and the Tarentorus Fish Culture Station. There are three main trail systems: the Crystal Creek system with five trails; the Lookout Trail System (locally known as the Pinder System after the family who donated the land), which includes four trails; and the Red Pine Trail System, with four trails. All three systems branch out in different directions from the corner of 5th line east and Landslide Road.

The Crystal Creek System includes the 2km (1mi) **Kinsmen Lit** loop, a flat, easy trail beside the children's playground. This trail has lights to enable skiers to practice at night. The 5km (3mi) **Crystal Creek Trail** is also easy. It offers the best scenery, including good views of Crystal and Minnehaha falls. There's also a 2.5km (1.6mi) **Hiawatha Extension Trail**, a 2km (1mi) **Inner Loop**, and a 2.5km (1.6mi) **Olympic Extension**, which are all for intermediate skiers who want to extend their runs. You may also want to continue along **Mabel Lake Backcountry Trail**, a 15km (9.3m) extension of the Crystal Lake Trail past Crystal Lake to Mabel Lake.

Groomers always trackset the Lookout Trail System (Pinder System) first, since it includes the most popular trails. Trails attract mainly intermediate and advanced skiers, and include the 4km (2.5mi) **Lookout Trail**, with red markers; the 2km (1mi) **White Pine Extension**, with white markers; the 2km (1mi) **Mockingbird Hill** loop, with blue markers; and the 1.5km (.9mi) **Sugar Bush Extension**, with yellow markers.

The Red Pine Trail System, which also attracts intermediate and advanced skiers, gets its name from the main **Red Pine Trail**, a 5km (3mi) loop through a forest of red pine that was planted in the 1930s. Those who want to ski for longer periods can continue over Cold Water Creek to the **Fish Hatchery Extension** for an additional 5km (3mi) loop. Trail markers are in green. After that, choose between the blue marked **Cold Water Creek Extension** (indicated in blue), a 2.5km (3mi) loop, or the 2km (1mi) looped **Wishart Park Extension**, which is marked in purple and leads to a lookout over Root River.

Getting There

Take Highway 17 north of Sault Ste. Marie to 5th Line East. Follow the road until it meets Landslide Road, where you'll find parking at a small lot on the corner.

Further Information

Hiawatha Lodge
767 Landslide Rd.
Sault Ste. Marie, ON
☎*(705) 945-6444*

Sault Trails and Recreation Inc.
PO Box 580
Sault Ste. Marie, ON P6A 5N1
☎*800-361-1522*

Sault Ste. Marie Community Services Department
☎*(705) 759-5310*

Sault Ste. Marie Region Conservation Authority
1100 Fifth Line E.
Sault Ste. Marie, ON P6A 5K7
☎*(705) 946-8530*
www.city.sault-ste-marie.on.ca/links/conservation/lands.shtml

Travis Reed, Park Manager
The Kinsmen Club
PO Box 22050
44 Great Northern Rd.
Sault Ste. Marie, ON P6B 4Y5
☎*(705) 759-1920*

Searchmont Ski Resort

Location:	North of Sault Ste. Marie
Number of trails:	4
Total distance:	10km (6mi)
Level of difficulty:	● ■ ◆
Groomed:	100%
Trackset:	100% classic and skating
Interesting features:	Goulais River Forest
Fee:	$7/day
Other activities:	Alpine skiing, snowboarding
Services:	**(R)**
Amenities and other services:	Parking, toilets, telephones, lodge, snack bar, maps, waxing centre

Getting There

From Sault Ste. Marie, take Highway 17 west to Regional
Road 556. Take Regional Road 556 north to Regional Road
532 north. Searchmont is on the right, just before Wabos.

Further Information

Searchmont Resort
PO Box 146
Searchmont, ON P0S 1J0
☎*(705) 781-2340*
☎*800-663-2546*
✆*(705) 781-2483*
www.searchmont.com

Smoothwater Ecolodge

Location:	North of Temagami
Number of trails:	10
Total distance:	60km (37mi)
Level of difficulty:	● ■ ◆
Groomed:	100%
Trackset:	100% classic, 30% skating
Interesting features:	James Lake, old growth forests with 700yr-old trees, frozen marsh, cedar groves
Fee:	$10/day
Other activities:	Meals of organic food, sauna, lodge-to-lodge skiing, massage therapist, dog sledding
Services:	**(R)** *($15/day)*, **(A)**
Amenities and other services:	Parking, toilets, telephones, lodge, snack bar, maps, waxing centre, gift shop

Getting There

From Temagami, take Highway 11 north. Turn left at Smoothwater Road.

Further Information

Smoothwater Ecolodge
PO Box 40
Temagami, ON P0H 2H0
☎*(705) 569-3539*
⇆*(705) 569-2710*
www.smoothwater.com

South Shore Rim Nordic Ski System

Location:	Sudbury
Number of trails:	3 systems
Total distance:	35km (22mi)
Level of difficulty:	● ■ ◆
Groomed:	100%
Trackset:	100% classic and skating
Interesting features:	Wetlands
Fee:	$5/day
Other activities:	Doran Planetarium, arboretum
Amenities and other services:	Parking, toilets, warm-up chalet and Canadian Ski Patrol

The Lake Laurentian Conservation Area, the Idlewylde Golf and Country Club and the Laurentian University Nordic Ski Trails interconnect to create the South Shore Rim Nordic Ski System.

Lake Laurentian Conservation Area has some additional trails, for a total of 55km (34mi) on site.

Trail passes can be purchased at any of the three locations or from the ski patrol on the trail.

Getting There

Enter the system from Laurentian University, Idylwylde or Lake Laurentian Conservation Area.

Further Information

Laurentian University
Ramsay Lake Rd.
Sudbury, ON P3E 2C6
☎ *(705) 675-1151*
www.laurentian.ca

Idylwylde Golf Course
400 Walford Rd. E.
Sudbury, ON P3E 2G9
☎*(705) 523-1006*
(705) 522-0173
www.golfsudbury.com

Lake Laurentian Conservation Area
South Bay Rd.
Sudbury

Nickel District Conservation Authority
Civic Sq.
200 Brady St.
Sudbury, ON P3E 5K3
☎*(705) 674-5249*
(705) 674-7939
www.ndcf.com

Stokely Creek Lodge and Ski Touring Centre (♥)

Location:	North of Sault Ste. Marie
Number of trails:	42
Total distance:	130km (81mi)
Level of difficulty:	● ■ ◆
Groomed:	96%
Trackset:	96% classic, 58% skating
Interesting features:	Stokely Creek, Goulais River, Norm Bourgeois's Cabin, Canadian Shield, views of Batchewana Bay and Lake Superior
Fee:	$14/day or free with accommodation
Other activities:	sauna, library, videos, reading
Services:	**(R)**, **(L)**, **(A)** *(Stokely Creek Lodge plus 6 chalets; non-smoking)*
Amenities and other services:	Parking, toilets, telephones, heated lodge with sauna, restaurant in lodge

Getting There

From Sault Ste. Marie, take Highway 17 north for 34km
(21mi). Drive past the Goulais River Bridge and Joseph's
Homestead barn. (Stop at the Timberland store on the way
to use the phone to call the lodge for a parking lot
pickup). Turn right (east) onto Old Highway 17. The
Stokely Creek parking lot is on the right. You'll now climb
into a sled or someone will take your luggage while you
ski in.

Further Information

Stokely Creek Lodge and Ski Touring Centre
RR 1
Goulais River, ON P0S 1E0

PO Box 507
Sault Ste. Marie, MI 49783

☎*(705) 649-3421*
(705) 649-3429
www.stokelycreek.com

Temiskaming Nordic Ski Club

Location:	South of New Liskeard
Number of trails:	6
Total distance:	20km (12mi)
Level of difficulty:	● ■ ◆
Groomed:	100%
Trackset:	100% classic and skating
Interesting features:	Rolling eskers
Fee:	$7/day
Services:	(L)
Amenities and other services:	Parking, toilets, heated lodge, maps, waxing centre, snack bar (on occasion)

Getting There

Take Highway 11 south from New Liskeard to the Portage Bay Road turnoff on the right (west). Take Portage Bay Road west for about 2km (1mi) until you reach the Barr Forest Access Road. Turn left to get to the parking lot.

Further Information

Temiskaming Nordic Ski Club
PO Box 2019
New Liskeard, ON P0J 1P0
☎ *(705) 679-5106*

Walden Cross-Country Fitness Club

Location:	Sudbury
Number of trails:	3 systems: Beaver Lake, Naughton and Lively
Total distance:	20km (12mi)
Level of difficulty:	● ■
Groomed:	100%
Trackset:	100% classic
Nightlit:	2.5km (1.6mi)
Interesting features:	Canadian Shield, red oak stands, poplar
Fee:	$5/day, $30/year
Services:	(L)
Amenities and other services:	Parking, toilets, Naughton Ski Chalet

Getting There

The trail system connects Beaver Lake in Walden, the old community of Naughton and the golf course in Lively. All three communities are just west of downtown Sudbury on Highway 17.

Further Information

Walden Cross-Country Fitness Club
RR 1
Worthington, ON P0M 3H0
www.town.walden.on.ca

Friends of Walden Trails
77 Field St.
Lively, ON P3Y 1B4

West Nipissing Nordic Ski Club

Location:	West of Sturgeon Falls
Number of trails:	10
Total distance:	25km (15mi)
Level of difficulty:	● ■ ◆
Groomed:	100%
Trackset:	100% classic
Interesting features:	Moonlight skis
Fee:	$6/day, $40/year
Amenities and other services:	Parking, toilets, heated lodge

Getting There

From Sturgeon Falls, take Highway 17 west. Turn right
(north) onto LeBlanc Road and continue for 5km (3mi) to
the entrance.

Further Information

West Nipissing Nordic Ski Club
☎*(705) 753-1082 (Jeanette Holland)*

Discovery Routes Partnership
North Bay-Mattawa Conservation Authority
701 Oak St. E.
North Bay, ON P1B 9T1
☎*(705) 474-5420*
(705) 474-9793

Windy Lake Lodge (♥)

Location:	Mile 122.5 on the Algoma Central Railway
Number of trails:	9
Total distance:	50km (31mi)
Level of difficulty:	● ■ ◆
Groomed:	100%
Trackset:	No
Interesting features:	Callahan Lake, Agawa River, ice falls, mountain top lookouts, Laurel Lake, Yesi Lake, Pike Lake, Hotshot Lake and Stovepipe Lake
Fee:	Free, with accommodation
Other activities:	Ice fishing
Services:	(R), (A)
Amenities and other services:	Parking, toilets, telephones, lodge, snack bar, maps, waxing centre, gift shop

After a scenic 5hrs on the Algoma Central Railway, you'll arrive at the 122.5 flag marker that indicates the Windy Lake Lodge. Stepping off the train, you'll begin skiing right away, heading towards the main lodge and Lake Callahan, while lodge employees take care of your luggage (and your food if you've decided to cook your own meals.) From then on, your only decision is whether to leave your cabin for snowshoeing, ice fishing, to explore one of the groomed cross-country trails or to blaze your own backcountry trail. There are several trails, ranging from the shortest **Scenic Trail**, which is 5km (3mi), to the longest 25km (15.5mi) **Hotshot Lake Loop**. An outpost cabin splits the Hotshot Lake loop in two, for those who prefer two leisurely days to one tough haul. In between are the **Main Trail**, the **Small Plantation Loop**, the **Pike Lake Loop**, the **North Plantation Loop**, the **Laurel Lake Trail**, the **Yesi Lake Loop** and the **Stovepipe Lake Trail**.

Getting There

Take the Algoma Central Railway from Sault Ste. Marie to mile marker 122.5. Your trip passes the Agawa Canyon's north portal, which features rock walls less than 15m (50ft) apart and a close-up view of the Agawa River.

Further Information

Windy Lake Lodge
Mile 122 and 1/2 ACR
Sault Ste. Marie, ON P6A 5N9
☎*(705) 781-3236 or 856-7086*
☎*800-771-5495*
www.windylake.com

Northwestern Ontario

Northwestern Ontario has the longest snow season in Ontario. Skiing and snowshoeing can begin as early as November and almost always continue until mid-April, and at times into the first week of May.

Snowshoeing and backcountry skiing are popular activities in just about any green space in this region, although count on skirting trees that have fallen onto trails for at least part of your trip. Other skiers should stick to trails that are maintained by the many clubs in the region, city officials or conservation authorities.

One of the most popular skiing centres in northwestern Ontario is **Kamview Nordic Centre** (see p 336). The Thunder Bay Nordic Trails Association (TBNTA) grooms 28km (17mi) of trails for both classic and skating techniques at Kam-

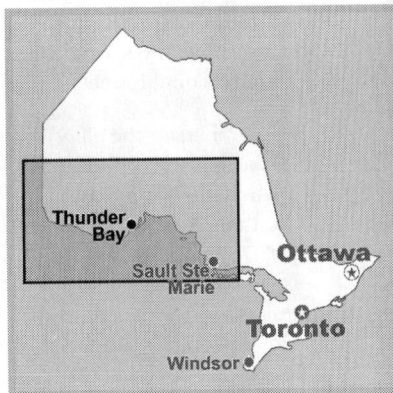

view, including 5.5km (3.4mi) that are lit until 10pm every night. The same association also benefits other area skiers too, since its volunteers are essential for maintaining the trails at **Kakabeka Falls** (see p 334), **Mink Mountain Resort** (see p 339), and **Sleeping Giant Provincial Park** (see p 343). Membership in the TBNTA costs $110/season.

Club members also participate in running the Sibley Ski Tour, a major race held at Sleeping Giant Provincial Park every March. More than 800 participants compete in this event, which is known as the most important cross-country ski event in northwestern Ontario and also rates as Ontario's top cross-country skiing loppet.

Members of the TBNTA can also choose to pay a surcharge for inclusion in the **Lappe Nordic Centre** (see p 337). Lappe was started by ex-Olympian Reijo Puiras, who extends his already longer-than-usual season by covering his trails in sawdust and holding a ski race in September.

The **Dryden Ski Club** (see p 332), which has a reputation for great alpine skiing, also specializes in cross-country skiing with more than 20km (12mi) of trails that are groomed for both classic and skating techniques. The **Superior Cross-Country Ski Club** (see p 345), operates two locations along the Trans-

Canada Highway, including one within Rainbow Falls Provincial Park. **Red Lake District Cross-Country Club** (see p 342) has the most northerly groomed ski trails in Ontario, which are located on McKenzie Island, a location that can only be accessed via an ice road in the winter. Other clubs in the region include: **Beaten Path Nordic Trails (Atikokan)** (see p 330), **Club Minaki** (see p 332), **Marathon Cross Country Ski Club** (see p 338) with 3km (2mi) of night-lit trail, **Nipigon Ski Club**, and **Nordic Nomads Ski Club** (see p 341) in Sioux Lookout. There's also the possibility that the Rendezvous Ski Club will reopen in Nipigon.

Independent skiers and snowshoers in the Thunder Bay area also visit the conservation authority lands of **Hazelwood Lake Conservation Area** (see p 333) and **Mission Island Marsh Conservation Area** (see p 340) and city parks, such as **Centennial Park** (see p 331).

The private sector is represented by forestry

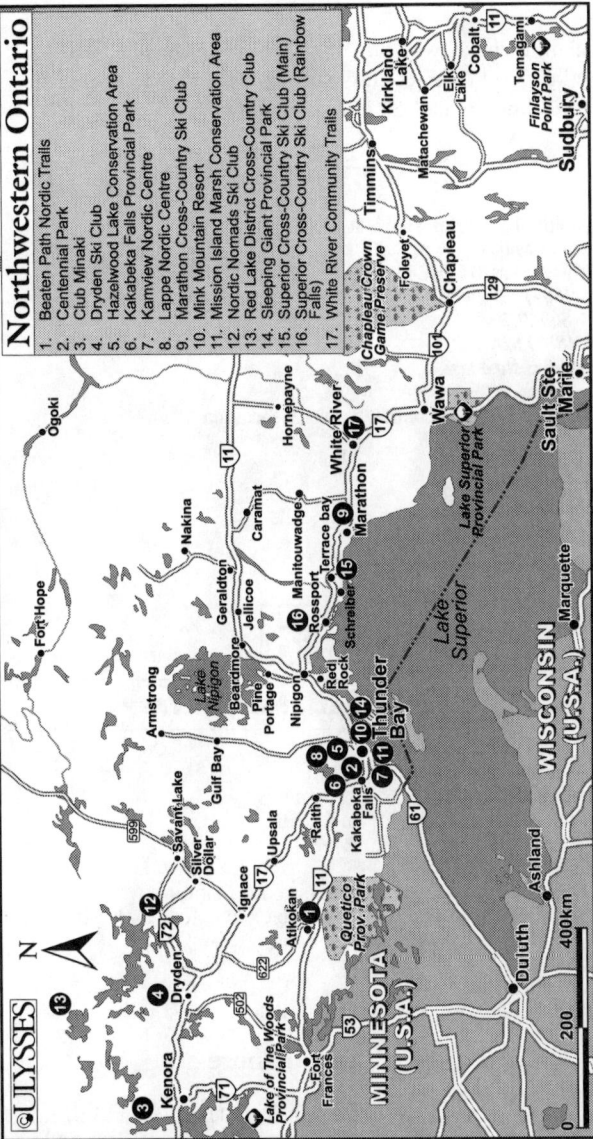

© ULYSSES

Northwestern Ontario

1. Beaten Path Nordic Trails
2. Centennial Park
3. Club Minaki
4. Dryden Ski Club
5. Hazelwood Lake Conservation Area
6. Kakabeka Falls Provincial Park
7. Kamview Nordic Centre
8. Lappe Nordic Centre
9. Marathon Cross-Country Ski Club
10. Mink Mountain Resort
11. Mission Island Marsh Conservation Area
12. Nordic Nomads Ski Club
13. Red Lake District Cross-Country Club
14. Sleeping Giant Provincial Park
15. Superior Cross-Country Ski Club (Main)
16. Superior Cross-Country Ski Club (Rainbow Falls)
17. White River Community Trails

giant Domtar, which maintains good cross-country ski trails known as the **White** **River Community Trails** (see p 346) in the town of the same name.

Tourist Information

North of Superior Tourism
1119 Victoria Ave. E.
Thunder Bay, ON P7C 1B7
☎ *(807) 626-9420*
☎ *800-265-3951*
⇄ *(807) 626-9421*
www.nosta.on.ca

Ontario's Sunset Country Travel Association
102 Main St., Suite 201
Kenora, ON P9N 3X6
☎ *(807) 468-5853*
☎ *800-665-7567*
⇄ *(807) 468-5484*
www.ontariossunsetcountry.ca

Beaten Path Nordic Trails

Location:	Atikokan
Number of trails:	6
Total distance:	28km (17mi)
Level of difficulty:	● ■ ◆
Groomed:	100%
Trackset:	100% classic and skating
Interesting features:	Jim Lake, deer, red fox, horseshoe hares
Fee:	$20/year
Services:	**(L)**
Amenities and other services:	Parking, toilets

Getting There

Take Regional Road 622 north from Highway 118 to Atikokan and stop in the visitor centre parking lot. The trails begin just behind the centre.

Further Information

Beaten Path Nordic Trails
☎*(807) 597-4399 (Arlene Robinson)*

Lake Superior Ski Division Cross Country
lssdxc.baynet.net

Centennial Park

Location:	Thunder Bay
Number of trails:	3
Total distance:	28km (17mi)
Level of difficulty:	● ■ ◆
Groomed:	100%
Trackset:	100% classic and skating
Interesting features:	Current River, bluffs
Fee:	No
Other activities:	Sleigh rides, logging-history musem
Amenities and other services:	Parking, telephones, chalet with snack bar and toilets

Getting There

Take Hodder Avenue south off Highway 11/17. At the four-way stop at the bottom of the hill, turn left on Arundel Street. Turn right into the park.

Further Information

Tourism Thunder Bay
500 E. Donald St.
Thunder Bay, ON P7E 5V3
☎*800-667-8386*
www.city.thunder-bay.on.ca/tourism

Club Minaki

Location:	Minaki
Number of trails:	7
Total distance:	25km (17mi)
Level of difficulty:	■
Groomed:	100%
Trackset:	100% classic, 3km (1mi) skating
Interesting features:	Gunn Lake
Fee:	$2/day, $25/year
Other activities:	Ice-skating with lights, tobogganing, winter camping in yurts (heated tents)
Services:	**(R)** *(very limited, call ahead)*, **(L)**, **(A)** *(bed and breakfast)*
Amenities and other services:	Parking, wilderness centre yurt with toilets and two bed-and-breakfast rooms available

Getting There

Take Highway 17A to Minaki. Turn to head north onto Trailhead Road, which ends at the tri-level yurt.

Further Information

Minaki Yurt Adventures
Trailhead Rd.
Minaki, ON P0X 1J0
☎ *(807) 224-2203 (Nadene or Jordy McBride)*
www.minaki.ca/ski.htm

Dryden Ski Club

Location:	Dryden
Number of trails:	3
Total distance:	21.5km (13mi)

Level of difficulty: ● ■ ◆
Groomed: 100%
Trackset: 100% classic and skating
Interesting features: Bloomer's Bluff
Fee: Donation
Other activities: Alpine Skiing, snowboarding
Services: (R) *(weekends and holidays)*, (L) *(weekends and holidays)*

**Amenities and
other services:** Parking, heated lodge with snack bar, toilets, telephones and waxing centre on weekends and holidays, Canadian Ski Patrol

Getting There

From Dryden, take Highway 601 north. When the highway turns, continue driving straight ahead on the gravel road to the Dryden Ski Club sign. Turn right and then follow the road past the steep hill until you see a sign that indicates the club entrance on the left side.

Further Information

Dryden Ski Club
PO Box 25
Dryden, ON P8N 2Y7
☎ *(807) 937-5449 (Brian Lockyer)*

Hazelwood Lake Conservation Area

Location: Thunder Bay
Number of trails: 3
Total distance: 7km (4mi)
Level of difficulty: ●
Groomed: No
Trackset: No
Interesting features: Hazelwood Lake
Fee: Donation
**Amenities and
other services:** Parking, toilets, lodge with fireplace for rent

Northwestern Ontario

Getting There

Take Highway 102 (Dawson Road) north past Country Fair Plaza to Hazelwood Drive. Turn right (east) and follow the road until it ends at the conservation area.

Further Information

Lakehead Region Conservation Authority
PO Box 10427
Thunder Bay, ON P7B 6T8
☎(807) 344-5857
⇌(807) 345-9156
www.lakeheadca.com

Kakabeka Falls Provincial Park

Location:	West of Thunder Bay
Number of trails:	7
Total distance:	13km (8mi)
Level of difficulty:	● ■ ◆
Groomed:	100%
Trackset:	100% classic and skating
Interesting features:	Kakabeka Falls, views of Kaministiquia River
Fee:	$6/vehicle, TBNTA membership (see p 327)
Services:	**(L)** *(Jackrabbit program)*
Amenities and other services:	Parking

Kakabeka Falls Provincial Park has protected one of the most beautiful waterfalls in the north since 1957. The falls are 71m (234ft) wide and drop 39m (128ft) from the Kaministiquia River into a gorge where fossils as old as 2.1 billion years have been found. As indicated by their nickname "Niagara of the North," these falls share some similarities with their southern counterparts. Both absolutely must be seen. Ontario Hydro controls both, making them appear most impressive on holidays and weekends. Both have an ancient history depicted in Ojibway oral tradition. Kakabeka Falls' legend is that of Greenmantle, a 17-year old woman who led Sioux captors to their deaths over the falls, although no one seems to know whether Greenmantle swam safely to shore or if her spirit still floats above the "thundering water." That's where the similarities end, however, for Kakabeka Falls has a much more rustic setting than its southern version. Winter visitors will have to view the falls first and then head over to the cross-country ski trails, which are accessed from a parking lot on the Whispering Hills Campground side of the park just off of Harstone Road.

The ski trails form three loops that are roughly parallel to the 4km (2.5mi) **Poplar Point** (which used to be called the Circle Trail), 5.6km (3.5mi) **Beaver Meadows** and 3.6km (2mi) **River Terrace** hiking trails. Expect to see the tracks of chipmunks, snowshoe hares, white-tailed deer and red fox.

Getting There

To see Kakabeka Falls, take Highway 11/17 west, past the town of Kakabeka Falls, and follow the signs. To get to the parking lot beside the cross-country ski trails, turn onto Highway 590 at Kakabeka Falls and take it south to Harstone Road. Turn left and then make an immediate left into the parking lot.

Further Information

Thunder Bay Nordic Trails Association (see p 337)

Kakabeka Falls Provincial Park
Lynda Horman, Park Superintendent
PO Box 252
Kakabeka Falls, ON P0T 1W0
☎ *(807) 473-9231*
⇌ *(807) 473-5973*
www.ontarioparks.com

Kamview Nordic Centre (♥)

Location:	Thunder Bay
Number of trails:	11
Total distance:	28km (17mi)
Level of difficulty:	● ■ ◆
Groomed:	100%
Trackset:	100% classic and skating
Night lit:	5.5km (3.4mi)
Interesting features:	Cliffs, lookout over Lake Superior and the Kaministiquia River Valley, Bucky's Creek
Fee:	TBNTA membership (see p 327)
Services:	**(R)**, **(L)** *(Jackrabbit, junior and masters programs)*
Amenities and other services:	Parking, toilets, telephones, warm-up lodge with snack bar and waxing centre

The trail system at Kamview is diverse enough to attract a variety of skiers. Five easy trails, totalling roughly 10km (6.2mi) give young children, families and skiers who need to warm-up plenty of entertainment. All the skiing trails that are lit at night, which include the 2.2km (1.4mi) **Sundown Trail**, the 2.1km (1.3mi) **Sun Up Trail** and the 1.5km (.9mi) **Northern Lights Trail**, are easy. Additional easy trails include the 3.2km (2mi) **Tamarack Trail** and the 1.1km (.7mi) **Roadway Rambo**.

Intermediate skiers can continue for roughly another 9km (5.5mi) on the 3km (1.9mi) **Aspen**, the 1.9km (1.2mi) **Poplar** and the 3.8km (2.4mi) **Jackrabbit**.

Avid skiers, racers and those with advanced skills will enjoy the 6.8km (4.2mi) **Lookout**, which can be accessed from the Tamarack Trail via the .3km (.1mi) **Uppercut Trail**, and the 2.5km (1.6mi) **Woodland Wander** on the east side of Sideroad 20.

The design and grooming of these trails is so excellent that several groups of skiers meet regularly here during the season. They include the Lakehead University Nordic Ski Club on Mondays, jackrabbits from Big Thunder Nordic Ski

Club on Thursday nights and Saturday mornings, Big Thunder Nordic Ski Club's masters on Thursday nights and the Kamview Jackrabbit Ski League on Saturday mornings.

Getting There

Take Highway 61 west from downtown Thunder Bay to Sideroad 20. Turn right and continue for about 5km (3mi) past the airport.

Further Information

Thunder Bay Nordic Trails Association
RR 3, Site 2
PO Box 9
Thunder Bay, ON P7C 4V2
☎*(807) 475-7081*
☎*(807) 625-5075 (snowphone)*
⇝*(807) 577-9772*
www.nordictrails-tb.on.ca

Lakehead University Nordic Ski Club
955 Oliver Rd.
Thunder Bay, ON
flash.lakeheadu.ca/~lunordic

Lappe Nordic Centre

Location:	North of Thunder Bay
Number of trails:	10
Total distance:	11km (7mi)
Level of difficulty:	● ■ ◆
Groomed:	100%
Trackset:	100% classic and skating
Night lit:	5km (3mi)
Interesting features:	North-facing slope—skiing lasts until April
Fee:	$140/year
Other activities:	Sawdust Run in September
Services:	(R), (L)
Amenities and other services:	Parking, barn clubhouse with ski waxing area, change rooms, saunas, snack bar

Ex-Olympian Reijo Puiras started Lappe in a location with a north-facing slope that holds the snow, thereby extending the season until April or early May. Puiras extends his lengthy season even further by covering his trails in sawdust so he can hold a ski race in September.

The centre is also known for its snack bar, which serves delicious Finnish pancakes, and for 5km (3mi) of night-lit trail.

Getting There

Take Highway 102 west from Thunder Bay to Highway 589 (Dog Lake Road). Turn right and drive for about 10km (6mi) to Concession 4. Turn left (west) and continue for about 4km (2.5mi) to the Lappe Nordic Centre parking lot.

Further Information

Lappe Nordic Ski Club
c/o Lappe Ski Centre
Thunder Bay, ON
http://flash.lakeheadu.ca/~lnordic

Marathon Cross-Country Ski Club

Location:	Marathon
Number of trails:	10
Total distance:	15km (9mi)
Level of difficulty:	● ■ ◆
Groomed:	100%
Trackset:	100% classic and skating
Night lit:	5km (3mi) until 9:30pm
Interesting features:	Red fox, scenic view of Lake Superior
Fee:	$10/day, $20/day family, $110/year, $200/year family
Services:	**(R)** *(no charge)*, **(L)** *(Jackrabbit and adult programmes)*
Amenities and other services:	Parking, warm-up lodge with fireplace, snack bar, pro-shop, board games, toilets and waxing centre

The Marathon Cross-Country Ski Club's trail system has three segments, the Jackrabbit Trails, the Challenge Trails and the Olympic Trails. The Jackrabbit Trails include **two Northern Lights** loops that are lit daily from dusk until about 9:30pm, a **Prospectors' Loop** and a **Riverview Loop**. The Challenge Trails include the **Discovery Loop**, the **Cascade Loop**, **Ransoms' Romp** and **Renney's Run**, which is named after a short form for renard, the French word for fox. The Olympic Trails include only one loop, which is known as the **Vortex Loop**.

Getting There

From Highway 17, take Peninsula Road south into Marathon. After about 3km (1.9mi), turn right into the Peninsula Golf Course. The lodge and parking lot are a short drive along.

Further Information

Marathon Cross-Country Ski Club
PO Box 1587
Marathon, ON P0T 2E0
☎ *(807) 229-0288*

Northwestern
Ontario

Mink Mountain Resort

🛏 **Access to trails reserved for overnight guests**

Location:	Thunder Bay
Number of trails:	10
Total distance:	28km (17mi)
Level of difficulty:	● ■ ◆
Groomed:	100%
Trackset:	100% classic and skating
Interesting features:	Lake Superior, Mink Mountain, lookouts
Fee:	No, TBNTA membership is required (see p 327)
Services:	**(R)**, **(A)** *(cabins)*
Amenities and other services:	Parking, toilets, warm-up area, restaurant

Getting There

Take Highway 61 south from Thunder Bay about 32km (20mi) to Sturgeon Bay Road. Turn left (east) towards Lake Superior and drive to the entrance next to the lake.

Further Information

Mink Mountain Resort
RR 7, Site 8, Comp. 23
Thunder Bay, ON P7C 5V5
☎ *(807) 622-5009*
www.superiornorth.com

Thunder Bay Nordic Trails Association (see p 337)

Mission Island Marsh Conservation Area

Location:	Mission Island, Thunder Bay
Number of trails:	4
Total distance:	2km (1mi)
Level of difficulty:	●
Groomed:	No
Trackset:	No
Interesting features:	Marsh, views of Lake Superior, McKellar River
Fee:	Donation
Amenities and other services:	Parking, toilets

Getting There

Take either Empire Avenue or Arthur Street south to Syndicate Avenue, which runs from east to west. Turn south onto 106th Avenue, which leads across the Jackknife Bridge and ends at the conservation area parking lot.

Further Information

Lakehead Region Conservation Authority
PO Box 10427
Thunder Bay, ON P7B 6T8
☎*(807) 344-5857*
✆*(807) 345-9156*
www.lakeheadca.com

Nordic Nomads Ski Club

Northwestern Ontario

Location:	Sioux Lookout
Number of trails:	5
Total distance:	33km (20mi)
Level of difficulty:	● ◆
Groomed:	100%
Trackset:	100% classic, 3km (1.8mi) skating
Interesting features:	Rocky terrain, Pelican Lake, Duck Lake, scenic lookout
Fee:	Donation, $20/year
Other activities:	Tobogganing hill
Services:	**(L)** *(Jackrabbits)*
Amenities and other services:	Parking, toilets

Getting There

Current access is through Cedar Bay Riding Stables on Eighth Avenue or Ojibway Golf and Curling Club on Third Avenue.

Further Information

Nordic Nomads Ski Club
Roger Zilkowsky, President
PO Box 2037
Sioux Lookout, ON P8T 1J7
☎*(807) 737-7448*

Red Lake District Cross-Country Club (♥)

Location:	North of Red Lake
Number of trails:	7
Total distance:	30km (18.6mi)
Level of difficulty:	● ■ ◆
Groomed:	100%
Trackset:	100% classic and skating
Interesting features:	Eagles, old gold mine site, bear, wolf and wolverine tracks
Fee:	$40/year, $60/year family
Services:	**(L)** *($10 members, $20 non-members)*, **(A)** *(cabin)*
Amenities and other services:	Parking, warm-up lodge with toilets (Sundays only)

Getting There

Take Highway 11/17 to Vermillion Bay. Head north on Highway 105, which ends at Red Lake. Just prior to Red Lake, you'll see the turnoff for Highway 125. Take it north past Cochenour and it continues right onto the ice road to McKenzie Island. Take a left once you reach the island. You'll see a large brown building where the trails begin.

Further Information

Red Lake District Cross-Country Ski Club
PO Box 40
Red Lake, ON P0V 2M0
☎ *(807) 662-1149 (Catherine Mochrie)*
http://lssdxc.baynet.net

Sleeping Giant Provincial Park (♥)

Location:	Sibley peninsula, east of Thunder Bay
Number of trails:	4
Total distance:	59km (37mi)
Level of difficulty:	● ■ ◆
Groomed:	100%
Trackset:	100% classic and skating
Interesting features:	The Sleeping Giant, The Sea Lion, Silver Islet Silver Mine
Fee:	$8.50/vehicle plus $2/person, $1/youth or $25/season; TBNTA membership (see p 327)
Amenities and other services:	Parking, toilets, telephones, visitor centre with two fireplaces and hot drinks (weekends only)
Other:	Park closed Nov, Dec and Apr

Ski trails at Sleeping Giant Provincial Park are nowhere near the Gulliver-shaped stone landmark that the park is now named for. Instead, the park's skiing fame harks back to the park's pre-1998 name with a famous loppet called The Sibley Ski Tour. Every year, on the first Saturday in March, more than 800 cross-country skiers, including a good many families, take 10km (6.2mi), 20km (12mi) and 50km (31mi) tours across the Sibley Peninsula. The event is so popular, it's become *the* cross-country skiing event in northwestern Ontario.

Skiers enjoy trails skirting the Sibley Peninsula the rest of the year too. Four trails lead out from the trailhead, visitor centre and parking lot next to Marie Louise Lake in the park, which is south of Pass Lake on the north shore of Lake Superior. The 2km (1mi) **Beginner Trail** connects with every other trail, which includes: a 10km (6.2mi) **Intermediate Trail** on the east side of Highway 587; the 18km (11mi) **Marie Louise Lake Trail** that enables intermediate skiers to circle the lake; and a 29km (18mi) difficult trail that connects the **Burma** and **Pickerel** trails into a loop. The Pickerel Lake portion takes up about one third of the total trail and falls to the east of Highway 587, where some of the park's largest white pines are located.

Sleeping Giant
Provincial Park

0 — 4 — 8km

Thunder Bay

N

Bay's End

Milkshake Lake

Caribou Island

Wiswell Lake

Squaw Bay

Pounsford Lake

Joe Creek

Lizard Lake

Joeboy Lake

Thunder Bay Bog

Piney Wood Hills

Rita Lake

Burne Trail

Addison Lake

Sifting Lake

Pickerel Lake

Thunder Bay

Twinpine Lake

Gardner Lake

Pickerel Lake Trail

Black Bay

Marie-Louise Lake Trail

Marie-Louisa Lake

Ferns Lake

Foster Point

Horizon Bay

Habitat

Plantain Lake

Finlay Bay

Sawyer Bay

Sawbill Lake

Middlebrun Bay

Nanabosho

The Sea Lion

Silver Islet

Lake Superior

The Sleeping Giant

Thunder Mountain

The Chimney

Lehtinen's Bay

Thunder Cape Bird Observatory

©ULYSSES

Courtesy of Ontario Parks

Getting There

Take Highway 17 east from Dorion or west from Thunder Bay. Turn right on Highway 587 towards the town of Pass Lake. Drive 32km (20mi) past a railway suspension bridge. The park boundary begins just after the town of Pass Lake and ends before the town of Silver Islet.

Further Information

Thunder Bay Nordic Trails Association (see p 337)

Sleeping Giant Provincial Park
Pass Lake, ON P0T 2M0
☎ *(807) 475-1531 or 977-2526*
☎ *800-667-1940*
⇌ *(807) 977-2583*
www.ontarioparks.com

The Friends of Sleeping Giant Park
PO Box 29031
McIntyre Centre Postal Outlet
1186 Memorial Ave.
Thunder Bay, ON P7B 6P9

Northwestern Ontario

Superior Cross-Country Ski Club

Locations:	Hwy. 17 West, between Schreiber and Terrace Bay
	Rainbow Falls Provincial Park
Number of trails:	8
Total distance:	30km (19mi)
Level of difficulty:	● ■ ◆
Groomed:	100%
Trackset:	100% classic and skating
Interesting features:	Scenic view of Lake Superior, grosbeaks, gray jays
Fee:	$5/day, $25/year, $40/year family
Services:	**(R)**, **(L)** *(occasional programs)*
Amenities and other services:	Parking

Getting There

To get to the main Superior Cross-Country Ski Club trails,
take Highway 17 west from Terrace Bay or east from
Schreiber and watch the south side for the sign.

To get to the Rainbow Falls location, drive 7km (4.3mi)
east from Schreiber or 5km (3mi) west from Rossport along
Highway 17 to the main entrance of Rainbow Falls Provincial Park. The main entrance road is plowed to the park
gate. After that, follow the tracks to the trails.

Further Information

Superior Cross-Country Ski Club
Terrace Bay, ON P0T 2W0
☎ *(807) 825-9143 (Clark Stuttard, president)*

White River Community Trails

Location:	White River
Number of trails:	4
Total distance:	20km (12.4mi)
Level of difficulty:	● ■ ◆
Groomed:	100%
Trackset:	100% classic
Interesting features:	Beaver dam, wolf tracks
Fee:	No
Amenities and other services:	Parking

There are four trails on this Domtar site: the 4km (2.5mi)
looped **Jackrabbit Trail**, the 4km (2.5mi) **Whisky Jack Trail**, the
2km (1.2mi) **Beaver Trail** that connects the Jackrabbit and
Whiskey Jack trails, and the 10km (6.2mi) looped **Timber-
wolf Trail**, which leads up and down a boreal forest ridge.

Getting There

Drive east of the information centre on Highway 17 in
White River to Highway 631. Drive north for 2km (1.2mi)

towards Hornepayne. The parking area and sign are on your right.

Further Information

Domtar Forestry Centre
18655 Kenyon Rd.
PO Box 21
Apple Hill, ON K0C 1B0
☎ *(613) 528-4430*
⇌ *(613) 528-4819*

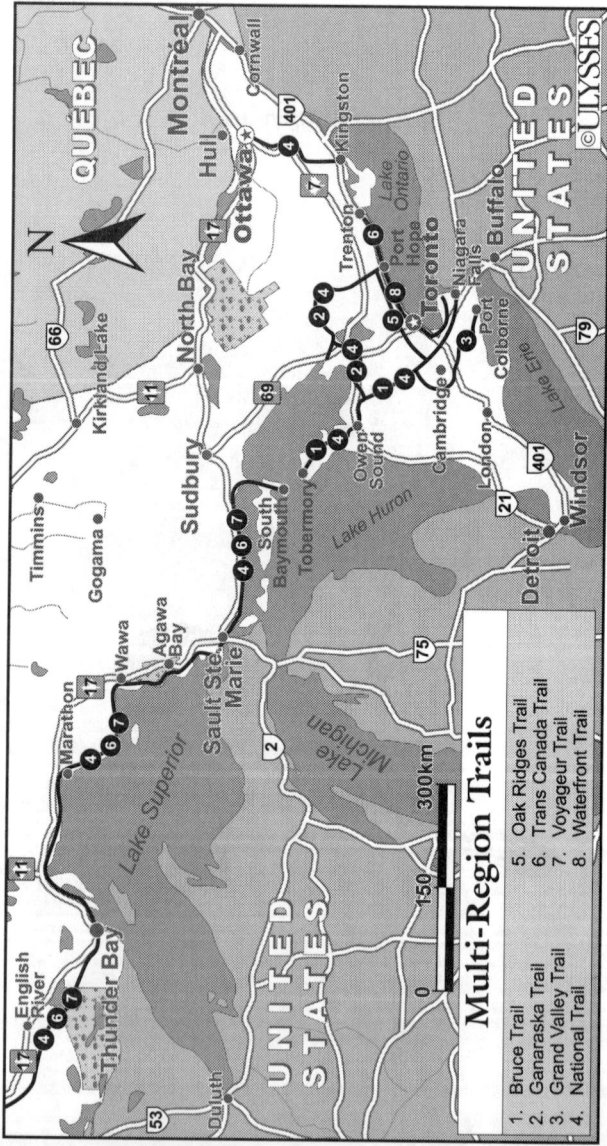

Multi-Region Trails

1. Bruce Trail
2. Ganaraska Trail
3. Grand Valley Trail
4. National Trail
5. Oak Ridges Trail
6. Trans Canada Trail
7. Voyageur Trail
8. Waterfront Trail

© ULYSSES

Multi-Region Trails

Snowshoers and cross-country skiers are welcome on several long-distance hiking trails located throughout Ontario.

The sections in each of these trails that are groomed for cross-country skiing are mentioned in other chapters of this guide, but for the interest of backcountry skiers and snowshoers, this chapter outlines the trails in full.

The oldest multi-region trail is the **Bruce Trail** (see p 351), a 1,100km (682mi) footpath along the ridge of the Niagara Escarpment from Tobermory to Niagara-on-the-Lake. The initial 700km (434mi) were completed in 1967, just in time for Canada's 100th birthday.

The popularity of the Bruce Trail inspired several other Ontario groups to begin blazing trails in the early 1970s.

Two of the trails—the **Ganaraska Trail** (see p 357) and the **Grand Valley Trail** (see p 361)—naturally link with the Bruce by following the routes of major rivers flowing from the Niagara Escarpment. A third, the **Oak Ridges Trail** (see p 366) copies the Bruce example by leading snowshoers across the top of another major landform, the Oak Ridges Moraine, which fortuitously intersects with the Niagara Escarpment.

The success of the Bruce Trail also inspired a group of volunteers to begin thinking about a trail along the northern border of Lake Superior in 1973. The landscape the northerners face is a lot more rugged than that faced by southern trail blazers, but they're still at it. About half of the **Voyageur Trail's** (see p 371) anticipated 1,100km (682mi) have been completed so far, but every year the trail gets a bit longer.

The Bruce Trail also inspired like-minded folks in other provinces to try and develop ties across the nation. The Alexander Mackenzie Voyageur Canoe and Portage Trail follows the first recorded crossing of the country from Montréal, Québec to Bella Coola, British Columbia. Then in 1971, efforts to try and blaze a footpath called the **National Trail** (see p 364) began. Although the National Trail hasn't yet been completed, it has been somewhat overshadowed by the **Trans Canada Trail** (see p 369), a 16,000km (9,920mi) multi-use trail open to cross-country skiers, cyclists, equestrians, hikers and snowmobilers. Some 9,000km (5,580mi) have thus far been completed.

The cross-country Trans Canada Trail effort has inspired further efforts in Ontario. A group of municipalities located along the shore of Lake Ontario, for instance, has been busy building a trail to link 28 different cities, towns and villages, which is now known as the **Waterfront Trail** (see p 372). So far, some 325km (202mi) of a potential 700km (434mi) have been completed. Eventually, it's hoped that the Canadian side of the trail will link with similar trails on the U.S. side so that ambitious skiers will be able to ski all the way around Lake Ontario.

Further Information

Hike Ontario
1185 Eglinton Ave. E., Suite 411
Toronto, ON M3C 3C6
☎*(416) 426-7362*
☎*800-422-0552*
⇥*(416) 426-7045*
www.hikeontariocom

Bruce Trail (♥)

Location:	Niagara to Tobermory
Number of sections:	9
Total distance:	800km (497mi) plus 300km (186mi) of side trails
Markers:	White blazes, blue blazes for side trails
Groomed:	35%
Trackset:	35% classic, 15% skating
Interesting features:	Niagara Escarpment, 300 bird species
Fee:	Donation, $40/yr

Canada's oldest, longest marked trail began in 1960, when Raymond Lowes, a member of the Hamilton Naturalists Club, proposed that the Federation of Ontario Naturalists build a footpath across the entire Niagara Escarpment. Since then, the idea has become reality. The main trail was established in 1967, four years after the incorporation of The Bruce Trail Association. Today, the association in-cludes nine member clubs, with a total membership of 7,500. Members mark blazes, build bridges, stiles and boardwalks, negotiate with park administrators and land-owners to maintain more than 1,000km (620mi) of trail, and work to add or replace more every year. Actually, 700 active volunteers maintain the trail; the other 6,800 provide the funding that helps make it possible.

Less than half of the Bruce Trail crosses public lands, which include one national park, seven provincial parks, 40 conservation areas and 43 public parks or nature re-serves. The rest of the trail crosses private property.

Multi-Region Trails

Protecting the unusual beauty of the Niagara Escarpment itself has been an international priority since 1990, when the United Nations named it a Unesco World Biosphere Reserve. The recognition came, in part, because the area is home to more than 300 bird species, 53 mammals, 35 reptiles and amphibians and 90 fish species, many of which can be viewed in the winter.

The Bruce Trail Association offers a fabulous trail guide complete with colour maps and descriptions of camping areas along the trail. The Peninsula Bruce Trail Club has also produced a mini-map to the Tobermory region.

Getting There

A variety of conservation areas and nature reserves provide access to the trail. Please see access points for each section.

Further Information

Bruce Trail Association
PO Box 857
Hamilton ON L8N 3N9
☎ *(905) 529-6821 or 800-665-hike (4453)*
📠 *(905) 529-6823*
www.brucetrail.org

Niagara Section

Location:	Queenston to Grimsby
Level of difficulty:	■
Distance:	84km (52mi) linear plus 64km (40mi) along 10 side trails
Access points:	Balls Falls Conservation Area, Brock University, Decew House Park, Fireman's Park, Glendale Ave., Kinsmen Community Park, Louth Conservation Area, Morningstar Mill, Pelham Rd., Rockway Community Centre, Rockway Conservation Area, Short Hills Provincial Park (see p 141), Thorold Old Stone Rd., Quarry Rd., Woodend Conservation Area

This part of the trail is covered with Carolinian forest. Look for ash, beech, tulip trees and sassafras.

Iroquoia Section

Location:	Grimsby to Kelso
Level of difficulty:	■
Distance:	119km (74mi) linear plus 41km (25mi) along 35 side trails
Access points:	Battlefield Park, Beamer Memorial Conservation Area, Crawford Lake Conservation Area (see p 94), Devil's Punch Bowl Conservation Area, Dundas Valley Conservation Area (see p 128), Felker's Falls Conservation Area, Kelso Conservation Area, Gage Park, Mount Nemo Conservation Area, Mountainview Conservation Area, Rattlesnake Point Conservation Area, Rock Chapel Sanctuary, Snake Rd. (Halton), Spencer Gorge Wilderness Area, Tiffany Falls Conservation Area, Vinemount Conservation Area, Webster's Falls Park, Winona Conservation Area

This section of the trail begins just prior to Beamer's Point Bluff in Grimsby, an area known for spectacular fall hawk migrations. It then passes through Stoney Creek, Hamilton, Dundas, Burlington and Milton. You'll pass five waterfalls, Tiffany, Sherman, Webster's, Tews and Borer's. There's also a huge pothole, 34m (112ft) deep with a circumference of 180m (591ft), called Devil's Punch Bowl, just west of Battlefield Park.

Toronto Section

Location:	Kelso Conservation Area to Creditview Rd.
Level of difficulty:	■
Distance:	48km (30mi) linear plus 54km (33mi) along 13 side trails
Access points:	Dufferin Quarry Bridge, Halton Country Inn, Hilton Falls Conservation Area, Limehouse Conservation Area, Scottsdale Farm, Terra Cotta Conservation Area

This trail begins at Highway 401, near Campbellville Road and then travels along the edge of the Niagara Escarpment past small 500-year-old cedars and over the Dufferin Quarry Bridge.

Multi-Region Trails

Caledon Hills Section

Location: Creditview Rd. to Mono Centre
Level of difficulty: ■
Distance: 83km (51mi) linear plus 58km (36mi)
                          along 13 side trails
Access points: Albion Hills Conservation Area (see p 91),
                          Belfountain Conservation Area, Caledon
                          Administration Centre, Forks of the Credit
                          Provincial Park (see p 160), Glen Haffy
                          Conservation Area, Ken Whillans Re-
                          source Management Area (east side of
                          Hwy. 10), Inglewood Arena, Resource
                          Management parking lot in Alton Village

This trail begins north of Creditview Road at the Chelting-
ham Badlands, a series of ridges of rock-hard red and grey
soil that resemble the Alberta Badlands. From there, it
passes the ruins of McLaren Castle, an 1864 neo-Norman
stone building that was destroyed in a fire in 1964 and a
view of the 1885 hydroelectric mill at Cataract Falls. Part of
the trail follows the Caledon Trailway through a sheep
farm. After leaving the old railway bed, the path leads
north past Albion Hills (see p 91) and Glen Haffy to the
Hockley Valley.

Dufferin Hi-land Section

Location: Mono Centre to Lavender
Level of difficulty: ■
Distance: 51km (32mi) linear plus 12km (7.5mi)
                          along 4 side trails
Access points: 1st Line East Hurontario St. (south of
                          Dufferin Rd. 17, Mono Cliffs Provincial
                          Park

This trail begins through Mono Cliffs and continues north
past Boyne Valley Provincial Park, Pine River Fishing Area
and through an area of Honeywood loam known as one of
Ontario's best farming regions.

Blue Mountains Section

Location: Lavender to Craigleith
Level of difficulty: ■
Distance: 59km (37mi) linear plus 19km (12mi)
                       along 13 side trails
Access points: Devil's Glen Provincial Park, Nottawasaga
                       Bluffs Conservation Area, Petun Conserva-
                       tion Area

This trail passes a series of drumlins, Best Caves, an old
Petun Aboriginal settlement, Petun Conservation Area,
Singhampton Caves (moss-covered crevices open to the
sky), Nottawasaga Bluffs, the Blue Mountain ski slopes and
the Scenic Caves.

Beaver Valley Section

Location: Craigleith to Blantyre
Level of difficulty: ■
Distance: 88km (55mi) linear plus 14km (9mi) along
                       8 side trails
Access points: Beaver Valley Lookout, Blantyre Commu-
                       nity Hall, Duncan Crevice Caves Provin-
                       cial Nature Reserve, Epping Lookout, Old
                       Baldy Conservation Area

This trail begins on Maple Lane and follows the Niagara
Escarpment through many woods and pastures to the sum-
mit of Metcalfe Rock, which offers a good view over
Kolapore Creek. It then descends through a rocky gorge to
the valley and the base of Pinnacle Rock, a large chunk of
limestone that has separated from the edge of the escarpment. The trail then leads along several side roads to Old
Baldy Conservation Area. Old Baldy is the 152m-high
(500ft) section of the escarpment that's known locally as
Kimberley Rock. The trail then leads to Epping Lookout, an
area managed by the Grey Sauble Conservation Authority,
and Anthea's Waterfall.

Multi-Region Trails

Sydenham Section

Location:	Blantyre to Wiarton
Level of difficulty:	■
Distance:	117km (72mi) linear plus 22km (14mi) along 13 side trails
Access points:	Bruce Caves Conservation Area, Grey-Bruce Tourist Information Office (Hwy. 6 and 21), Harrison Park, Indian Falls Conservation Area, Ingis Falls Conservation Area, Pottawatomi Conservation Area, Skinner's Bluff Conservation Area, Walters Falls Conservation Area

This trail crosses and parallels Rocklyn Creek in Blantyre and then goes through the Bighead and North Spey river valleys through Walters Falls and Inglis Falls (see p 230) conservation areas. From there, it travels alongside Owen Sound to the Pottawatomi Conservation Area for a look at Jones Falls. The trail follows the shore of Owen Sound past Indian Falls Conservation Area to Kemble Mountain Management Area, a highland that separates the Owen Sound valley from the Colpoy's Bay valley. It continues past a wetland called the Slough of Desponds to an overhanging lookout known as Skinner's Bluff and continues to Bruce Caves Conservation Area.

Peninsula Section

Location:	Wiarton to Tobermory
Level of difficulty:	◆
Distance:	157km (98mi) linear plus 50km (31mi) on 29 side trails
Access points:	Bruce Peninsula National Park (see p 155), Cape Croker Park, Colpoy's Bluff, Hope Bay Forest Provincial Nature Reserve, Lion's Head Provincial Nature Reserve, Smokey Head-White Bluff Provincial Nature Reserve, Spirit Rock Conservation Area

This section of the Bruce Trail is definitely the most difficult. It also includes a variety of unusual rock formations that can't be seen elsewhere along the trail, including Devil's Monument—also known as Devil's Pulpit—a 14m

(46ft) flowerpot-shaped pillar between Cape Chin and Dyer's Bay. You'll also see the ruins of the Corran, a 17-room mansion built by Alexander McNeil in 1882.

Ganaraska Trail (♥)

Location:	Port Hope on Lake Ontario to Glen Huron, south of the Blue Mountains
Number of sections:	8
Total distance:	500km (310mi)
Markers:	White blazes for main trail, blue blazes for side trail
Groomed:	50%
Trackset:	50% classic, 35% skating
Interesting features:	Ganaraska River, Moore Falls, Fenelon Falls
Fee:	Donation, $15/yr family
Amenities and other services:	Parking, toilets

Volunteers from 10 different clubs maintain the Ganaraska Trail, which was started in 1967 to connect Port Hope with the Bruce Trail. Today, the trail goes through Lindsay and Orillia, passing the drumlin fields of Peterborough, the Oak Ridges Moraine, some of the Kawartha Lakes, the Minesing Swamp and a series of sand dunes east of Wasaga Beach.

The volunteers have also organized a wonderful inn-to-inn service with 17 bed and breakfast operators along the route. Skiers and snowshoers stay two nights at each inn, with the inns providing breakfast prior to each day's activities. The inns will also provide box lunches, suppers or luggage shuttle service to the next location.

Getting There

Choose any of the trailheads or access points mentioned under each section.

Multi-Region Trails

Further Information

Ganaraska Trail Association
PO Box 693
Orillia, ON L3V 6K7
www3.sympatico.ca/hikers.net/ganarask

Pine Ridge Section

Level of difficulty: ●
Distance: 66km (41mi) linear
Access points: Port Hope town hall, Port Hope Conser-
                      vation Area, Sylvan Glen Conservation
                      Area, Fudge's Mill, Ganaraska Forest (see
                      p 101), Hwy. 7 between Lindsay and
                      Omemee

This section leads from the Port Hope town hall along the
west and then east shore of the Ganaraska River to
Corbett's dam and a fish ladder near Highway 401. The
trail passes the Ganaraska Forest and over the Hogsback
drumlin.

Peterborough Section

Level of difficulty: ●
Distance: 77km (48mi) linear
Access points: Crosswinds Rd., Old Mill Rd., Post Rd.,
                      Hillhead Rd., Logie St., McDonnel Park,
                      Carew Park and boardwalk, Pottinger St.,
                      Victoria St., Lindsay St. in Fenelon Falls,
                      Buller Rd., Moore Falls, Ken Reid Conser-
                      vation Area (see p 232)

The Peterborough section of the Ganaraska Trail begins on
the rail trail between Dranoel and Lindsay through the
Peterborough drumlin field. It then travels along the shores
of the Scugog River to King Street, then to Lindsay Street
and south, past Lock 33 of the Trent Canal. It continues
through McDonnel and Carew parks to the Victoria Rail
Trail. Visits to the Ken Reid Conservation Area, an 1885
Grand Trunk Railway station, the 7m-high (23ft) Fenelon
Falls, Cameron Lake, and Corben Lake are also worthwhile.

Orillia Section

Level of difficulty: ●
Distance: 70km (43mi) linear
Access points: Sadowa, Lake Couchiching, Lightfoot
                   Trail, Tudhope Park, Leacock Estates,
                   Sagebush Estate Rd.

Orillia-area volunteers maintain a trail that begins in
Sadowa and continues to a limestone plain known as an
"alvar," after an island off the Swedish coast, past limestone
outcrops called "karst" towards a marsh. They have to
build bridges to enable snowshoers to cross the narrows
between Lakes Simcoe and Couchiching and continue to
Tudhope Park. They also help clear the path through to
the Sagebrush Estate.

Barrie Section

Level of difficulty: ●
Distance: 50km (31mi) linear
Access points: Huron Heights Rd., Copeland Forest,
                   Craighurst, Midhurst Community Centre,
                   Horseshoe Valley Ski Resort (see p 228),
                   Minesing swamp, Hwy. 90

The Barrie section runs through the Copeland Forest Resources Management Area, a mixed forest, swamp and
meadow that attracts songbirds and white-tailed deer. Follow the markers through the villages of Craighurst and
Midhurst, through the Simcoe County Forest and through
the Minesing swamp.

Mad River Section

Level of difficulty: ●
Distance: 55km (34mi) linear
Access points: Bruce Trail west of Glen Huron,
                   Carruthers Memorial Conservation Area,
                   New Lowell Conservation Area, Creemore

This portion of the trail leads along the shores of the Mad
River, where trout spawn in the spring. There are two
lookouts, one from Ten Hill and the other from McKinney's

Multi-Region Trails

Hill. The trail then leads through New Lowell and Car-ruthers Memorial conservation areas. It ends in the village of Creemore, home of Canada's smallest jail, which is no longer used.

Midland Section

Level of difficulty: ●
Distance: 35km (22mi) linear
Access points: Copeland Forest, Wye Marsh (see p 255)

This section of the trail leads snowshoers through the Copeland Forest and north through the Sturgeon River Valley, known as "pretty valley" by the locals. It then con-tinues north along a rail trail to the Wye Marsh (see p 255).

Tiny Trails Section

Level of difficulty: ●
Distance: 18.5km (11.5mi) linear
Access points: Balm Beach Rd., Concession 12, Perkins-field, Wyeville, Bluewater Beach

This trail is still under construction. Currently, it begins at Concession 12 and follows a rail trail south to Balm Beach Road. The trail will eventually lead snowshoers through the village of Perkinsfield, into Wyevale and on to Bluewater Beach.

Wasaga Section

Level of difficulty: ●
Distance: 50km (31mi) linear
Access points: Allanwood Beach, Wasaga Stars Arena, 11th Concession Rd. in New Wasaga Beach, Wasaga Beach Provincial Park

This section connects Wasaga Beach and the Wasaga Beach Provincial Park with the Mad River section. Skiers will particularly enjoy the 13km (8mi) section through the Blueberry Trails (see p 208), although snowshoers will find staying off the ski trails a challenge. You'll also travel along the Nottawasaga River and through many of the McIntyre Creek's valleys.

Grand Valley Trail

Location:	Lake Erie to Alton
Number of sections:	4
Total distance:	254km (157mi)
Groomed:	No
Trackset:	No
Markers:	White paint blazes for main trail, blue for side trails
Interesting features:	Grand River, Monarch butterfly migration, spawning carp, migrating songbirds and waterfowl, Elora Gorge, Mennonite Pioneer Tower, Alexander Graham Bell Homestead, West Montrose covered bridge
Fee:	Donation
Amenities and other services:	Parking, toilets

The Grand Valley Trail began at a public meeting in Kitchener in January 1972. Since then, the trail has been extended along the Grand River several times, so that it now measures 254km (157mi).

The trail begins at Rock Point Provincial Park, a peninsula that juts into Lake Ontario and provides a refuge for migrating songbirds, waterfowl and monarch butterflies. Fossils found along the shore indicate that it may have been a tropical coral reef 350 million years ago. The path follows the Grand River through the Dunnville Marsh, along the Gordon Glaves Memorial Pathway in Brantford, past Paris, through the Doon Pioneer Village and Chicoppe Hills Conservation Area in Kitchener, past the covered bridge in West Montrose, along the Elora Gorge in the Elora Gorge Conservation Area (see p 158) and through Belwood Lake Conservation Area to the pinnacle in the tiny community of Alton.

Members organize volunteer work parties to maintain the trail, although some members have adopted sections of the trail that they maintain themselves. The club also organizes group outings and offers badges to any skier who skis from one end of the trail to the other. As with any other

Multi-Region Trails

long trail, members also deal with private landowners who graciously allow members to cross their land and others who ask that the trail be rerouted away from their properties.

Getting There

Bellwood Conservation Area, Bingeman Park, Brant Conservation Area, Byng Island Conservation Area, Churchill Park, Elora Gorge Conservation Area (see p 158), Highland Pines Campground, La Fortune Campground, Laurel Creek Conservation Area (see p 168), Pinehurst Conservation Area (see p 177) and Rock Point Provincial Park all adjoin the trail. The Avon (see p 152), Bruce (see p 351), Feeder Canal and Speed River trails also connect to this trail. Also refer to the access points under each section.

Further Information

Grand Valley Trails Association
75 King St. S.
PO Box 40068 RPO Waterloo Square
Waterloo, ON N2J 4V1
www.gvta.on.ca

Cayuga, Caledonia, Dunnville Section

Level of difficulty: ●
Distance: 56.5km (35mi) linear
Access points: Rock Point Provincial Park, Byng Island
                       Conservation Area, County Rd. 54 in
                       York, Caledonia Dam Riverside Park

This flat section begins along a 2.5km (1.6mi) trail in Rock Point Provincial Park and travels through Carolinian forests and along a portion of the Welland Feeder Canal, before heading to the Grand River Marsh in Dunnville. It then continues through Cayuga, along the Grand River to York, past a sawmill to Sims Locks, then to Seneca Park and the Riverside Park in Caledonia. Because of limited snowfall on this section, you'll be hiking frequently.

Brantford Section

Level of difficulty: ●
Distance: 84km (52mi) linear
Access points: Caledonia Dam, La Fortune Conservation
                       Area, Onondaga Town Hall, McLellan Rd.,
                       Hamilton Rd., Brant Conservation Area,
                       Hardy Rd., Curtis Ave. in Paris

This section of the trail begins at the Caledonia Dam and follows County Road 54 to Mine Road where it turns into an open meadow and then follows a meandering path through the La Fortune Conservation Area. From there, it follows the Six Nations Reserve boundary to Onondaga. Snowshoers will enjoy travelling along the Grand River shore from Onondaga to Brantford, and then along the Gordon Glaves Memorial Pathway. The trail splits at Wilkes Dam and leads below Highway 403 on the way to Paris.

Kitchener-Waterloo and Cambridge Section

Level of difficulty: ●
Distance: 56km (35mi) linear
Access points: Bingeman Park, Doon Conservation Area,
                       Chicopee Hills Conservation Area, West
                       Montrose Covered Bridge

The section of trail through Kitchener-Waterloo leads through Homer Watson Park, where Carolinian species grow, and through the white cedar swamps of Bingeman Park. It includes Hidden Valley and the Chicopee Hills Conservation Area through to Natchez Hill. From this point, it leads along a very scenic route through Mennonite country, and passes Ontario's only remaining covered bridge at West Montrose.

Elora Section

Level of difficulty: ●
Distance: 57km (35mi) linear
Approx. time: 3 days each way
Access points: Elora Gorge Conservation Area (see
                       p 158), Elora Bissel Conservation Area,
                       Beatty Line in Fergus, Belwood Lake Con-
                       servation Area

Multi-Region Trails

After seeing the 24.4m (80ft) cliffs at Elora Gorge, you'll pass the picturesque town of Fergus. You'll then pass a gravel quarry, a fish hatchery, and a cedar swamp near Hillsburgh. The trail then crosses the Credit River, leads past the pinnacle on the Millcroft Inn property and goes on to Alton.

National Trail

Location:	Canada—from the Atlantic Provinces to British Columbia
Number of trails:	4 in Ontario: Bruce, Ganaraska, Rideau and Voyageur
Total distance:	10,000km (6,200mi) when completed
Markers:	A stylized pedestrian logo
Groomed:	No
Trackset:	No
Interesting features:	Welcomes hikers, walkers, cross-country skiers and snowshoers along winding, rocky paths
Interesting features:	Niagara Escarpment, 300 bird species
Fee:	Donation

Volunteers have been trying to build a footpath across Canada since 1971, when National Trail visionary Doug Campbell and other activists met at a conference in Toronto. It took another six years before the National Trail Association of Canada was officially registered, and some 10 years after that before the first national trail marker made it onto a post.

In Ontario, Hike Ontario acts as an official representative of the association and directs people to the Bruce (see p 351), Ganaraska (see p 357), Rideau (see p 282) and Voyageur (see p 371) trails, which form part of the national trail within the province. You can't get from one side of Ontario to the other in any direction yet, but when the trails are done, they'll join Niagara Falls, near the New York border to Tobermory on the shores of Georgian Bay along the Bruce; Glen Huron, on the shores of Georgian Bay to Port Hope, near Toronto along the Ganaraska; Manitoulin Island in Georgian Bay to Thunder Bay, east of the Manitoba border on the Voyageur; and Ottawa, near the Quebec border to Kingston along the Rideau. There are still major gaps between Trenton and Kingston, between Thunder Bay and Rossport, between Pukaskwa National Park and Wawa, between Wawa and Lake Superior Provincial Park (see p 308), between Lake Superior Provincial Park and Goulais River, and between Elliot Lake and Espanola.

The Voyageur Trail offered 600km (372mi) of its trail—the portion between Sault Ste. Marie and Thunder Bay—to the Trans Canada Trail in 1998, initiating cooperation between the two organizations. Within a year, the Trans Canada Trail Foundation offered its shared-use trails to the National Trail, so that now the Trans Canada and the National are one and the same for much of their trans-Ontario route. Although many snowshoers would prefer a non-motorized route where possible, any off-road trail is better than the alternative.

Unfortunately, gaps still exist, but it's hoped that trails will connect all three coasts of Canada very soon.

Getting There

Although traversing Ontario from one side to the other is not yet possible, most of the province can be covered along the Bruce, Ganaraska, Rideau and Voyageur trails.

Further Information

The National Trail Association of Canada
PO Box 8063
Canmore, AB T1W 2T8
www.alpineclubofcanada.ca/trails

Hike Ontario
1185 Eglinton Ave. E., Suite 411
Toronto, ON M3C 3C6
☎ *(416) 426-7362 or 800-422-0552*
⇰ *(416) 426-7045*
www.hikeontario.com

Multi-Region Trails

Oak Ridges Trail (♥)

Location:	Along the Oak Ridges Moraine between Caledon and the Northumberland Forest
Number of sections:	11
Total distance:	160km (99mi), 135km (84mi) completed so far
Markers:	White blazes
Groomed:	No
Trackset:	No
Interesting features:	Witch hazel, black oak savanna, boreal and mixed forests, kettle lakes, swamps
Fee:	Donation
Amenities and other services:	Parking

When finished, the Oak Ridges Trail will cut across the top of the Oak Ridges Moraine, a ridge running from the Niagara escarpment in the west to Trent River in the east. High points along the moraine include the Caledon Hills, Mount Wolfe, Happy Valley Sandhills and Glenville Hills. The ridge is large enough to be seen from space and contains the headwaters of more than 60 rivers draining into Lake Simcoe and Lake Ontario. The most important of these include the Don, Duffin, Ganaraska, Holland, Humber, Nonquon, Nottawasaga, Pigeon and Rouge. Twenty-five percent of the Oak Ridges Moraine is forested, primarily by sugar maple and beech, although white pine and red oak are also common. Black oak savanna also grows on the moraine, in a sandy area south of Rice Lake.

Volunteers have been working on a trail across the ridge since the Great Pine Ridge Trail was established in 1973, although efforts to blaze the current footpath officially began in 1992. Members are now divided into nine chapters: Aurora, Caledon, Clarington, Hope-Hamilton, King, Northumberland, Scugog, Stouffville and Uxbridge. Together, these chapters help maintain, promote and extend the trail. When the trail is completed, it will connect to the Bruce (see p 351), Ganaraska (see p 357), Humber, Rouge and Trans Canada (see p 369) trails.

Getting There

Several parking lots and conservation areas access the trail.
Refer to the access points within each section.

Further Information

Oak Ridges Trail Association
PO Box 28544
Aurora, ON L4G 6S6
☎ *(416) 410-2601 or 877-319-0285*
www.interlog.com/~orta

Caledon/King West Section

Level of difficulty: ●
Distance: 17km (10.5mi) linear plus 1.5km (.9mi)
                 unopened road allowance
Access points: Hall Lake sideroad, 10th Concession at
                 18th sideroad

This trail leads south on the Albion Trail and then south-
east across the West Holland River and past Puck's Farm
family entertainment facility.

King East Section

Level of difficulty: ●
Distance: 22.5km (14mi) linear
Approx. time: 9hrs
Access points: 8th Concession, 7th Concession, Weston
                 Rd. at 16th sideroad, Seneca College King
                 Campus

Part of this section runs through Happy Valley Forest, the
largest upland forest on the moraine. It then passes an
orchard where apples are sold in the fall and Sacred Heart
Church, the only remaining symbol of a Catholic colony,
where 35 families worked together to survive the Depres-
sion. You'll also pass the Augustinian Monastery, located in
a brick barn built by Sir Henry Pellatt in the early 1900s
and Eaton Hall, a home built for Sir John and Lady Flora
McCrae Eaton in the 1930s.

Multi-Region Trails

Aurora Section

Level of difficulty: ●
Distance: 10km (6.2mi) linear
Access points: 16th Side Rd. east of Bathurst, Wellington St. East at Larmont, Sheppard's Bush Conservation Area, Vandorf Sideroad at Bayview Ave., "Newmarket B" Go bus from Finch subway station

The Aurora section passes by Salamander Pond in a 17ha (42-acre) forest called Case Woodlot, Tamarac Green and Confederation Park. It also crosses Yonge Street and then passes through Sheppard's Bush Conservation Area and the Vandorf and Alliance woodlots.

Whitchurch-Stouffville Section

Level of difficulty: ●
Distance: 14km (8.7mi) linear
Access points: Woodbine Ave. south of Aurora Rd., Whitchurch Conservation Area, Lakeshore Rd. at Hwy. 48

This section of the trail passes by the 1947 Slaters Mill and through the Whitchurch Conservation Area. It also passes through three (Robinson, Dainty and Clark) of the 18 York Regional Forest Tracts that were planted in the 1920s to prevent soil erosion. The Whitchurch-Stouffville section ends at Musselman Lake, a kettle lake named after a Pennsylvanian family that settled nearby in 1807. The area became very popular with vacationers in the 1920s.

Uxbridge Section

Level of difficulty: ●
Distance: 25.5km (15.8mi) linear
Access points: Hillsdale Rd., Secord Forest and Wildlife Area, Durham Regional Forest

The Uxbridge section begins at Musselman Lake and continues through wetlands and forests to the Durham Regional Forest. Veterinarian Dr. Alan Secord once operated a pet cemetery in Secord Forest and Wildlife Area.

Scugog West

Level of difficulty: ●
Distance: 17km (10.5mi) linear
Access points: Durham Regional Forest, Purple Woods
                       Conservation Area

The Scugog West section begins at the Durham Regional Forest and continues to Ocala Orchards Farm Winery. It passes the old rail bed of the "nip and tuck" railway that ran from Whitby to Port Perry in 1871 and on to Lindsay in 1876. The railway was thus named because passengers had to jump off the train so it could climb the Oak Ridge Moraine. The portion of the trail along Old Simcoe Road follows an 18th century route used by the Mississauga, who trapped beaver in Osler Marsh to trade with the French in current-day Oshawa. The trail also passes through Purple Woods Conservation Area.

Scugog East/Clarington Section

Level of difficulty: ●
Distance: 19.5km (12.1mi) linear
Access points: Byers Rd., Boundary Rd., Long Sault Conservation Area

This trail goes through the Long Sault Conservation Area, a 336ha (830-acre) forest, meadow and cedar swamp reserve with 14km (8.7mi) of trails.

Trans Canada Trail

Location:	Newfoundland, Nova Scotia, P.E.I., New Brunswick, Québec, Ontario, Manitoba, Saskatchewan, Alberta, British Columbia, N.W.T., Yukon and Nunavut
Total distance:	16,000km (9,920mi) linear
Markers:	Trans Canada logo
Groomed:	100% (by snowmobiles)
Trackset:	No

Interesting features: Multi-use trail for cross-country skiing, snowmobiling, walking, cycling and horseback riding
Fee: Donation
Amenities and other services: Parking, toilets

More than 1.5 million people have been working to build the Trans Canada Trail along ancient railway beds and new trails that link Canada from east to west as well as northward. Eventually, it will be the longest trail of its kind in the world, running for about 16,000km (9,920mi). The trail attracts cross-country skiers and snowshoers in the winter as well as hikers and cyclists in the summer. Where possible, horseback riders and snowmobilers will also be welcome.

The Ontario route goes through Hamilton, Kenora, Kingston, Ottawa, Niagara Falls, North Bay, Peterborough, Sault Ste. Marie, Sudbury, Thunder Bay, Toronto, Tweed and Windsor, with links to Belleville, Chatham, Cornwall, Kingston, London, Owen Sound, Pembroke and Stratford. More than 75 different existing trails, including 600km (372mi) of the Voyageur Trail (see p 371) and the Waterfront Trail (see p 372) will be part of the final trail.

Getting There

Most Ontario communities have a Trans Canada Trail or a spur trail to it somewhere nearby. Check with the local tourist information office or the contacts below.

Contact Information

Ontario Trails Council
Trail Studies Unit
Trent University
Peterborough, ON K9J 7B8
☎*(705) 748-1419*
www.trentu.ca/academic/trailstudies/otc

Trans Canada Trail Foundation
6104 Sherbrooke St. W.
Montreal, QC H4A 1Y3
☎*800-465-3636*
⇰*(514) 485-4541*
www.tctrail.ca

Voyageur Trail

Location:	Thunder Bay to South Baymouth, Manitoulin Island
Level of difficulty:	◆
Number of trails:	16
Total distance:	1,100km (682mi) when completed, 550km (372mi) at present
Markers:	White blazes for main trail, blue blazes for side trails, yellow blazes for loop trails
Groomed:	100% (by snowmobilers)
Trackset:	No
Interesting features:	Rolling terrain, coastal bluffs, secluded beaches and coves
Fee:	Donation, $20/yr
Other activities:	Snowmobiling
Amenities and other services:	Parking, toilets

Volunteers began planning the Voyageur Trail at a meeting in Sault Ste. Marie in March 1973. By late 1975, they had completed the Saulteaux section between Gros Cap and Mabel Lake. A year later, the Desbarats section between Tower Lake and Rydal Bank was completed, and additional sections were added as local volunteers were recruited. Volunteers from 24 clubs (eight currently inactive) have been maintaining and blazing trails for almost 30 years. They also organize daytrips for local members, produce a fabulous guidebook and liaise with the various Aboriginal communities, private landowners, public parks and municipalities along their proposed route which follows the north shores of Lake Superior and Georgian Bay.

There are currently 16 different trails that make up the route, including the Nipigon River Recreation Trail, 3km (1mi) of which is groomed for cross-country skiing by the Rendezvous Cross-Country Ski Club, the Casque Isles Trail, the Marathon Peninsula Harbour Coastal Trail, the Pukaskwa National Park Coastal Hiking Trail, the Michipicoten Trail, the Lake Superior Provincial Park Coastal Hiking Trail, the Harmony Trail, the Stokely Creek Lodge Trail (see p 321), the Goulais River Trail, the

Multi-Region Trails

Salteaux section, the Echo Ridges section, the Desbarats section, the Thessalon section, the Iron Bridge section (see p 302), the Penewobikong section, and the Coureur de Bois section.

Anyone interested in hiking the Voyageur Trail should obtain a copy of the *Voyageur Hiking Trail Guidebook* and consider joining the Voyageur Trail Association. Potential members are permitted to do one group hike with association members before membership is required.

Getting There

Completed sections of the trail are accessible from Nipigon, Terrace Bay, Marathon, Wawa, Goulais River, Elliott Lake or at Pukaskwa National Park, Lake Superior Provincial Park (see p 308) and Rainbow Falls Provincial Park.

Further Information

Voyageur Trail Association
PO Box 20040
150 Churchill Blvd.
Sault Ste. Marie, ON P6A 6W3
☎ *(705) 253-5353 or 800-393-5353 x9999*

Waterfront Trail

Location:	Canadian shore of Lake Ontario
Number of sections:	26 total, 14 major
Total distance:	700km (434mi) when completed, currently 350km (217mi)
Markers:	Stylized logo
Level of difficulty:	●
Interesting features:	Lake Ontario
Groomed:	No
Trackset:	No
Fee:	Donation
Other activities:	Snowmobiling

The Waterfront Trail leads along the north shore of Lake Ontario from Niagara-on-the-Lake to Trenton, with plans to extend to Kingston soon. The trail links 184 nature reserves, 161 parks and 84 marinas and yacht clubs.

Plans to build the trail began with a short section from Burlington to Trenton in 1995. Since then, the Seaway Trail in western New York and additional communities have joined the trail. It's hoped that one day the Waterfront Trail will loop around the coast of Lake Ontario.

Birders particularly appreciate the migrating and nesting waterfowl seen in the area, including black-crowned night heron, caspians, common terns, herring gulls and ring-billed gulls. Good birding spots include the East Hamilton Harbour and the Burlington Skyway Bridge, among others.

Getting There

Visit the coast of any community on the trail and ski as far as you like.

Further Information

Waterfront Regeneration Trust
PO Box 129
207 Queen's Quay W., 5th Floor
Toronto, ON M5J 1A7
☎ *(416) 943-8080*
⇌ *(416) 943-8068*
www.waterfronttrail.org

Ajax

Distance: 8.6km (5.3mi) linear
Access points: Rotary Park, Pickering Beach

This section leads from Liverpool Beachfront Park in Pickering to the Lynde Shores Conservation Area in

Multi-Region Trails

Whitby. It passes through Duffins Marsh, a prime water-fowl viewing area.

Brighton

Distance: 38km (5.3mi) linear
Access points: Presqu'ile Provincial Park

This section leads from Colborne village to Hanna Park in Trenton. It passes through Presqu'ile Provincial Park.

Burlington

Distance: 18km (11mi) linear
Access points: Beachway Park, Burloak Park, LaSalle Park, Royal Botanical Gardens, Spencer Smith Park

This section runs from the canal/liftbridge to Shell Park in Oakville. It passes through Bayshore Park, Port Nelson Park, McNichol Park and the Sioux Lookout.

Clarington

Distance: 33km (21mi) linear
Access points: Darlington Provincial Park, Ontario Power Generation-Darlington Nuclear, Bowmanville Harbour Conservation Area, Bondhead Park

This section runs from the General Motors of Canada headquarters in Oshawa to downtown Port Hope. It passes through the Wilmot Creek Provincial Fishing Area.

Etobicoke

Distance: 14km (8.7mi) linear
Access points: Colonel Samuel Smith Park, Humber Bay Park, Marie Curtis Park

This section, which travels along the shore of Lake Ontario between Lakefront Promenade Park in Mississauga and the Sir Casimir Gzowski Park in Toronto, links the Etobicoke Creek, Humber Bay, and Tommy Thompson trails.

Hamilton

Distance: 10.5km (6.6mi) linear
Access points: Confederation Park, Canal Liftbridge

This trail leads from the intersection of Frances and Millen avenues in Stoney Creek, through Confederation Park to the Canal Liftbridge.

Haldimand Township

Distance: 27.8km (17.2mi) linear
Access points: Lakeport, Nawautin Shores Nature Sanctuary, Wicklow Beach Boat Launch

This section passes some very rural areas. It also links to a series of trails at the Nawautin Shores Nature Sanctuary.

Mississauga

Distance: 23.5km (14.6mi) linear
Access points: Jack Darling Memorial, Lakefront Park, Lakeside Park, Port Credit Harbour, Marie Curtis Park, Rattray Marsh, Rhododendron Gardens

This section leads from Gairlock Gardens in Oakville along the lake to Marie Curtis Park in Etobicoke, passing several waterfront parks, gardens, and Rattray Marsh.

Niagara-on-the-Lake

Distance: 6km (3.7mi) linear
Access points: Fort George

This section runs from Fort George to the intersection of Mary and Dorchester streets and then along Lakeshore Road from Town Line to Read Road. It also links with the Niagara River Recreational Trail (see p 134), which leads to the Niagara Glen and Dufferin Islands.

Multi-Region Trails

Oshawa

Distance: 11.4km (7.1mi) linear
Access points: Lakeview Park, Lakefront West Park

This section leads from Heydenshore Kiwanis Park in Whitby to Darlington Provincial Park. It passes tthe Pumphous Marsh Wildlife Reserve, Oshawa Habour, the Second Marsh Wildlife Reserve and the Oshawa Community Museum.

Pickering

Distance: 12.7km (7.9mi) linear
Access points: Beachfront Park, Conmara Ave. (Squires Beach), Petticoat Creek Conservation Area, West Shore Community Centre

This section leads from Rouge Beach Park in Scarborough to Rotary Park. It passes Frenchman's Bay and the Ontario Power Generation—Pickering Nuclear station.

St. Catharines

Distance: 9.8km (6mi) linear
Access points: Happy Rolph Bird Sanctuary, Spring Gardens Park, Welland Canals Parkway, Westcliffe Park

This section runs along Lake Ontario between Port Dalhousie and the Happy Rolph Bird Sanctuary. It also connects with the Bruce (see p 351) and Merritt trails.

Stoney Creek

Distance: 2km (1.2mi) linear
Access points: Confederation Park in Hamilton

This section provides a safe passage from Hamilton, across the Queen Elizabeth Way to the intersection of Frances and Millen avenues in Stoney Creek.

Toronto

Distance: 22.5km (14mi) linear
Access points: Ashbridge's Bay Park, Balmy Beach, Cherry Beach, Coronation Park, Harbourfront, High Park, Kew Beach, Sir Casimir Gzowski Park at the Humber Bridge, Ontario Place, Sunnyside Park, Tommy Thompson Park

This trail leads along Lake Ontario from the Beaches area of Toronto in the east to Humber Bay Park in Etobicoke on the west. You'll pass wilderness bird reserves and a music garden development by YoYo Ma and other Toronto musicians. This section links to the Lower Don, High Park and Tommy Thompson trails.

Whitby

Distance: 10.6km (6.6mi) linear
Access points: Port Whitby Harbour, Rotary Sunrise Lake Park, Kiwanis Heydonshore Park and Pavillion

This section starts at the Ajax Waterfront Park and ends at Lakefront West Park in Oshawa. It passes the Iroquois Sports Centre, Station Gallery and Intrepid Park.

Appendix – Winter Bird Checklist

The birds you can expect to see in Ontario during the winter season include:

American goldfinches (*Carduelis tristis*), in central, eastern and southern Ontario, in Toronto, and in the Niagara area;

American kestrels (*Falco sparverius*), in southern and central Ontario, in Toronto and in the Niagara region;

American robins (*Turdus migratorius*), in southern Ontario;

barn owls (*Tyto alba*), along the shores of lakes Erie and Ontario;

barred owls (*Strix varia*), throughout Ontario;

Bewick's wren (*Thryomanes bewickii*), along the shore of Lake Erie;

black-backed three-toed woodpecker (*Picoides arcticus*), throughout Ontario;

black ducks (*Anas rubripes*), along the shores of lakes Erie, Huron and Ontario;

black-capped chickadees (*Parus atricapillus*), throughout Ontario;

bobwhites (*Colinus vierginianus*), along the shores of lakes Erie, Huron and Ontario;

bohemian waxwings (*Bombycilla garrulus*), in northwestern Ontario;

boreal chickadees (*Parus hudsonicus*), in central, northeastern and northwestern Ontario;

boreal owls (*Aegolius funereus*), in central, northeastern and northwestern Ontario;

buffleheads (*Bucephala albeola*), along the shores of lakes Erie, Huron and Ontario;

Canada geese (*Branta canadensis*), along the shores of lakes Erie and Ontario;

canvasbacks (*Aythya valisinteria*), along the shores of the Great Lakes;

cardinals (*Cardinalis cardinalis*), in southern Ontario;

Carolina wren (*Thryothorus ludovicianus*), on the shore of lakes Erie and Ontario;

cedar waxwings (*Bombycilla cedorum*), along the shore of lakes Erie and Ontario;

common crows (*Corvus brachrhynchos*), along the shore of lakes Erie, Huron and Ontario;

common goldeneyes (*Bucephala clangula*), in central, southern and eastern Ontario, in Toronto and in the Niagara region (look for their head-back, feet first, screaming display during courtship in late winter);

common flickers (*Colaptes auratus*), along the shores of the Great Lakes, and in central, eastern, northeastern and southern Ontario;

common loons (*Gavia immer*), along the shores of the Great Lakes;

common mergansers (*Mergus merganser*), along the shores of lakes Erie, Huron and Ontario and in eastern Ontario;

common ravens (*Corvus corax*), in central, eastern, northeastern and northwestern Ontario;

common redpolls (*Carduelis flammea*), throughouth Ontario;

common scoters (*Melanitta nigra*), along the shores of the Great Lakes;

Cooper's hawks (*Accipiter cooperii*), in the Niagara region and southern Ontario;

dark-eyed juncos (*Junco hyemalis*), in Toronto, the Niagara region and in central, eastern, northwestern and southern Ontario;

downy woodpeckers (*Picoides pubescens*), throughout Ontario;

evening grosbeaks (*Hesperiphona vespertina*), throughout Ontario;

fox sparrows (*Passerella iliaca*), on the shore of Lake Erie;

Glaucous gulls (*Larus hyperboreus*), along the shores of the Great Lakes;

Golden-crowned Kinglet (*Regulus satrapa*), throughout Ontario;

golden eagles (*Aquila chrysaetos*), in northeastern and northwestern Ontario;

Goshawks (*Accipiter gentiles*), in central, eastern, northeastern and northwestern Ontario;

gray jays (*Perisoreus canadensis*), in central, northeastern and northwestern Ontario;

gray partridges (*Perdix perdix*), along the shores of the Great Lakes, throughout southern Ontario, in Toronto and in the Niagara region;

great black-backed gulls (*Larus marinus*), along the shores of Lake Ontario;

great gray owls (*Strix nebulosa*), in central, eastern, northeastern and northwestern Ontario;

great horned owls (*Bubo virginianus*), throughout Ontario;

greater scaups (*Aythya marila*), along the shores of lakes Erie and Ontario;

gyrfalcons (*Falco rusticolus*), in central, eastern, northeastern and northwestern Ontario, in Toronto and in the Niagara region;

hairy woodpeckers (*Picoides villosus*), throughout Ontario;

hawk-owls (*Surnia ulula*), in central, eastern, northeastern and northwestern Ontario;

hoary redpoll (*Carduelis hornemanni*), in northwestern Ontario;

horned larks (*Eremophila alpestris*), along the Great Lakes, and in southern, central and eastern Ontario;

house sparrows (*Passer domesticus*) that were descended from a few birds released in New York's Central Park in 1850, throughout Ontario;

Lapland longspur (*Calcarius lapponicus*), in southern and eastern Ontario, in Toronto and in the Niagara region;

lesser black-backed gulls (*Larus fuscus*), along the shores of Lake Ontario;

lesser scaups (*Aythya affinis*), along the shore of Lake Erie;

long-eared owls (*Asio otus*), in the Niagara region, in eastern, central and southern Ontario and in Toronto;

mallards (*Anas platyrhynchos*), along the shores of lakes Erie and Ontario;

marsh hawks (*Circus cyaneus*), in southern Ontario, in Toronto and in the Niagara region;

northern shrikes (Lanius excubitor), in a band that covers southern, central and eastern Ontario, Toronto, the Niagara region and a southern portion of northeastern and northwestern Ontario;

northern three-toed woodpecker (*Picoides tridactylus*), throughout Ontario;

oldsquaws (*Clangula hyemalis*), along the shores of lakes Ontario and Erie;

pileated woodpeckers (*Dryocopus pileatus*), throughout Ontario;

purple finches (*Carpodacus purpureus*), throughout Ontario;

red-billied woodpeckers (*Centurus carolinus*), along the shore of Lake Erie and in southern Ontario;

red-breasted mergansers (*Mergus serrator*), along the shores of the Great Lakes;

red-breasted nuthatches (*Sitta canadensis*), throughout Ontario;

red crossbills (*Loxia curvirostra*), throughout Ontario;

redheads (*Aythya Americana*), along the shores of lakes Erie, Huron and Ontario;

red-tailed hawks (*Buteo jamaicensis*), in the Niagara region, southern Ontario and Toronto;

ring-necked pheasants (*Phasianus colchicus*), along the shores of the Great Lakes and throughout southern Ontario;

rock doves (*Columba livia*), throughout Ontario;

rough-legged hawks (*Buteo lagopus*), in southern and eastern Ontario;

ruffed grouse (*Bonasa umbellus*), throughout Ontario;

Rufous-sided towhee (*Pipilo erythrophthalmus*), along the shore of lakes Erie and Ontario;

Saw-whet owls (*Aegolius acadicus*), throughout Ontario;

screech owls (*Otus asio*), in the Niagara region, southern Ontario and Toronto;

sharp-shinned hawks (*Accipiter striatus*), in central and southern Ontario, in the Niagara region and in Toronto;

sharp-tailed grouse (*Pedioecetes phasianellus*), northeastern and northwestern Ontario;

snow buntings (*Plectrophenax nivalis*), throughout Ontario

snowy owls (*Nyctea scandiaca*), throughout Ontario;

song sparrows (*Melpspiza melodia*), along the shore of lakes Erie and Ontario;

starlings (*Sturnus vulgaris*), throughout Ontario;

swamp sparrows (*Melospiza Georgiana*), in southern Ontario;

surf-scoters (*Melanitta perspicillata*), along the shores of the Great Lakes;

tufted titmouse (*Parus bicolour*), in southern Ontario and the Niagara region;

tree sparrows (*Spizella arborea*), in southern and central Ontario, in Toronto and in the Niagara region;

white-breasted nuthatches (*Sitta carolinensis*), in central, eastern and southern Ontario, the region of Niagara and Toronto;

white throated sparrows (*Zonotrichia albicollis*), along the shore of Lake Erie;

white-winged crossbills (*Loxia leucoptera*), throughout Ontario;

winter wrens (*Troglodytes troglodytes*), on the shore of lakes Erie and Ontario and in southern Ontario.

Index

Index

Travel Notes

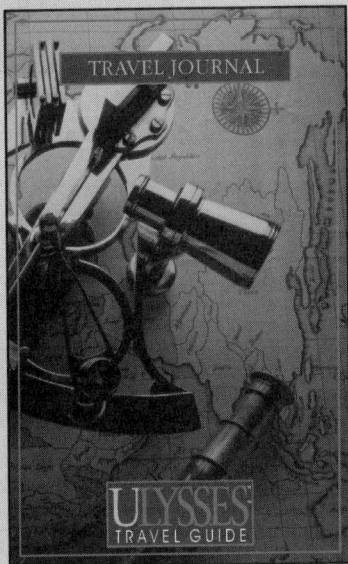

Travel Notes

Travel Notes

Order Form

Ulysses Travel Guides

☐ Acapulco . . . . . \$14.95 CAN
$9.95 US
☐ Alberta's Best Hotels and
Restaurants . . . \$14.95 CAN
$12.95 US
☐ Arizona– . . . . . \$24.95 CAN
Grand Canyon $17.95 US
☐ Atlantic Canada \$24.95 CAN
$17.95 US
☐ Beaches of Maine \$12.95 CAN
$9.95 US
$10.95 US
☐ Belize . . . . \$16.95 CAN
$12.95 US
☐ Boston . . . . \$17.95 CAN
$12.95 US
☐ British Columbia's Best
Hotels and . . . \$14.95 CAN
Restaurants $12.95 US
☐ Calgary . . . . . . \$17.95 CAN
$12.95 US
☐ California . . . . . \$29.95 CAN
$21.95 US
☐ Canada . . . . \$29.95 CAN
$21.95 US
☐ Cancún & . . . . . \$19.95 CAN
Riviera Maya $14.95 US
☐ Cape Cod, ... \$24.95 CAN
Nantucket and
Martha's Vineyard $17.95 US
☐ Cartagena . . . . . \$12.95 CAN
(Colombia) $9.95 US
☐ Chicago . . . . . . \$19.95 CAN
$14.95 US
☐ Chile . . . . \$27.95 CAN
$17.95 US
☐ Colombia . . . . . \$29.95 CAN
$21.95 US
☐ Costa Rica . . . . \$27.95 CAN
$19.95 US
☐ Cuba . . . . \$24.95 CAN
$17.95 US
☐ Dominican . . . . \$24.95 CAN
Republic $17.95 US
☐ Ecuador and . . \$24.95 CAN
Galápagos Islands $17.95 US
☐ El Salvador . . . . \$22.95 CAN
$14.95 US

☐ Guadalajara . . . \$17.95 CAN
$12.95 US
☐ Guadeloupe . . . \$24.95 CAN
$17.95 US
☐ Guatemala . . . . \$24.95 CAN
$17.95 US
☐ Haiti . . . . \$24.95 CAN
$17.95 US
☐ Havana . . . . . . \$16.95 CAN
$12.95 US
☐ Hawaii . . . . \$29.95 CAN
$21.95 US
☐ Honduras . . . . . \$24.95 CAN
$17.95 US
☐ Huatulco– . . . . \$17.95 CAN
Puerto Escondido $12.95 US
☐ Inns and Bed & Breakfasts
in Québec . . . . \$14.95 CAN
$10.95 US
☐ Islands of the . . \$24.95 CAN
Bahamas $17.95 US
☐ Jamaica . . . . . . \$24.95 CAN
$17.95 US
☐ Las Vegas . . . . . \$17.95 CAN
$12.95 US
☐ Lisbon . . . . \$18.95 CAN
$13.95 US
☐ Los Angeles . . . \$19.95 CAN
$14.95 US
☐ Los Cabos . . . . . \$14.95 CAN
and La Paz $10.95 US
☐ Louisiana . . . . . \$29.95 CAN
$21.95 US
☐ Martinique . . . . \$24.95 CAN
$17.95 US
☐ Miami . . . . \$9.95 CAN
$12.95 US
☐ Montréal . . . . . \$19.95 CAN
$14.95 US
☐ New England . . \$29.95 CAN
$21.95 US
☐ New Orleans . . \$17.95 CAN
$12.95 US
☐ New York City . \$19.95 CAN
$14.95 US
☐ Nicaragua . . . . . \$24.95 CAN
$16.95 US
☐ Ontario . . . . . . \$27.95 CAN
$19.95US

☐ Ontario's Best Hotels and Restaurants . . . $27.95 CAN $19.95US
☐ Ottawa–Hull . . . $17.95 CAN $12.95 US
☐ Panamá . . . . . . $24.95 CAN $17.95 US
☐ Peru . . . . $27.95 CAN $19.95 US
☐ Phoenix . . . . . . $16.95 CAN $12.95 US
☐ Portugal . . . . . . $24.95 CAN $16.95 US
☐ Provence & the Côte d'Azur $29.95 CAN $21.95US
☐ Puerto Plata– . . $14.95 CAN Sosua $9.95 US
☐ Puerto Rico . . . $24.95 CAN $17.95 US
☐ Puerto Vallarta . $14.95 CAN $9.95 US
☐ Québec . . . . . . $29.95 CAN $21.95 US

☐ Québec City . . . $17.95 CAN $12.95 US
☐ San Diego . . . . $17.95 CAN $12.95 US
☐ San Francisco . . $17.95 CAN $12.95 US
☐ Seattle . . . . $17.95 CAN $12.95 US
☐ St. Lucia . . . . . . $17.95 CAN $12.95 US
☐ St. Martin– . . . . $17.95 CAN St. Barts $12.95 US
☐ Toronto . . . . . . $19.95 CAN $14.95 US
☐ Tunisia . . . . $27.95 CAN $19.95 US
☐ Vancouver . . . . $17.95 CAN $12.95 US
☐ Washington D.C. $18.95 CAN $13.95 US
☐ Western Canada $29.95 CAN $21.95 US

budget.zone

☐ Central America $14.95 CAN $10.95 US
☐ Western Canada $14.95 CAN $10.95 US

Ulysses Travel Journals

☐ Ulysses Travel Journal (Blue, Red, Green, Yellow, Sextant) . . . . $9.95 CAN $7.95 US
☐ Ulysses Travel Journal (80 Days) . . . . . $14.95 CAN $9.95 US

Ulysses Green Escapes

☐ Cross-Country Skiing and Snowshoeing . . $22.95 CAN in Ontario $16.95 US
☐ Cycling in France $22.95 CAN $16.95 US
☐ Cycling in . . . . . $22.95 CAN Ontario $16.95 US
☐ Hiking in the . . . $19.95 CAN Northeastern U.S. $13.95 US

☐ Hiking in . . . . $22.95 CAN Québec $16.95 US
☐ Hiking in . . . . $22.95 CAN Ontario $16.95 US
☐ Ontario's Bike Paths and Rail Trails . $19.95 CAN $14.95 US

Ulysses Conversation Guides

☐ French for .... $9.95 CAN
Better Travel $6.50 US

☐ Spanish for Better Travel in
in Latin America $9.95 CAN
$6.50 US

Title	Qty	Price	Total
Name:		Subtotal	
		Shipping	$4.75CAN $3.75US
Address:		Subtotal	
	GST in Canada 7%		
		Total	
Tel:		Fax:	
E-mail:			

Payment: ☐ Cheque ☐ Visa ☐ MasterCard

Card number_____

Expiry date_____

Signature_____

ULYSSES TRAVEL GUIDES

4176 St. Denis Street,
Montréal, Québec,
H2W 2M5
☎(514) 843-9447
Fax: (514) 843-9448

305 Madison Avenue,
Suite 1166,
New York, NY 10165

Toll-free: 1-877-542-7247
Info@ulysses.ca
www.ulyssesguides.com